Universities
For A Changing World

Universities For A Changing World

THE ROLE OF THE UNIVERSITY
IN THE LATER TWENTIETH CENTURY

Edited by
Michael D. Stephens and Gordon W. Roderick

A HALSTED PRESS BOOK

JOHN WILEY & SONS
New York

Published in the USA
by Halsted Press, a division
of John Wiley & Sons Inc New York

Printed in Great Britain

Library of Congress Cataloging in Publication Data
Main entry under title:

Universities for a changing world.

 'A Halsted Press book.'
 Includes bibliographical references.
  1. Universities and colleges. 2. Education,
Higher—1965– I. Stephens, Michael Dawson.
II. Roderick, Gordon Wynne.
LB2322.U488 1975 378.1'009'047 75-6567
ISBN 0-470-82209-0

Contents

Introduction

MICHAEL D. STEPHENS AND GORDON W. RODERICK

Never before in their long histories have universities been subjected to so many conflicting pressures. Ashby in a recent paper[1] drew an analogy between universities and systems existing in nature; they both exhibit 'phylogenetic' inertia. Universities, he stated, existed originally to conserve and transmit the cultural inheritance. They are subjected both to internal forces of traditional educational values and objectives and to external forces of 'customer' demand. At times of relative calm there is an unstable equilibrium between these forces, but in times of rapid changes in social environment higher educational systems are forced to adjust to these changes, if somewhat reluctantly. Ashby claimed that 'at present there is a worldwide instability and higher education systems are shifting towards fresh equilibria. But we do not know where the new equilibria will be.' All this is evident in the chapters which follow.

At a time when ideas are rapidly transmitted globally and changes in thought and attitudes in one country spread immediately to others, international movements are created which may affect several countries simultaneously. The student revolts of the late 1960s were an instance of this. But, of course, open communication of ideas is not universal, barriers still exist and transmission is often resisted. Further, even where 'open' two-way communication is found the same willingness to change will not be present everywhere. We would expect to find in the relatively open societies of Western countries certain similarities. The same pressures may be operating but their impact is tempered by differing traditions, for university education, having evolved over centuries, may still to some degree reflect the traditions and conditions peculiar to those countries. In addition, not all countries within this group have advanced to the same economic level and this will be a further factor leading to diversity. Among the countries of the Communist bloc, on the other hand, one would anticipate a less diverse higher education, a greater degree of rigidity and a resistance to outside influences. Finally, one might predict that the countries of the Third World would adopt and borrow freely from both East and West those features which would assist them along the path of economic progress, provided they were consistent with their particular political ideologies.

Much of this is found to be the case, but the differences which exist between industrialised countries of the West are greater than anticipated. As one American writer has said: 'When we pass beyond the facts of exponential growth and student disorders any resemblance between the American universities and universities elsewhere is purely coincidental.'[2] Further, almost as great a diversity can be found within the United States itself as exists between America and the others.

In the past, countries of the West have been dominated by what the authors term the 'English', 'German' and 'Scottish' models of university education. These have influenced countries as widely divergent as Japan and those of the Caribbean. So important are these models in the history of university development that the authors' allusions to them require some simplification. Both the English and German models were elitist, but in other respects were very different. Central to the English model was the concept of 'liberal education'; this stressed the individual's needs, the quality of teaching and the special value of the tutor-student relationship. Since the early nineteenth century the central concept of the German model, in contrast, was *Wissenschaft*, best translated as the empirical approach to all knowledge; and it was the concern for knowledge – its increase and dissemination – which characterised the Prussian universities. Superficially, one might be tempted to see the two models in terms of a polarisation, one as student-oriented and the other as subject-oriented, but such a description would be inadequate, if not misleading. Neither country concentrated on one to the exclusion of the other.

As state institutions, the German universities were intended to serve the professional needs of the state. That universities should be concerned with servicing the professional needs of society was not a new idea and was indeed present during the early days of the universities at Bologna and Padua, but the Germans reaffirmed this function and extended the definition of 'professional' needs to include the economic and industrial requirements of a technologically based society.

It took some time for German attitudes to permeate English thinking on the role of universities and England, meanwhile experiencing the turmoil of the First Industrial Revolution, was heavily reliant on the products of Scottish universities which supplied scientists, engineers and medical men in comparative profusion. The Scottish universities were more democratic than either the English or German, but shared the meritocratic outlook of the latter. Emphasis was placed on both research and teaching but perhaps what is of greater significance is their willing acceptance of the new sciences and technologies and, as a result, the crucial part they played in servicing the manpower needs of industrial Britain.

The English provincial universities established in the late nineteenth century looked to both the German and Scottish universities for inspiration. A quotation from the Aberdare Report on university education in Wales in 1896 will serve to illustrate the change in attitude which had come about in England during the nineteenth century, the causes of which were the demands of international industrial competition and the fears it induced. 'It is important,' said the commissioners, 'that the colleges should be adapted, as regards their management and the course of instruction given, to the particular circumstances of the country. The more practical the education, the more it takes account of the requirements of commercial or professional life, the more will it be in demand amongst a people . . . [who] have very definitely before them the importance of fitting themselves for a career. Science, therefore, especially in its application to arts and manufactures, should occupy a prominent place in the curriculum of the colleges, and . . . a leading position must be given to those modern languages, the knowledge of which . . . is found most conducive to commercial success.'[3]

A far cry, then, from the 'ivory towers' of the Oxford and Cambridge of 1800. At that time knowledge, mind and the interaction of one with the other were important, but so were nobility of spirit and character to which Newman later added aesthetic taste and feelings. Such intangibles could only be developed by means of a close, person-to-person relationship. In the German and Scottish view, on the other hand, modern knowledge and the needs of the state had a higher priority. This duality of function, represented by individual needs on the one hand and social needs on the other, is a constant theme throughout this book. University systems vary in the degree to which they stress one at the expense of the other.

In the present context of rapid change it is no longer foolish to pose the question, 'What is a university?' It might be argued that the principal function of a university is to provide intellectual leadership; it must be a centre of independent thought, criticism and judgement. Such a view is found almost everywhere, but over and above this wide disparities exist. Lord Annan, though conceding social need, lays more stress on the university's duty to promote the life of the mind and to transmit high culture. The American author, Dr Wilcox, speaks of intellectual roles but also takes pain to emphasise social adaptation in a technological society. Research and scholarship are mentioned in the chapter on Australian universities by Professor Walker, but so are 'preparation for the professions' and 'service to society'. Subtle, albeit significant shades of emphasis are found in the role of the university in Western countries but these differences are insignificant compared to the difference in fundamental outlook between West and East. The Soviet view is that 'higher education constitutes and develops as an organic component of the unified system of socialist economy' and 'all work in the institutions of higher learning is subordinate to one task – education in the spirit of communist morality'. And in Communist China slogans appeared in 1958 which declared that 'education must serve proletarian politics'. Education should be integrated with 'productive labour' and those receiving it should 'become labourers with socialist consciousness and culture'.

During the 1950s and 1960s universities in the industrialised countries were under constant strain from the demands imposed by the so-called 'cold war' in terms of manpower and research expectations – government and industrial research contracts changed the nature of scientific research and led to what has been called 'mission-oriented' research, creating an imbalance in university studies towards science and technology and infringing university autonomy – from the constant striving of societies after economic growth and from the implications of the technological revolution. Science, technology and military considerations underpinned most thinking about university education. Further, the belief that economic success was equated with higher education systems was more strongly adhered to than ever before.

In the last few years the intensity of these factors has weakened and it is even suggested that efficient higher education systems may not be a necessary precondition for technological breakthroughs. Thinking in the

West at least is no longer conditioned, as Lord Annan points out, by the urgent need to train scientists and technologists; the industrial machine no longer mops them up as it once did. To state that pressures that were intense not so long ago have now somewhat diminished is very different from suggesting they are no longer operative and, indeed, throughout these essays the manpower needs of technology and the economy form a constant theme. But a new factor has emerged: the state of society brought about by the headlong progress of the unfettered technological revolution is now causing alarm and there is little doubt that the 'environmental conservation' crisis will markedly affect university developments.

In the short term, the most acute problem that universities have to face stems from the insatiable demands of societies for university expansion. But there are some exceptions. Such examples as Egypt are not included here but within these essays India and Latin America, where only 7 per cent of primary school children go on to secondary schooling and only 3 per cent of secondary school children enter higher education, fall into this category. So does South Africa where, surprisingly, the pressure of expansion does not seem to be acute even in the 'whites only' universities and certainly not in the black ones where, because of the poor quality of schools and low level of literacy, increased demand is going to be slow in developing. There are parallels between several countries, for example India and black South Africa (where school systems have been inadequately developed) and England in the nineteenth century. Indian and black South African universities for a long time yet will have to go on doing work which is normally done in secondary schools.

The above examples notwithstanding, the problem of expansion is now almost universal. Economic growth, the spread of egalitarian views and the increased material aspirations of the young have all contributed to this. It is said in these essays that the United States, Japan and Australia are moving from mass higher education to universal higher education and that several other countries, Britain among them, are moving from elitist systems to mass higher education. The acuteness of the problems such a trend causes will vary according to the economic level of each country. One consequence of this is that too much attention has been directed at the problem of how to get bigger systems and how to pay for expansion. This, according to Lord Ashby, has tended to divert attention from the real problem for, 'We are assuming that growth, diversification of curricula and changes of mode of government will solve our problems. What we should be doing is asking whether the system should change and what is to be its new function.'[4]

The present rates of expansion will continue and in many countries actually increase in momentum. To what extent can this continue before a crisis occurs? At some stage countries will be unable to finance expansion any further and this will bring about a situation of zero growth; it is at this point, Lord Annan considers, that drastic rethinking will be called for.

The escalating costs which governments have to bear have already led to a demand for 'public accountability'. Every country in the Western bloc finds it necessary to claim that its universities are autonomous almost as if this were the defining characteristic of a university. Infringing this sacred cow of autonomy will jeopardise relations between the universities and the state. None the less it is seriously being questioned whether society is getting value for money and it is suggested that universities be subjected to cost-benefit analysis. Although it is a simple matter to demonstrate that for the individual in most countries there is a substantial economic return to be gained from university education – borne out, for instance, by the higher salaries of university graduates – it is more difficult to assess the economic return to a country of a particular course or element of university study. Charles Carter, Vice-Chancellor of Lancaster University, considers that the search for a social return is a wild-goose chase.[5] Cost-benefit analysis and manpower planning criteria, he claims, which are based on the assumption that the prime purpose of all societies is to get richer, have led us up blind alleys and as a result we have forgotten the proper purpose of higher education. 'We have damaged the true cause of civilization and culture,' he says, 'by trying to convince people that universities are "good business" and that education has a yield as good as that of a jam factory.' Higher education should not be reduced to an economic matter. 'The point in time at which a developed country can afford mass higher education is simply that point at which this purpose has a sufficient political priority, that is, when people want it enough to sacrifice other things to obtain it.'

Expansion in the numbers attaining university education has led to the slogan 'more means worse'. This has evoked the response that it is not a case of more means worse but 'more means different'. Some would claim that there has not been a lowering of standards but a widening of expectations and requirements. The universities have become all things to all people and the functions demanded of universities have increased. Knowledge, especially highly specialised knowledge, expands exponentially and universities are still expected to carry out their traditional role, that of its increase and dissemination. In addition they serve as production belts for skilled manpower and service the manpower needs, social, economic and industrial, of society. There has, too, been a growing insistence that universities should help to offset the impact on society of the increasing complexity of the modern technological world. Further, the terms 'useful' and 'relevant' are now frequently heard. Dr Eric Williams says that there is a call now for 'relevant' studies in the Caribbean which in practice means Caribbean studies. Also, 'the governments of the West Indies,' he states, 'are certain to pay attention in future years to emphasising the relationship between study and work'. A recent book by a Nigerian on Nigerian education ends by saying that in Nigeria even Shakespeare's Sonnets must be taught with a view to the light they may shed on contemporary African life and contemporary African dilemmas.

Several of the following authors point out that in order to meet changing conditions and an enlargement of function it has been necessary to develop a variety of institutions all of which come within the term 'university'. In the United States some universities have been likened to a service station or department store. The view is that what society wants the university will do, provided society is prepared to pay for it. 'Some critics argue,' declares Robert Hutchins,[6] President of the Center for the Study of Democratic Institutions, 'that any subject, interest or activity is as good as any other. Nothing is more important or trivial than anything else . . . Whereas other countries have an idea of a university, however inadequate, vague, or even erroneous, we have none. All we have to do is to decide whether there is anything imaginable that would seem inappropriate in an American institution of higher learning.' One way of meeting present-day complexities is to develop institutions having different functions at different levels. In the United States we find a whole complex of colleges ranging from community or junior colleges at one end of the spectrum through to the prestigious private establishments such as Johns Hopkins which emphasise postgraduate work. But many colleges are multipurpose and Clark Kerr, former President of the University of California, speaks of them as 'multi-versities'. Doubtless such institutions as these will proliferate in the future. In Britain and Australia 'binary systems' have evolved but this latter will probably move closer to the 'pyramid-like' structure of the United States. The Australian Central Advisory Council for Education suggests five categories of institutions and states that, 'No single model will in the future be able to cope with such diverse aspirations and motivations as will exist in the future.'

A striking feature of recent years has been the growing disaffection of the young, highlighted by the student revolts of the 1960s. During this period there were student revolts in over two dozen countries. Studies have shown, however, that it is only a small minority, perhaps 5 per cent of students, who are actively engaged in riots and many of these are first-year students from good socio-economic backgrounds studying sociology or political science. Further, in the United States many protests were over Vietnam and the draft, but leaving aside the traditional role of student riots as a form of political protest the students in many cases were protesting about academic matters or about sincerely held views concerning the fundamental nature of society.

There has been a breakdown in the traditional acceptance of authority, hostility to and scepticism about the predictive value of entrance qualifications and doubts about the appropriateness of certification. Again, the cry for participation and involvement will affect internal governmental procedures and bring about a greater flexibility in disciplines and teaching methods. But of greater significance is the disenchantment of the young with the university in other areas such as social change and social and educational underprivilege and with its close identification with the economic and technological basis of modern societies whose servants universities all too often appear to be.

The university is frequently central to the aspirations of the young for social change, but many of them tend to view it as an instrument bolstering up the inequality they wish to see eliminated. They argue that greater equality can be brought about by changing the universities and by throwing their doors open to a wider clientele. Such a process is clearly taking place in some countries but in others, such as India, South Africa, Latin American and Caribbean countries where the university population is very small, an emphasis on free higher education may merely subsidise the privileged classes; such a step perpetuates the hegemony of the elite and negates the social function which it is intended to serve.

A concern with the underprivileged leads to a demand for easier entry at eighteen years of age but also, and more significantly, the right of entry to university of people of mature years. In the United States 'open admissions' and 'continuing' education were popular slogans in the 1960s. 'With that single-minded idealism which will be remembered of the Americans when Watergate is forgotten universities and colleges all over the country have tried to make opportunities of higher education for those who most need the extra chance of advancement and personal enrichment which it provides . . . I see a weakness in our thinking . . . throughout the British system. We do not plan imaginatively to bring opportunity where it is most needed.'[7] In the Soviet Union it has for long been made easy for workers and other adults to enter university in later life. In China, too, adult workers are highly favoured as students for when the universities re-opened following the Great Proletarian Cultural Revolution of 1969 (see Dr Price's essay) they chose workers, peasants and soldiers. The policy of part-time study on the other hand is, it seems, taken too far in the Latin American countries where the majority of students hold jobs while studying and the staff also are frequently on a part-time basis. This has its defects, as Dr Hewlett points out.

Whereas Swedish universities allocate 25 per cent of their places to adults, many of whom do not have formal qualifications, only 3 per cent of British undergraduates are over the age of twenty-five at entry. There is now an increasing awareness generally that by no means all those wishing and able to study at university level manage to get into such institutions at the age of eighteen. For a variety of reasons countless individuals are either not strongly motivated or 'opt out' at critical stages in the educational process. Many are lost for ever but others come to realise their 'error' at a later stage and wish to get back into higher education, only to find doors are often barred to them. In Britain the Open University has exposed this problem and its success indicates that traditional methods such as external degree programmes and correspondence courses have been inadequate. Some critics go as far as to argue that eighteen is not necessarily the best age for university entry and claim that the stronger motivation and greater maturity of judgement of older adults help to compensate for their lack of formal qualifications.

The Wright Commission of Ontario in its report[8] on post-secondary education has grasped this particular nettle in both hands and produced radical proposals. It intends to hasten the change from elitist to mass higher education (in 1971 over 50 per cent of the nineteen-year-old age group in Ontario were attending institutes of higher education) and at the same time eliminate social discrimination. It proposes an 'open sector' which will include an open university, libraries and museums, easier entry requirements, grants to students pursuing self-education and periodic re-certification. If nothing more comes of this 1972 report, it will still have served a purpose in stimulating thought on this problem. Likewise the implications of the French concept of *education permanente* and the stress now being put everywhere on lifelong or continuing education will keep attention focused on this area.

Finally, there are already signs of a growing distaste among the young towards certain aspects of the modern competitive and technological society. This has led to changes in demand: engineering and technology are giving way to the creative arts and communication sciences, social sciences and medicine. The physical sciences, for so long very much to the fore, are yielding to biological, environmental and earth sciences. A revolution is quietly taking place; man and his interaction with his immediate environment are being put at the centre of things, whereas matter, machines and the wider universe – the concerns of science and technology – are retreating to the periphery (shades of Copernicus!). 'We are witnessing,' says Ashby, 'a greater emphasis by the young on skills with people rather than with ideas.' This has led to an incongruity between 'mission-oriented' teaching and 'discipline-oriented' teaching which 'is one of the great discontents with higher education'.[9]

But how far can this process continue? A high economic growth rate is still a major goal of most countries and the 'service function' of a university, ie its duty to produce scientists, engineers, lawyers, economists and all the 'experts' that society needs, has to keep pace with economic growth and the increasing complexity of society. The 'socio-cultural' function, on the other hand, has to be adjusted to student demand. This raises intriguing questions about the rates of expansion in relation to these two functions and niceties of judgement as to the balance between them. What factors will operate in producing answers to these problems? How far removed are we from the situation in China where an attempt is made to regulate student numbers in the different specialties to match projected needs of the economy? Students are also directed into employment when they graduate, with minimal arrangements for the expression of choice.

The view that a high economic growth rate is the major purpose is being seriously questioned and it may be that the challenge will be accommodated without any radical alteration of the system. But what if societies do have a serious change of heart and turn their backs on the economic Jerusalem and seek instead the 'convivial' society as proposed by Illich?[10] To put his argument simply and briefly: he states that society is suffering from a sickness in which human relationships are being eroded and destroyed. He seeks instead a society in which human relationships will be strengthened and enhanced. According to Illich we impose inhumanities on ourselves in the name of growth, efficiency and progress and we must examine afresh what makes for conviviality. He speaks of 'addiction to growth', withdrawal from which will be painful. There has been too much formalised education and overprogramming, he says, and a growing dependence on specialist expertise acquired by expensive training. Such views may be unpalatable to those countries which have witnessed a century of struggle to achieve universal higher education and even more unwelcome to those poorer countries who are seeking salvation through economic growth.

It may be that Illich's views at the moment are in advance of the times but if they were to spark off the idealism of the young, societies might alter radically and universities would become very different institutions from their present form. There are few signs of such a revolution yet but one of the opinions expressed by several authors is that because of the unstable state that our societies are now in, it is difficult, if not impossible, to forecast the future.

I

The
University in Britain

LORD ANNAN

There really is no mystery about the roles of the university. For the past century there has been no dispute about its two main functions. It exists first to promote through reflection and research the life of the mind; second to transmit high culture to each generation. Whatever is thought to be intellectually important and of concern to society it teaches to new students.

But immediately one asks, well, what *is* thought to be of concern to society, the debate grows warm. How far should universities teach vocational subjects, trim their courses to the changing needs of society – how do they or anyone else identify those needs? Which market do they intend to trade in? – the market of jobs, adapting their graduates to the requirements of professions and business, or the market of the school leavers, who often have no idea for what job they are destined, detest utilitarian subjects and protest that their mission is to understand society – perhaps to destroy it and build it again in three days? Despite the fact that many of the civic universities founded in Victorian times were firmly turned towards vocational subjects – to the study of textiles at Leeds and of metallurgy at Sheffield – British universities have never seen themselves in the role of the American land-grant colleges. The dons do not picture themselves as vocational teachers. They regard themselves as dedicated to the task of discovering new knowledge or re-drawing the map of existing knowledge. Those who teach medical or law students are often researching on abstruse topics far removed from the routine teaching of the subject to undergraduates. Certainly their teaching is not all that often concerned with improving the quality of professional practice. Give any subject to a don and he will make it academic. Dons in the humanities and in pure science have not lost their belief, as some have in America, that academic study is the best way to train and expand the mind.

Universities have also by custom undertaken a third role. They certificate the young. In British universities this is done by awarding after three years' study the bachelor's degree, and by declaring that students have been placed in the first, upper or lower second or third class in that degree. Each university runs a careers advisory service from which prospective employers can get the results of the examination, and a confidential assessment by the student's teachers of his abilities. Since certification, and the degree itself, is thought to have become the passport for a job suitable for a graduate, all sorts of consequences have followed: a mounting pressure to go to a university, and hence a groundswell of resentment against the qualifications that are required to obtain a place and the examinations set to obtain a degree; a mounting envy of the meritocracy who make it, and hence a demand to abolish the A and O level examinations at school which are the keys to university entry; a mounting scepticism about the appropriateness of certification when it is not specifically linked to entry into a profession, and hence a hint that examinations themselves are out of date. These resentments and doubts have not risen very high as yet, but they remind us that universities are for ever being asked by the public to play more roles: to mix nationalities and races and so promote better understanding; to reduce the gap in knowledge between the children of the poor and the well-to-do; to lay on post-experience courses for teachers, policemen, industrialists and social workers; to introduce the young to the visual arts and music, and offer refuge to creative artists. Such demands are characteristic of the belief of our age that everything is possible and the nation's ills could be cured if only politicians were wiser and the establishment could be shattered. The fact that such a belief is an illusion does not make the task of the university any easier.

THE INFLUENCE OF OXFORD AND CAMBRIDGE
Anyone who intends to look into the future had better first consult the past; and the history of British universities spotlights the peculiarities which differentiate them from universities on the Continent.

Only 10 per cent of university students go to Oxford and Cambridge.

But, just as a dominant social class imposes its style of life upon the rest of society, so the ancient universities have imposed a style upon all British universities. Oxford and Cambridge were always national universities, drawing their students from all over the country. Like them, every British university claims to be a national institution. In 1920 more than 50 per cent of the students in Manchester, Birmingham or Leeds came from their home town: today only 10 per cent or less do so. Whereas French universities are zoned, and a Lyonnais must study at Lyons or a boy or girl living at Maisons Lafitte must go to Nanterre and cannot opt for the Sorbonne, in Britain a student can choose his university. The style of living at Oxford and Cambridge has been the model for the civic universities, who built halls of residence and hostels in which 40 per cent of students now live.

Oxford and Cambridge gave British universities their special traditions in teaching. When the medieval method of examination by disputation became inappropriate and the study and translation of Greek and Latin became all-important, the colleges provided the necessary individual tuition; and in the Victorian age the tutorial became, under the influence of Newman and Jowett, the training not only of a man's mind but of his character. For many dons the tutorial took precedence over their duty to research and add to knowledge; so much so that Abraham Flexner referred to them contemptuously as finishing schools. German scholars sniffed. When the great Williamowitz-Moellendorf, on a summer's afternoon, was taken to the top of the tower of Magdalen College chapel and saw below him Matthew Arnold's young barbarians punting on the river or sauntering towards the parks swinging their tennis racquets, he recalled the dons sitting over their wine the night before and uttered a fearful judgement: 'So . . . eine Luststadt.'

No one could call Oxford or Cambridge mere pleasuredromes today, but due to their example British students expect not merely lectures but tutorials, seminars and small-group teaching. They expect graduate students and junior academic staff to be available to help them in the laboratories. This tradition of teaching has been responsible for the exceedingly favourable staff/student ratio, which at present is 1:8 over the universities as a whole. But this ratio is misleading. Most universities have some small departments and research units where the ratio is even more favourable; for instance clinical medical schools are exceptionally well staffed. Other departments compensate for them and the ratio in popular departments is nearer 1:12 and will go to 1:15 over the next decade. Even so, the ratio will still be markedly better than in continental universities. It brings results: 87 per cent of students admitted obtain degrees. British universities see their role as being to teach students so successfully that they obtain their first degree in a short period, and not to admit as many students as want to try for a degree.

British universities have inherited another role from Oxford and Cambridge – that of being self-governing institutions holding their liberties directly from the crown which gave them their charter and statutes. The relations of universities to the state have always been equivocal. Even if one of the incidents in James II's loss of his throne was his ill-judged interference in the affairs of Oxford, the ancient universities in the days of the Whig ascendancy were treated as yet another arena of crown patronage; and the succession of royal commissions and committees upon the ancient universities and London in the nineteenth and twentieth centuries established what was really never in doubt: that the state can and will interfere, even in the details of the curriculum or the costs of student board and lodging, when it considers reform to be necessary. Nevertheless, enormously as the area of state control of higher education has grown, it is still, where the universities are concerned, remote control. Universities are not directly answerable to a minister and the dons are not civil servants capable of being disciplined by dismissal as they are in many continental countries. No one can require a don to move from his present post to another university; whereas a civil servant must expect these days to be told to leave London for Newcastle.

But the influence of Oxbridge is more pervasive than this. The Oxbridge dons govern themselves. No layman sits on their councils. Government is by committee, and though inevitably there are some *ex officio* members of the important committees, a don is not appointed by the vice-chancellor to serve on a committee: he is elected by his colleagues. It is true that no university has followed Oxbridge in submitting all important decisions of their councils to approval by the whole electorate of dons. But British universities have moved closer to Oxbridge democracy in recent years – a democracy where heads of departments and the professoriate are not all-powerful and where non-professorial staff have a chance to be heard. The Privy Council and the University Grants Committee (UGC) no longer require laymen to be in a majority on the councils of civic universities; indeed, they may prefer academic staff to be in a majority, and in many universities, old as well as new, the council has become in effect a rubber-stamp, an authenticating body which like a constitutional monarch regards its role as to encourage, advise and warn the senate which is the true source of power. This is not yet true of the new technological universities, the former colleges of advanced technology, which retain their tradition of effective lay control through the council to which they were accustomed when they belonged to the public sector.

THE INFLUENCE OF LONDON

British universities, however, draw upon another tradition for their roles. Even if for seven and a half centuries Oxford and Cambridge were the only English universities, there were for hundreds of years five Scottish universities in which the students were poorer and lived not in colleges but at home or in lodgings – the majority of Glasgow's university students still live at home. They kept humane studies alive in the eighteenth century during Oxbridge's deep decline, and it was from them as much as from Germany that the founders of University College, London, drew their inspiration and established two traditions which were to affect the development of the civic universities: first, that research was an essential function of a university – conducted with all the seriousness and professionalism that characterised a German university; and second, that researchers should be free to follow whatever line they saw fit and that they themselves and their pupils should be of any race, religion or creed. The English liberal university was born in London, and it was there that the first departments of modern studies such as European languages, engineering and medicine were formed.

The laymen who founded the London colleges and the civic universities were determined to retain ultimate control over their institutions. They wanted to be sure that scholarship did not preclude the study of 'useful' subjects and that Greek, Latin and mathematics were not the only subjects fit for students. The founders were suspicious that, left to themselves, dons might revert to their old ways; and since fees, and not endowments, were their main source of income, the laymen kept tight control of finances. Gradually there emerged the principle, which was enshrined in the constitution of Manchester University in the first decade of this century, that while laymen should remain in control of the strictly financial affairs of the university, the dons should control its academic development. Thus the two-tier system of university government came into being. It symbolises a significant role. The council symbolises through the lay members the recognition that the university ultimately must serve the needs of society; and the senate symbolises the freedom of the university to order its academic life without outside interference and to be the sole judge as to whom it admits, how and what they are taught and how they are examined.

London gave more to English universities than lay government. It became the practice in this century for an institution aspiring to become a university to be obliged to adopt the London curriculum and conform through the London external degree to London academic patterns during its chrysalis stage as a university college. The intention was honourable enough: to ensure that no place should become a university which had not proved itself to be academically respectable. But in retrospect this tutelage to London was deplorable. For half a century it inhibited academic experiment, and the dons in the university colleges, restricted and hogtied, were unable to find a specific academic role for themselves in their locality. It was only after World War II, with the foundation of Keele, that a new university could work out its own curriculum and way of life, and only in the fifties that the system was brought to an end. The sterility which Bruce Truscot[1] diagnosed in his controversial analysis of the redbrick universities was induced by the London tutelage.

THE UNIVERSITIES' VIEW OF THEIR STUDENTS

This tutelage was inseparable from the way they defined the role of their students. The days had passed when, in the early years of the nineteenth century, the role of Oxbridge would be summed up as producing men who would be of service to church and state; although nothing so utilitarian as specific courses in the techniques of government were ever envisaged, the universities thought of themselves as educating those who would probably rise to the highest posts in the civil service and the professions – including teaching in the secondary schools.

The authorities still regarded themselves as standing towards their students *in loco parentis*. The old ideal, propagated by John Henry Newman, that universities existed primarily to shape the mind and character of their pupils still existed vestigially in the shape of regulations governing student activities that would have been regarded on the Continent (though not in America) with astonishment. As late as the early 1960s, these restrictions, and summary proceedings against students who broke them, were accepted without question.

At that time the universities were educating about 4 per cent of the adolescent age group, and only 10 per cent received some form of full-time higher education. Suddenly all this was to change. By the 1970s, 25 per cent of the age group were receiving some form of full-time higher education. The universities were educating 8 per cent of them. By the 1980s, according to present plans, 30 per cent of the age group will be receiving full-time education of which 15 per cent will be in the universities.

We are foolish not to realise, as Martin Trow has observed, that if a nation moves from small-scale to mass higher education, it must expect the customs, ideals, organisation and behaviour of its universities and other institutions to change. All the technical and economic organisations in society – no longer only the higher professions – expect to recruit graduates from the universities and colleges. Soon entry to a university, formerly regarded as a privilege (which could be forfeited by failure to obey its rules), comes to be regarded as a right. Soon the state, which has previously been a benevolent and distant provider of funds, becomes intimately implicated in planning the growth of universities. The dons themselves (a higher proportion of whom in a period of rapid growth are young) no longer have the same cohesion and consensus; they no longer are so sure what precise knowledge a man educated in their subject should possess when he takes his degree. Universities do different things: what unifies them today is not the curriculum but the fact that they receive their funds from the University Grants Committee, ie from central government. The unity of universities is guaranteed by the binary system.

THE NEW UNIVERSITIES

Universities became more variegated during the 1960s. The new universities built on green fields were inspired by a belief in interdisciplinary studies. The enemy was the department, with its specialised courses, inflexible staffing and a tyrannical professorial stranglehold over the curriculum, staff and students. The new ideal was to relate the old disciplines to each other and knowledge to society. Since competition to get into universities had forced sixth forms, indeed the whole of grammar-school education, into premature specialisation, the universities should enable their students to see the connection between disciplines instead of further driving students to become even more specialised. So the new universities built bridges between arts and sciences, and between different parts of the social sciences, and emphasised that knowledge had a social context and learning was not to be divorced from the needs of society. Indeed, one particular type of new university – the colleges of advanced technology which, having been promoted to that status in the 1950s now found themselves upgraded again to university status – had been particularly dedicated to vocational study. Some speedily got rid of their part-time students and sandwich courses. But others retained their commitment to the sandwich-course degree in which students alternated periods in the university with periods in business or industry.

The foundation of the new universities invigorated the whole system. The orderly, decorous expansion of the system in the 1950s really meant the development of what was already there within the framework as the dons returning from the war found it. The fifties will probably be judged as the golden age of the British universities – when they enjoyed the maximum prestige, support and privileges. Their public reputation was immense – boosted particularly by the reputation which scientists had acquired during the war. To many young men, the life of the don was the desirable life: a life dedicated to the pursuit of knowledge and truth, with reasonable financial reward, free – as they saw it – from the compromise of politics or the harsh rat race and narrow, false values of the world of industry or business. Entry to the university carried status and was thought to carry a passport to the inner circle of jobs. The universities shared in the prosperity of that decade and, in terms of the national income, their comparatively modest demands upon the Exchequer were met so nearly in full that their main financial worries were the effects of the oscillations of stop-go economic policy upon their quinquennial allocations. But by the end of the decade a small number of dons had begun to ask whether the size of the privileged group of children who moved from public and grammar school to university, and the scope of what they did when they got there, was adequate. The founders of the new universities were determined to re-interpret the role of the university.

THE ROBBINS REPORT AND UNIVERSITY GROWTH

But did they re-interpret it? Like several commissions set up to effect change and mass the guns which would blast the positions of the unthinking, the Robbins Commission[2] spent a great part of its energy winning a battle against an enemy that had retreated from the field. The commissioners believed that they had to convince a sullenly conservative academic profession and a sceptical Conservative government that their academic standards could still be preserved if universities expanded, because the growing sixth forms in the secondary schools would fill to overflowing the pool of ability in whose existence the opponents of growth declined to believe. But in fact the progress of the inquiry itself convinced the government, who accepted the expenditure envisaged in the Robbins Report overnight, and the diehards decamped. As it turned out, the pioneer projections in the report of the demand for higher education were underestimates. But that was not its weakness. The weakness lay in one assumption and one omission. It assumed that university status should be the goal of aspiring institutions: hence university staffing ratios and salary scales and what universities did – subject to their degree courses being more broadly based – constituted, broadly speaking, the yardstick. It omitted consideration of governmental and administrative problems which this transformation of the scale of higher education would create. This was the weakness that forced Anthony Crosland, when Secretary of State for Education, to announce that not every institution could enter the university sector with all its costly standards of capital and recurrent expenditure, staff establishments and supporting services merely because it had established a readiness on its part to move and the willingness of a university to receive it. Partly in self-defence and partly to confirm other institutions of higher education in their own roles, the government pronounced the existence of the binary system.

Was the Robbins Report wrong to envisage universities as being the first institutions to double in size? Certainly some critics, not all of them diehards, have thought so. According to them the role of the university has been distorted ever since the Robbins Report. Instead of remaining a small, privileged sector of high prestige, untroubled by Treasury controls by virtue of its comparatively small budget, it is now suffering from all the follies and constraints of Whitehall supervision, however

27

discreetly applied through the University Grants Committee. Since the UGC chooses to abide by the hypocrisy – so the argument runs – that all universities are equally distinguished and should receive the same degree of support, mediocrity will in the end be the order of the day, and the classic status of Oxford and Cambridge and a handful of other institutions will be eroded. The role of the university will not so much change as decay. The number and size of universities should have been limited; the expansion should have taken place in other specially created institutions such as the polytechnics.

This thesis will not stand up to examination. The model on which it is based is higher education in the USSR where there are proportionately few universities and many specialised institutes; a pattern which follows logically in a country which puts faith in manpower predictions and national plans. Britain would have followed the Russian pattern only if a decision had been taken immediately after World War II not to found Keele or proceed with the upgrading of the university colleges, such as Leicester or Exeter, which within a few years were to achieve university status. Everything in the climate of opinion at that time made such a decision inconceivable. In fact the pattern of higher education, and the placing of the university at the apex of that pattern, was determined long before the Robbins Commission was ever set up, just as the decision in 1958 to found seven new universities was taken before the commission ever sat. We certainly do not live in a planned economy. A cynical observer might well ask whether the Robbins Commission was not established to justify at great length the decisions that officialdom had been taking without proper foresight.

SCIENCE IN THE UNIVERSITIES

So when we ask whether the founders of the new universities re-interpreted the role of the universities, the answer must be that, if by re-interpretation anything radical or startling is meant, they achieved very little. Sir Alec Cairncross has expressed the indecent thought that among other ventures in which Britain invested far beyond her means in the twenty years after World War II, such as groundnuts, ocean liners, the aircraft industry, atomic-energy plant and a pile of defence missiles and equipment, was big science. The achievements of the boffins in the war, the romance surrounding their response to some crucial technical challenge when brilliant scientific inventiveness came up with the answer

28

and saved thousands of lives, Patrick Blackett's successes in operational research, indeed the story of the invention of the atomic bomb itself, made a deep impression upon many minds, not least that of Churchill. To invest in science seemed to be a way of investing in industrial success. But, in fact, so Cairncross argues, it was in harsh economic terms little more than another attempt to keep up with the Joneses across the Atlantic. Our Nobel Prizemen were our credentials for parity of esteem in the world of big science and foundation grants, but there was all too little spin-off into workaday industry.

The prestige, moreover, which attached to the Fellowship of the Royal Society was such that university scientific teaching and research was geared to that goal. Whereas the dons in the humanities had always acknowledged that only a handful of their students would become professional scholars, the goal of a science student was solely to learn how to become a good research worker. Rightly conscious of the reproaches that British industry lacked the technical know-how of American industry and was insufficiently aware of the value of research, the government poured money into scientific plant in the universities and polytechnics, only to find that by the 1970s schoolchildren, for a variety of reasons, were no longer prepared to opt for sciences and technological courses in higher education. The government has reacted. In 1962 the minister of education, for the first time, refused to accept the bill which the UGC handed to him and cut its estimates. In 1972, for the first time, the government questioned the amount of money to be spent on fundamental scientific research. Lord Rothschild, a boffin, Fellow of the Royal Society, one-time chairman of the Agricultural Research Council and former head of scientific research in Shell, issued a report, accepted in the main by the government, which laid down that a proportion of research council funds should be available only for research which a customer had commissioned. The dons bitterly resent these arguments and make eloquent defences of research; but the Treasury has rarely been moved by eloquence alone.

STUDENT POWER

Things in Britain change too slowly. But occasionally there is something to be said for imperturbability. In the late sixties the convulsions of student unrest induced North American and European countries to grant real power to the students. In West Germany there is *Drittel-*

paritaet; in France students have powerful representation on the governing bodies and committees of the universities; and the smaller European
countries seem likely to follow one or the other pattern. At American
universities staff-student committees pullulate at every level.

The British, however, have not abandoned their traditional conception of the role of the student in university affairs. Students have been
brought on to committees concerning their welfare in strength; on to
committees concerning their curriculum and methods of assessment in
moderation; on to committees concerned with overall policy and the
allocation of financial resources in small numbers if at all; and on the
admission of students, the appointment of staff and the annual assessment
of students through examination, in no circumstances. One explanation
is the good conditions under which university students study in Britain.
Another is that, by and large, the dons retain the confidence of the
politicians and civil servants. The vindictiveness with which M Fauré
introduced his reforms in France revealed a long-felt contempt for the
conservatism of the professoriate and a determination to humiliate an
interest group which had for so long blocked educational reforms.
Again, the root-and-branch reforms in West Germany reflect the guilt
felt by the professoriate there for the failure of their predecessors to stand
up to Hitler. In Britain there were no moral and political issues such as
the Vietnam war which divided America and set light to the campuses.
Nor were the dons either too intransigent or too craven in their response
to student disturbances. But universities are not exempt from the pressures which erupt in other parts of British society. The recent erosion of
the Anderson principle, whereby students in need are awarded grants
which cover all their reasonable expenses including maintenance, could
produce a demand by students to play a far greater part in controlling
the finances of the university. Why should they not attempt to compensate themselves for the losses which they have sustained through the
effect of inflation upon their grants?

THE FUTURE

The erosion of the student grants – the inability of the government to
finance the expansion of higher education at the level to which a generation of dons and students have become accustomed – raises a multitude
of questions about the role of the university in the future. Lord Ashby's
well-known aphorism – 'More does not mean worse; but it certainly

means different' – challenges the view that universities can go on doing what they have done in the past. Universities, as has been pointed out, nowadays offer courses and options that only twenty years ago would have been thought beneath their dignity, and as institutions they have diversified in a way which would have astonished the professoriate in the immediate postwar periods. Late as the British were to recognise the need to expand higher education, their tardiness has enabled them to avoid some follies and to permit the system to evolve at a pace which, if it has led to some dilution of the standards of being a don, has not swamped the profession with new recruits who neither understand nor accept the conventions of their calling. Nevertheless, they will need to change still further. To double numbers in one decade and to plan nearly to double them in the next must mean some shift of emphasis: for unlike the 1960s when, for the first time, numbers of highly able school-leavers were finding a place, the expansion of the seventies is going to mean admitting for the most part increased numbers of less able students, some of them perhaps sucked into the system by convention, unmotivated, bewildered as to why they are there.

The universities will also be facing another challenge – competition from the polytechnics. By the eighties the numbers of full-time students in the local authority institutions is to be equal to that in the universities. The polytechnics will be offering courses directly related to a multitude of jobs – leading to specific qualifications. In the ever tougher situation governing grants and accommodation in which students will find themselves, there could well be genuine competition between universities and polytechnics, the prestige of the former by no means compensating for the fact that the latter will offer entry on easier terms and courses more geared towards careers.

But does the university exist solely to educate school-leavers? Will the handful of mature students today be augmented by the end of the century by large numbers of men and women in middle age either returning to university, or possibly entering it for the first time, highly motivated and understanding what a university has to offer? There is much talk of *education permanente* and practically no thought given to it. How is such a system to be financed? Is it to be partly by the state and partly by business and industry? Is the idea of issuing everyone at eighteen in theory with a coupon for some kind of higher education practical?

Directly finance is mentioned spectres begin to rise. By the eighties, at present prices and on present assumptions, we shall be spending £1,000 million a year on higher education; and if the aspirations of students regarding grants and accommodation were to be fulfilled the sum could be half as much again. They will not be fulfilled. It is inconceivable that any government will give such priority to this particular sector of the economy. Faced with economic difficulties, both a Labour and a Conservative government in effect cut students' grants, and more people are coming to believe that a system of grants supplemented by loans – or, as indeed is now the case, by earning in the vacation at whatever job can be found – will emerge when student numbers have again doubled. If students cannot be adequately financed the whole nature of the bachelor's degree could change. In Britain a degree is still inseparable from a period of time: three or sometimes four years for a first degree; one, two or three years for higher qualifications. The practice rests on the assumption that the student is totally supported, if necessary, by the state. But if this were to change, there would be irresistible pressure for a continental or American system of credits picked up over years of part-time study.

Nor is the present organisation of higher education likely to remain unchallenged. It has always been fashionable to decry the binary system, and this in turn has led people to ask whether it is wise any longer to organise higher education nationally. Should it not be organised regionally? Should not the University Grants Committee be swept away and regional councils allocate funds between all the competing institutions within their area, so that local influence could decide whether or not colleges of further education were not in more need – because in greater demand – than polytechnics or universities? Regionalisation could well change the role of universities. In Ontario the Commission on Post-Secondary Education[3] published a profoundly anti-intellectual report, and the province then appointed its chairman to consider public comment and draft legislative instruments for reform. The implications of the report are certain to turn the universities within the province more towards the role of service stations.

There may, of course, appear to be countervailing forces. If there were to be a significant change in the tide of opinion in Westminster and Whitehall on the role of the universities, it would sweep against some new groynes that have been erected in recent years in the universities – the more active trade unionism of the Association of University

Teachers and of the Association of Scientific, Technical and Managerial Staffs. But unionism, being, of course, a conservative force within whatever sphere it operates, is more likely to make it more difficult rather than easier for universities to modulate yet preserve their essence. The demands for conditions of work and professional structure which the unions will make could stifle the tiny band of intellectual creators and stimulators who give universities their *raison d'être*.

But no one can predict the future of this remarkable institution. Popes, kings, bishops, ministers of state at different times and in different countries have taken universities under their patronage, or tried to control or suppress them; but they break out of state control even under tyrannical regimes precisely because they trade in skills which cannot develop under too severe constraints. They have their ups and downs, and other intellectual centres, such as the Inns of Court under the Tudors or the research institute today, can rob them of their prestige and their best intellects either because such men find other sources of patronage and a more stimulating atmosphere elsewhere as English and French intellectuals and scholars did in the eighteenth century, or because the dons become too inward-looking, and what seems to them the essence of scholarship becomes regarded by the world as pedantry. Who can say whether the peremptory need for managerial talent and techniques will transform them into vocational factories? Or whether the egalitarian movement in its fear of meritocracy will lower their status, abolish their intellectual standards and relieve them of their role of certificating the young? After all, it is not going to pass unnoticed for much longer that higher education is provided largely for the children of the middle classes by taxation drawn, at any rate in part, from the working classes. The real test for some universities will come when they are no longer capable of further expansion, either because their sites are fully exploited or because further increases in student numbers or research facilities for whatever reason are not feasible. At this point they will become institutions of zero growth. That will be the hour of trial.

2

The University in the United States of America

WAYNE WILCOX

American colleges and universities have proved to be remarkably diverse and innovative since their founding, in part because they have been an integral part of a rapidly changing society. Eighteenth-century education in the colonies was conceived as a proper English training in the classics, theology or the law, but it was soon overtaken by the 'Scottish' view that education was a sober, practical business. This trend was more marked as higher education moved with the frontier, and state governments made land available to universities, charging them with the advancement of science, technology and agriculture. The Scottish imprint was further deepened in the late nineteenth century as the German-style graduate school arrived to wed research to teaching. The twentieth-century urban frontier of the European immigrants and later indigenous American minority groups created its own environment for unique schools and colleges, a development still vital with experimental vigour. The American 'ivory tower', always a myth, was in fact rejected not only as unattainable but as undesirable.

Socially sensitive higher education traditionally found itself with many tensions: academic autonomy versus state control, student socialisation as 'new man in America' versus training in universalist values, the social pillar versus the social critic. In gross terms, the educational process was characterised by a dialectic between the Scottish-German view of 'teach the subject, the student will take care of himself'

34

and the English-classical view of 'teach the student, the subject will take care of itself'. These approaches were institutionalised as the perpetual struggle between technical/professional and arts/humanities faculties, between elitist and democratic admissions standards, between the 'practical' and the 'civilising' curriculum, between 'publish or perish' and 'effective teacher' criteria for faculty selection and promotion.

The size, wealth and diversity of American higher education made it unnecessary to resolve these contradictions or evolve a national consensus. Various regional, ethnic, religious and nationality groups in the country could and did establish their own educational 'true church', and since education was a state rather than a national subject under the constitutional division of powers, the federal system encouraged diversity. The funding arrangements of higher education also insured against standardisation in a rich, capitalist America where money was presented to higher education in what can only be called, in terms of ideology, a highly random way.

Private endowments and the coffers of the church seeded the first colleges in the New World, and the former continue to be the most fertile source for new educational capital. As the scale and costs of higher education increased, however, the American state governments created and sustained the major university systems, while large foundations (institutionalised private philanthropy) and the federal government came increasingly to the assistance of beleaguered 'private' universities.[1]

World War II was the watershed in American higher education because war-time mobilisation 'nationalised' the university world, immensely strengthened the professional-technical bias inherent in the system, and both broadened and levelled the student and faculty 'intake'. The postwar 'GI Bill' generation of war veterans were beneficiaries of a national scholarship system, and university growth to accommodate them constituted a revolution in itself.

The 'cold war' years furthered these trends. The arms race required vast expenditures on applied science and technology, and for reasons unique to American government, it proved more convenient to 'contract' science and technology to universities than to create a governmental scientific establishment.[2] The National Defense Education Act recognised that the American superpower would need manpower skilled in foreign languages and area experience, much as the Ford Foundation's Foreign Area Training Fellowship scheme pioneered the university 'area expert' revolution. Science, social science and 'strategic languages' waxed fat with federal subsidies in the 1950s and 1960s, their Scottish-German ancestors no doubt cosmically pleased.

The World War II and cold war revolutions in higher education had the greatest impact on large, high-quality institutions, where they witnessed the strengthening of the graduate school/research function, often at the expense of the undergraduate school/teaching function. During this period, American scholarship rapidly increased in both quality and quantity. In the nature of such rapid growth, much esoteric and uneven research was also completed, and the proliferations of scholarly monographs came to testify to a kind of publishers' St Vitus's dance. None the less, systematic scholarship of the highest quality was accompanied by impressive social and technological inventiveness. One only has to think of the Thomas J. Watson Computing Laboratory of Columbia University in which the first large computer (built for the navy's Ordnance bureau) was developed, and which contributed to the growth and development of a revolutionary scientific and social tool.

These developments, coupled with the domination in faculty training of the twenty largest American universities, led to an increasing standardisation of faculty quality and training. The development of a critical academic press, and national journals of disciplinary importance, narrowed the range of 'acceptable' academic research. The historic American diversity in educational ideologies was largely removed from research and relegated to the teaching function, and more especially to marginal colleges supported by their own large parochial constituency. In a real sense, the higher-education system of the United States, by 1960, was largely 'nationalised' in content and in consensus about standards, even though it remained diverse in regional and management terms, and in self-professed goals. This development, naturally enough, was accompanied by institutional stratification and the emergence of at least a transitory national rank-ordering of 'good' colleges and universities.[3] This, in turn, led to a ferocious institutional competition among the front runners to gain a place in the top rank.

THE SECOND POSTWAR REVOLUTION

While the great American universities were becoming 'multiversities', or 'secular cathedrals', or agglomerations of scientifically trained manpower available to the 'contract state', or 'the shadow government of in-and-outers', American education was in fact being over-run by the children of the World War II generation. The 'baby boom' of 1945 arrived on the campus in the early 1960s. At precisely the same time, American economic growth and an egalitarian idiom in education made it possible for the lower-middle class to send their children to university (no doubt in part because of advertisements that argued that the university graduate would make much more money than the high-school graduate).

The growth of the graduate schools and university research excellence in the 1950s would no doubt have pleased the German founders of the system, but it would have worried the Scots. On the other hand, the 1960s broadening of the student class intake would have produced the reverse reaction. Certainly the intellectual 'descendants' of these two founding educational philosophies expressed such concerns. Small college teachers in the English tradition probably viewed both trends as a form of misguided enthusiasm.

The numbers themselves reveal how far-reaching these changes really were:

CURRENT AMERICAN HIGHER EDUCATION STATISTICS

	Number	*Enrolment*
Public institutions		
(1970)	1,089	6,371,008
Private institutions		
(1970)	1,467	2,127,109
Public higher education budget		
(1972)	$20,800,000,000	
Private higher education budget		
(1972)	$10,700,000,000	
Number of students		
(1960)	3,570,000	
(1970)	7,413,000	
(1971)	8,087,000	
(1975 est)	10,664,000	
Federal support for higher education		
(1965)	$2,053 million	
(1970)	$3,814 million	
(1972)	$5,330 million	

Source: *Statistical Abstract of the United States, 1972,* op cit, pp 102–38

With the older East Coast universities increasingly dominated by a *de facto* 'German' approach – scholarly excellence, research orientation, professionalism, elitism, and the smaller good colleges loyal to their English roots – academic excellence, teaching orientation, college loyalty, civility, it was left to public higher education to expand to meet the student flood and it did so with the very relevant 'Scottish' ideology: educational pragmatism, professionally relevant programme, socially responsive organisation, greater egalitarianism.

In the 1960s, public higher education grew very rapidly. State normal schools (teacher training colleges) were incorporated into the state university systems and were revolutionised by growth and the expansion of faculties. Perhaps the State University of New York is the most impressive example of this phenomenon.

A second style of growth was the incorporation, into state systems, of larger but financially weak private universities. The bankruptcy of the University of Pittsburgh brought it into the Pennsylvania state system; the once high-flying University of Houston was quietly incorporated into the University of Texas after its fiscal future became bleak.

The third area of growth, and perhaps the most remarkable, was in community colleges. The City University of New York is, of course, the equivalent of a state system, but the community colleges that spread throughout the counties of the United States made higher education as accessible as secondary schooling. They were tax-supported and hence almost 'free', they were local and hence no residential costs arose. Their programmes could be directly relevant to the skills local people needed; their two-year structure allowed the weak or poor student to compile a record of ability with which to apply at a more prestigious four-year college or university.

These developments, as judged by some faculty observers, were considered irrelevant to the work of the older research universities and the well-established public universities. Expanding public systems were sometimes judged to be 'factories' by small college faculties, alumni and administrators. But 'open admissions' and 'continuing education' were the most potent ideologies for higher education in the late 1960s.

The growth of student numbers proved difficult to public universities caught between social (political) needs to be responsive, and faculty-administration elite pretensions (and, in schools such as the University of California, Berkeley, the University of Michigan and University of Wisconsin, realities). In the first instance, such universities could hold off the 'fall in standards' by internal stratification – less qualified students were admitted at newer campuses of the state university system. When the university system ran out of spaces (thereby ensuring at least a minimum standard), state and community colleges expanded to meet the demand.[4] The difficulty lay in the fact that state and city legislators saw all higher education as one category of expenditure, and believed in the system(s) being roughly equal. Since elite education is more expensive than mass education as practised in most systems (in 1970, the gross cost per student in public institutions was $3,265; in private schools, $5,080), the elite institutions were sure to feel the financial pinch. This was especially true as new university systems went 'star shopping' for famous professors to lend public relations lustre to new red brick.

At about the same time, the public, the foundations and the federal government were moving away from support for science, social sciences and the graduate/research universities. Student turbulence, most marked at elite 'German' schools, was part of the problem. It was also in part a function of decreasing demand for such products as atomic physicists, Mandarin Chinese speakers and anthropologists trained for field work in Upper Volta, and in part the accentuation of domestic American concerns that made the disciplines in vogue in the 1950s and 1960s less interesting. Americans wanted community relations experts, not international relations specialists; they wanted someone able to talk with the blacks and chicanos, not the Russians and Chinese; they wanted to change the relative availability of these different, useful skills.

Moreover, a new federal enthusiasm for the poor and for under-privileged minority groups meant that a 'means test' was applied for new federal fellowship schemes. Federal guidelines for colleges and universities receiving federal support also called for a larger representation of minority groups – leading to a sometimes comic-opera-like search for 'admittable' black students – at precisely the time when primary and secondary education in the black ghettoes was *decreasing* in quality. This paradox, like most other American paradoxes, was most easily seen in New York City, where average reading skills and mathematics scores were declining in the principally black secondary schools while the City University of New York was announcing minority groups programmes and 'open admissions', and was recruiting star professors at $36,000 a year. One could believe that for New York City blacks, only *higher* education was accessible.

With great consistency, the federal government's concern with student balance rapidly became one focused on faculty 'balance' and, as women's movements became important, with the balance between the sexes. Almost all of these new quasi-statutory requirements were easier to meet in public higher-education systems, which were expanding and in which many student and faculty standards, as measured by elite academic criteria, were low, or in which some units were low. It was the elite, private, higher-education institutions, especially the test-case university, Columbia, dependent upon federal and foundation support for their expensive graduate research establishments, that found it most difficult to comply with egalitarian regulations backed up by 'denial' sanctions.

While fashions and approaches changed, higher education's cost per student rose 3 per cent per year in excess of price inflation and had done so since 1930. In 1972 the bill was over $21,000 million and with no inflation but with the projected increased student population forecast for 1980, it will be $40,000 million.

In the second postwar revolution, therefore, hard-pressed resources were switched from cold war to 'civil war' priorities in a very short period, and at a time when the trends toward nationalisation and egalitarianism in American higher education were increasingly triumphant.

INTELLECTUAL ROLES FOR 1980–99

By 1985–90, the United States will probably have made the transition to almost universal higher education, including in its constituencies persons of rather indifferent intellectual ability and an increasing number of post-university adults, in new forms of higher re-education. New higher education programmes will be configured for 'drop-outs' and one can confidently expect 'remedial' higher education over a wide range of skills and personalities. This will be essential to maintain high levels of social creativity in a largely service-oriented, high technology society in which social adaptation will be increasingly important.[5]

The first requirement of this kind of expanded system will be the development of human potential and personality: 'teach the student'. A growing population, increasingly concentrated in urban centres, with increasing leisure and less arduous physical work, will require the capacity for self-amusement and self-understanding to an ever-greater degree. The intellect and the creative arts are likely to be much more important in the ordinary person's life, both as spectator and creator, and media growth will require and allow very high levels of communication skills on the part of the population as a whole.

This kind of society will allow individuals a greater range of choice, but it will also require greater specific discipline in work roles, due to the increasing complexity of technical industry. One need think only of the control over nuclear energy, public health systems and strategic weapons to see the magnitude of the need for a 'zero defect' personality as well as technology. Expressive individualism will also grow, however, to create a necessary freedom to offset increasing needs for urban discipline and social *Gleischaltung*.

This need can probably be best met in some variant of 'English' higher education in which interpersonal relationships and a reflective individualism are developed around, but are not necessarily intrinsic to, substantive education. This suggests a return to collegiate, or at least smaller-scale and decentralised undergraduate education. This has proved to be a high unit-cost form of education, however, and will probably therefore be available only to the elite (as it is then defined as the children of the wealthy, of the faculty, or of the extremely poor). In contrast, experiments such as the 'University Without Walls' may be able to develop 'low capital investment' small-unit education.[6]

It also suggests that the community college model of the 1960s and 1970s likely to become an increasingly attractive educational device for reducing scale, diffusing students and faculty resources, meeting localised needs and feeding more professionalised institutions where larger numbers and greater concentration are desirable or inevitable.[7] The community colleges will have to develop arts and humanities with as much effort as they have vocational subjects. Moreover, some forms of non-residential association life that lead to a deeper interpersonal experience will have to be developed. These may exist in such vehicles as 'The Living Theater', so-called group-therapy techniques involving sensitivity training, simulation of social experience for educational purposes, and the periodic residential experience at conference sites or even in Esalen-type seminars. Psychiatrists and pyschologists with group experience and educational interests would obviously be useful planning officers for this kind of higher education, as they have increasingly become useful supplementary staff in the universities of the 1970s.

A second important function for the higher education of the last two decades of the twentieth century in America is the creation and protection of the independent intellect. Universities, whether elite, practical or socially responsive, have a common interest in sustaining the kind of society in which inquiry and intellectual/artistic independence is protected. No other major social institution has such an interest. The suborning of truth is a historic tendency of all self-interested institutions, whether clerical, political or commercial. In each case, the influential of any organisation are pursuing normative values – the true faith, national interest, profit – but they are calculating in the short term as well as the narrow field.

Artists and intellectuals also have a narrow interest around a prime value – truth and its expression, as best they can see it – and in an organised and collectivised world, the only secure major forum for the expression of such a value is the free university. This does not mean that higher education cannot also serve the true faith, national interest, profit or personal interest, but it cannot do so at the expense of its internal autonomy and commitment. 'Take it or leave it' contracts are not threatening; statutory controls and external direction are potentially destructive.

The great cost of inquiry in the late twentieth century, especially in the sciences, and a seemingly intractable problem of raising the marginal productivity of teaching labour, combine to suggest that significantly more public money will be needed by 1985 for almost all higher education – at least all higher education that attempts to create knowledge as well as disseminate it. If this is so, the problem of maintaining university autonomy against the state will fall increasingly on faculties whose bargaining position is likely to decline. This is a potential problem area of great importance.

A third role in this era will be a historic one: the generation of new knowledge. Research and inquiry lie at the heart of the critical method and the scientific method; in different terms but the same reality, they lie behind artistic expression and creativity. This is so widely recognised that it appears unlikely that support for research will be threatened between now and the later twentieth century, although the balance between disciplines and fields will be changed from time to time to reflect social funding investments.

There may be dangers that an increasing amount of scientific research is done in state and private laboratories for proprietary rather than scholarly purposes, or that a particular field is starved while others prosper in the 'contrast state', but there seems no institution as likely as the university to dominate almost all fields of basic science and intellectual speculation. There are almost no other social institutions with an 'agnostic' approach to the interests of other groups in the society. Professional standards in the academy offer it an independence and a critical self-awareness that is unusual in other bodies.

A fourth function of higher education – also traditional – is the systematic diffusion of knowledge. It seems increasingly clear that students learn as much from effect in the teaching situation as from the substance conveyed, and the teacher therefore is unlikely to be rendered redundant by the hardware of educational technology that is increasingly evident in secondary education. The number of contact hours necessary for a teacher of, say, basic mathematics, languages, descriptive history and geography may be reduced; this will leave more time for other kinds of teaching and more interesting student-teacher relations.

As class, aptitude and experience criteria for admission cease to have a relatively narrowing effect, the range of student responses to traditional materials will vary greatly. A much more systematic review of method effectiveness will have to be done, and a more conscious effort paid to the psychological dimension of education across different social groups. Specialist teachers will probably emerge in all disciplines to deal with different kinds of education programmes.

Almost all higher education will probably be increasingly influenced by the social sciences. Physical sciences can, and probably will, be taught earlier than at present. Arts, humanities and social sciences, unlike basic tool disciplines, are more directly relevant to the 'humanscope', and to the kinds of interdependencies that will exist in the period. Social complexity will require greater social awareness; increasing egalitarianism will require the evolution of new kinds of conventions and consensus-creating myths and processes; increasing social turbulence will require new kinds of self-management and self-awareness skills.

In terms of historic university values, all four of these roles have ancient antecedents and there is a large measure of agreement, in academic circles at least, about their legitimacy. What is lacking is an educational system that can meet them all. Therefore, the relative balance given each of the factors becomes the critical variable. In a large and diverse society, there is probably no need to overstandardise institutions. There is, indeed, much to be said for a more explicit institutional commitment to one or two of these values, allowing the prospective student and supportive society at large to judge 'success' according to their own values.

The problem to be faced is forced by the sheer scale of universal higher education, its costs and its management. There is no way in which these problems can be successfully managed while maximising all of the roles of the university. So it cannot be forecast what choices governments, foundations, university administrators and faculties will make in responding to scarcity. To a degree, legal statutes are involved and they foretell greater egalitarianism and social heterogeneity in all institutions of higher education. To a degree, costs and resources are variable, but the greater the resource constraint, the more narrow the ability of the university to adopt high-cost values (development of student personality, research). The more dependent the university becomes on external resources, the less easily can it protect its autonomy although such support does allow maximum diffusion of some kinds of knowledge through teaching.

By 1990 the great wave of ever-expanding student numbers, at least younger undergraduates, will have receded because of the low birth rates in the early 1970s. Actual student numbers, however, are likely to continue to increase as higher education becomes a part of a normal professional life of 're-education'. A structured and systematic diffusion of the new knowledge will continue to be required, and it is likely that the higher-education world will provide it. Increasing leisure will provide more people with the time to pursue education-as-recreation, or as training for a second or third profession. Higher and middle management in the United States already is characterised by great flexibility and lateral movement across fields. This is likely to expand to other sectors of society. Higher education allows social mobility, a necessary function in a society dedicated to change and development.

As higher education becomes a near-universal system, it will almost surely develop greater specialisation/differentiation in order to meet its several demands. Colleges and universities for the young must emphasise social development as well as intellectual growth; schools for the disadvantaged must generate new kinds of teaching methods and evaluation procedures; research institutes require very special management and educational theory; the up-coming wave of mid-career and re-training education for older students requires different kinds of curriculum, approach and measurement.

In sum, American higher education near the turn of the century will probably be universal in scope, much more diverse in organisation and process than at present, more highly differentiated in function, and increasingly dependent upon governmental support. In undergraduate education there will be a greater emphasis on personal growth and less on early professionalisation/specialisation.[8] Research may be housed in universities and integrated into graduate instruction, but it will be increasingly autonomous. Teaching itself will continue to be the greatest part of the university enterprise, whether aspects of it are automated or not, although the prestige of the teaching profession will probably continue to slip *vis-à-vis* its professional peer-occupations of medicine, the law and management.

SOCIAL ROLES FOR 1980–99

In the 1960s major universities emerged as 'secular cathedrals'. They were lavishly endowed, monopolised certain important social functions, provided the country with its highest managers as well as its stock of ideas, and became for a generation of younger people a kind of attractive life-style.[9]

American universities became patrons of the arts. Many of the best buildings in modern architecture are on campuses; the Metropolitan Opera's tour season was dominated by college bookings; most major American sculptors are represented best on university plazas and sculpture gardens; modern dance groups can exist in profusion because colleges and universities constitute such a large 'market' for culture.

University health services constituted, after the military, the most successful 'socialised medicine' in the country; psychological counselling and services were more available, per capita, in higher education than anywhere else in society. Dieticians looked after the eating habits of students; university athletic directors looked after their competitive physical urges, campus police their security. Student groups were organised to look after social, recreational, political and economic needs. And the entire structure was relatively isolated from the constraints of family pressures, job-performance requirements and a large number of personal obligations.

Faculty members were also among the most privileged members of society. They had high status, and in the 1960s their income was rising much faster than many occupations. They were the last major professional group to have 'free time' over the summer and vacation holidays, during the week, when typically they spent only 15 hours in the classroom, and in terms of their own freedom of expression. In most universities, they were beneficiaries of the social-welfare system designed (and justified) for students.

It seems small wonder that so many bright students wanted to become professors in the 1950s and 1960s. The life was good, free, secure (if tenured) and intellectually invigorating. One could be a moralist/idealist in a well-paid search for truth, especially useful truth, and the activist professor would also have the opportunity to become a government consultant or television commentator. There was great mobility between institutions and from region to region in the country, and foundations and government made frequent research leave possible under the most desirable conditions.

The secular cathedral not only attracted would-be clerics; it attracted as well would-be believers and supplicants. The 'college town' became the most attractive address for stockbrokers and bankers. The middle classes found it difficult to move too far from alma mater and its concerts, library and community programmes. Better teachers in primary and secondary schools enjoyed teaching the children of educators, while earning additional degrees at the local teachers' college. The working classes enjoyed higher education's expansive years, because expansion created jobs as education became one of the nation's highest 'growth industries'.

By 1970 educational expansion, especially at the great universities of the country, had slowed to a walk, and for some to a recessional. Costs had skyrocketed as universities did more things for students and staff, as the information explosion led to groaning library shelves and weighty acquisitions budgets, as specialisation within the academy led to ever more courses of ever greater specialisation for fewer students, and as inflation attendant on the Vietnam era drove the costs of construction and services for the university to record heights.

The production of would-be professors exceeded the absorptive growth of colleges and universities as college after college restyled itself 'university' and began awarding graduate degrees, often with the most slender of pretexts. The only way to 'hold' good professors, it was argued, was to let them have their own graduate programme. This led to professors teaching fewer students, and graduate students teaching undergraduates. This system was viable only as long as the graduate students could become professors in their own right, and as universities ceased to expand, the system's logic collapsed. And thus appeared the much-feared 'PhD glut'. Newspapers carried stories of PhDs in engineering working as masons; of EdDs working as primary school teachers – even of PhDs in comparative literature driving taxicabs.

The federal government and foundations, having lavishly bought the universities into expensive scientific and area study programmes, lost interest in them, and cut back resources. The student turbulence of the 1960s, produced in part by the wider social tension of the period and partially by the vast growth in numbers and heterogeneity, cost the colleges and universities alumni support and general social approval. Parents of undergraduates were annoyed that their children, sent off to be taught by professors, found themselves with graduate students instead. The 'high life' of the university brought with it envy as well as appreciation. These several problems found the universities divided within and depressed without; human problems were compounded by resource problems in a country in which university prestige was rapidly declining.[10]

The poor and alienated of the society had by the 1960s determined to take advantage of higher education to earn access to its resources. The idea of 'community and neighbourhood services' was a historic one to minimise 'town versus gown' problems. When the civil-rights movement developed in the US, undergraduates quickly saw their own universities as potential allies in the struggle and attempted to commit their elders and administrators to the fray. Nothing could have been more foreign to most university professors and administrators. The working classes employed by universities also moved to better their position and used undergraduate egalitarian sentiments to demand higher wages and better conditions from their employers. Neighbours of universities laid siege to the special privileges of the university in an attempt to take advantage of the local 'fat'.[11]

This was a period in which the foundations and federal government became increasingly concerned with minority groups and the poor, and began using their resources, financial and legal, to 'encourage universities' to follow an external lead. The secular cathedral was asked to become the parish church of the masses.

This was also the period in which the state governments in the United States rapidly expanded their higher-education systems, and when county and city community colleges rapidly developed. Older universities found themselves competing for students in a situation in which their high tuition charges accompanied their high status, but in which fully subsidised state education was available and tax dollars were being used to raid professors from high-status private universities.

Whatever might have been the confusions of the period, the reality was an extraordinary diffusion of talent throughout the country and across an ever-broadening range of institutions. The financial squeeze within elite universities led to a greater commitment to teaching, especially cost-effective undergraduate teaching, while research languished. The financial squeeze with state and community colleges restricted new employment and held large numbers of professors at their rank and salary plateaux. Students unable to afford quality universities went to public institutions of indifferent standard or demoralised condition, and were often frustrated. Students attending the great private universities sometimes found their social services crimped and their teachers demoralised, especially the young who were unlikely to earn tenure in a zero-growth system. The crisis of contraction in American higher education was essentially among the clerics.[12]

In 1975 the American higher-education system begins to 'bottom-out' of its crisis. Ten years of constraints and the development of new philosophies and management approaches have created new kinds of institutions. The magnitude of the problem prompts both foundations and government to re-address the problems of funding for higher education. Private contributions will rise after the disasters of the 1960s. Public support for higher education broadens, and the capital plant of most universities will by the late 1970s and 1980s have been largely built to accommodate the kinds and numbers of students who will be entering the system. Faculty expectations will have been lowered, and fewer graduate students will seek an academic post. Inter-institutional mobility will be reduced, and there will be more faculty commitment to the kinds of institutions in which they serve.

In this period of post-consolidation development, university managers will have to develop new approaches to relevant education for a post-industrial society. Interclass educational experiences will have to be developed, and the university as a research centre will have to be able to address new kinds of problems, perhaps less technological and more social. Higher-quality universities will have to link themselves, and not in any lofty manner, to community colleges and to organisations in which mid-career education is decisive. Universities will have to develop the procedures of consultancy with their communities and neighbourhood groups, while maintaining the autonomy that their function requires.[13]

It seems almost inevitable that the departmental/disciplinary organisation, and its attendant degree structure,[14] of the historic university will have to be changed, and that the exclusivist/guild nature of faculty tenure and employment will also be changed to accommodate wider recruitment and the development of greater faculty capabilities.[15] This may be more easily accomplished in the new state universities and community colleges that have little commitment to a historic form in which their 'poor cousin' status is only too clear. The research universities have already developed multidisciplinary groups and nontenured research appointments that allow greater flexibility than traditional teaching appointments; the ratio between the two will shift toward the former.

The historic functions of the Western university will continue to characterise the American university in the later twentieth century. It seems equally likely that the same kind of talents will be necessary for their successful functioning, and that there will not be a revolutionary discontinuity in the process of higher learning.

It also seems likely that American higher education will continue to be characterised by diversity – in standards, styles, procedures, curriculum and success, by fragmentation and differentiation – due to funding sources, constituency and historical legacy, and by growth toward a near-universal higher-education system. The historic American bias toward egalitarianism will continue to be opposed by the elitism inherent in the goal of educational excellence and measured achievement.

The greatest changes likely in the next twenty years concern the students, who will increasingly include the poor, disadvantaged and older student groups. This will lead to the further development of social-welfare developments within higher education, and will alter its structure by destroying old expectation-levels. Universities are likely to become social microcosms of very representative characteristics, although this will be more marked in new colleges and universities than in elite schools.

Higher education will broaden its concerns and its practices, although probably different schools will specialise in various concerns and approaches, and the educational process will expand far from the guild rules and origins that have proved so persistent. The educational forms, therefore, will be hardly recognisable by the turn of the century, although their goals and functions will be remarkably similar to those of the past.

3
The University in Australia

W. G. WALKER

Australia should look towards the day when appropriate higher education can be provided for all who seek it . . . Australia needs a co-ordinated system of higher education. This will best be served by the development of a diversity of institutions offering a multiplicity of courses to cater for a wide range of individual needs and preferences. The system should not be constructed on the basis of two or three narrowly specified types of institutions, since students do not fall into simply defined groups such as those with analytical minds and those with practical minds, or those with vocational interests and those with non-vocational interests.

> Extract from *The Armidale Statement* issued by the Conference on Planning in Higher Education (August 1969)

The inner suburbs of Sydney and Melbourne, which house Australia's oldest universities, were built during the industrial and commercial boom of the late nineteenth century. They are strongly reminiscent of English big city suburbs developed during the same period. Mile upon mile of terraced and semi-detached houses, interspersed with rather grim factories, small pubs, corner shops and occasional skimpy parks, point high-pitched roofs, designed to shed snow, towards snowless skies.

The late-nineteenth-century citizens of the Sydney suburbs of Paddington and Lewisham ate, dressed and thought very much like their relatives in the suburbs of the same name in London. Their law, language and religions were those of Britain; their newspapers were modelled on those of 'home'; their entertainments were imported from 'the old country'. But 'home' for the Australians consisted not only of England, but of Wales, Ireland (as much as one-third of the population in the early nineteenth century was Irish) and Scotland. There were significant groups from other lands, but it was the convict, settler and gold-digger from Britain who played the major role in shaping Australian society. Yet there were fundamental differences in experience and outlook which, even in the colonial era, marked off the Australian as unique[1] and which, today, continue to puzzle the naïve observer of Australian society. Nowhere are these differences more marked than in approaches to formal education.

Education was a function of the colonial government long before the home government took any responsibility for formal schooling.[2] By 1848 New South Wales had established a 'national system' of public education with its roots in Irish practice. Later developments, especially in the twentieth century, had their roots in Scotland. From 1848 to the present day, and especially since 1900, 'state' or 'government' or 'public' education has been marked by an emphasis upon centralisation of administration and governance and a rampant egalitarianism. The ghosts of John Knox and Scottish democracy have never been far from the government schools.[3]

This has not been true of the 'independent' or 'non-government' schools and the universities, which have developed very much in the English upper-class tradition of decentralised governance and elitism. The government schools developed in a free, compulsory and secular ethos. The schools for the elite were anything but free, anything but compulsory and anything but secular. Significantly, one of the oldest of these in New South Wales is still named The King's School. Such schools for much of Australia's history provided the great mass of university students and especially of those destined for the high professions.[4]

As was to be expected, it was the social and economic elite of the colonies which called for the establishment of universities in Australia. These institutions, opened amid vice-regal pomp, were strongly reminiscent of 'home' and the arguments surrounding the oldest foundations reflected the Oxbridge-London schism of the period.[5] Would the proposed University of Sydney, for example, be a secular institution like London, or would it impose religious tests as did the ancient foundations? Ultimately the Act for the establishment of the University of Sydney (1850) took a middle path: the university was to be a secular teaching and examining institution which, however, was obliged to facilitate the establishment of residential colleges which might be religious foundations. By royal charter the infant university was granted the right to award degrees, to be regarded as equal to the degrees of the universities of the United Kingdom. Thus Sydney, and all universities founded subsequently, have inherited directly by charter the British traditions of academic freedom and academic autonomy. All have been state or national universities. None have been private or religious foundations. All have remained until recently very much under the influence of the British universities, though an important exception to this is the Australian emphasis on pass rather than honours degrees.

By 1911 there were six universities in Australia: Sydney (1850), Melbourne (1853), Adelaide (1874), Tasmania (1890), Queensland (1909) and Western Australia (1911).[6] Forty years later there had been no increase in this number, though two university colleges had been established, one at Armidale (1938) in association with the University of Sydney and one at Canberra (1929) in association with the University of Melbourne. These institutions became, respectively, the University of New England in 1954 and the Australian National University in 1960. One other university was established in Sydney during 1949. Originally entitled the New South Wales University of Technology, its title was changed to the University of New South Wales in 1958. This university in turn took responsibility for colleges at Newcastle (now the University of Newcastle), Wollongong (to become an autonomous institution in 1975) and Broken Hill, and for a faculty of military studies at the Royal Military College at Duntroon in the Australian Capital Territory.

Since the mid-1950s new universities have been established in Melbourne (Monash and Latrobe), Sydney (Macquarie), Adelaide (Flinders) and Townsville (James Cook University of North Queensland). New universities are at present being established in Brisbane (Griffith) and Perth (Murdoch) and there are long-range plans for a further university in New South Wales at Campbelltown near Sydney. There are also plans for another metropolitan university at Dandenong near Melbourne and a university at the new 'growth centre' of Albury-Wodonga which spans the New South Wales and Victorian borders on the Murray River. At the time of writing the Victorian government has announced plans for a university situated on three campuses in the provincial cities of Ballarat, Bendigo and Geelong. Further, the Australian government has expressed interest in an 'open university'.

After 125 years of history the role of the university in Australian society might reasonably be summarised as:

(1) preparation for the professions and quasi-professions;
(2) research and scholarship;
(3) service to society.

There was never a time in Australian history when more than a sprinkling of students in universities were there because they were interested in 'learning for its own sake'. They have almost invariably been heavily professionally and vocationally oriented. Research and scholarship, too, have been a major function of Australian universities, especially during the last twenty-five years. Indeed, a continuing theme of the last two decades has been a criticism of the university teacher's interest in research and his lack of interest in teaching.

With regard to service, the professors of the nineteenth century often played a major role in establishing scholarly and cultural societies, speaking at public lectures and in mechanics' institutes and schools of arts, and writing to the press on matters of public importance. With the coming of the Workers' Educational Association in the early twentieth century, an increasing number of university staff took part in adult education activities. In recent decades, university personnel also sit on a large number of governmental commissions and committees, act as consultants to individual organisations and provide varied forms of expert public service.

THE UNIVERSITY IN CONTEMPORARY SOCIETY

The role of the university in the future, as in the past, will inevitably be a function of its interaction with the society in which it exists. In an address to the Armidale Conference on Planning in Higher Education during 1969, Clark Kerr of the Carnegie Commission on Higher Education, speaking on the topic 'The Speed of Change: Towards 2000 AD',[7] adopted Peter Drucker's phrase 'the age of discontinuity'. Kerr referred to six discontinuities affecting higher education as the world approaches the year 2000. These discontinuities, which apply just as obviously to Australia as to the USA and most other Western societies, are:

(1) from elite to middle class to universal higher education;
(2) from ivory tower to public freeway;

(3) from workers versus capitalists to intellectuals versus the common man;

(4) from managerial to representative to participatory governance;

(5) from functions related to production to functions related to consumption;

(6) from libraries and laboratories to computers.

These are real discontinuities in Australian society; the existence of at least some of them will be obvious in the pages which follow. Kerr made no claims to prophecy but he emphasised that developments in the year 2000 will be substantially affected by the quality of decisions in the intervening period.

What are the tendencies in society which might influence the decisions of men 'in the intervening period' and hence the role of the university in the 1980s and 1990s? No less in Australia than in any other country, education is a political animal,[8] and in Australia at least, is becoming increasingly so. Fitzgerald[9] points out that in 1971 one sitting of the federal parliament saw 163 questions asked and 264 references about education recorded in the Hansard Index, while petitions on education were presented on twenty-six occasions. By comparison, in the two sittings of the federal parliament in 1965 only one petition was presented and fewer than half as many questions about education were asked.

Some parts of the political animal 'education' are extremely sensitive to the world around them; other parts are less sensitive, and among these has been the university, which as a result of its relative isolation from society and its high degree of autonomy has often proved remarkably resistant to change.

Yet pressures from both inside and outside the university are increasing, and some tendencies in society are crystal clear.[10] These tendencies include:

(1) the declining influence of Britain on Australia's economic, political and cultural life, following her withdrawal from South-East Asia and her relationship with the European Common Market; and a concomitant growing influence of, firstly, the USA and Canada as the English-speaking nations of the Pacific Basin form links in the face of Asian trading and military blocs, and, secondly, the Asian nations themselves, as they seek to develop trading and military links with Australia;

(2) the escalation of the knowledge explosion, coupled with the demand for

yet more and higher-level education and for formal qualifications to mark the completion of the various stages of education;

(3) the growing educational sophistication of the Australian population, with a concomitant decline in the mythology of education and a growing interest in, and demand for a say in, the development of educational policies;

(4) the growing recognition of the need to plan ahead for the development of national resources, including specifically human resources;

(5) the growing tendency to look to the Australian government rather than to the state governments for leadership in educational matters.

It would be naïve to pretend that these are the only forces likely to have a major impact on the development of Australian universities; it would be equally naïve to attempt to ignore any of them.

The first and second tendencies highlight the fact that the Australian universities, with those of New Zealand, very much part of the British university 'club' in the 1940s and 1950s, drew distinctly closer in the 1960s and 1970s to the North American university world. This tendency will, almost certainly, grow during the 1980s and 1990s.

The same tendency will affect curriculum. Schools of Asian studies or Asian civilisation, departments of Asian languages and the like, will surely grow in size and significance in universities. It is likely, too, that there will be increasing demands on university schools of anthropology, education, forestry, geology and agriculture, for example.

Australia is *in* the East, but is not *of* the East. The supersonic jet, cheap air fares and the English language will ensure that for the period under review, at least, the Australian university world will retain many links with Britain and will develop increasingly strong links with North America.

The second tendency suggests that the Australian people's concern for, and interest in, higher education will increase during the next two decades. By the 1970s Australian universities were admitting in proportion to the population aged seventeen to twenty-two, nearly twice the number of students entering United Kingdom universities. Further, large numbers of tertiary-education* institutions were being established or enlarged throughout the nation, and occupations which thirty years ago would never have recruited applicants with so much as university-

* Tertiary education is in this chapter defined as, to quote the 1971 *Report on Education in South Australia*, 'comprising courses the standard of entry for which involves the completion of full secondary schooling . . .'

entrance qualifications were calling for university degrees. The Australian penchant for formal pieces of paper to mark the end of stages of secondary education was rapidly producing a similar 'diploma elite' at the stages of tertiary education.

The demand for such education by Australians was already growing rapidly by the early 1970s. Borrie has predicted that the number of persons aged seventeen to twenty-two will reach 1,564,222 by 1986 (compared with 1,170,770 in 1966), but that in about the same period the number of students enrolling in tertiary studies will *double*.[11] If this is so, the total enrolment in tertiary-education institutions in 1986 should reach 350,000, of whom approximately half will be in universities. (In 1968 the total tertiary enrolment was only 144,548, the number in universities being 100,295.)

The pattern is similar in all states. The Government of South Australia report on Education in South Australia (1971) predicted that the number of tertiary students would rise from 18,500 in 1970 to about 36,000 in 1981 – an increase of about two-thirds in the propensity of seventeen to twenty-two year olds to attend tertiary institutions.[12] In that state the numbers enrolling from the seventeen to nineteen age group in 1981 would represent 32 per cent of a generation, though in terms of one calculation no less than 40 per cent of a generation by that year would enrol at one stage or another during their life-time.

In Western Australia forward planning for the 1980s had reached an advanced stage by 1972: the Tertiary Education Commission, influenced by Perth's Corridor Plan, was predicting 50,000 students by 1989 compared with only 19,000 in 1972.[13]

With regard to the third tendency, the 1970s have already seen the beginning of the end of the mythology of education. Increasingly, as the cost of higher education escalates, and the level of education in the community rises, the populace is asking embarrassing questions about whether education is really the social saviour which its protagonists claim and about the extent to which society is 'getting its money's worth'.[14]

This tendency reflects a healthy scepticism about the allocation and use of public funds, the decisions of 'autonomous' institutions in expending those funds and the apparent irresponsibility of a proportion of university staff in the face of demonstrated community needs. It also refers to the behaviour and attitudes of university students, whose outspoken criticisms and demonstrations, especially in the 1960s, aroused the anger of large sections of the population and, as in North America and Europe, produced some demands for reductions in the funds allocated to universities until they learned to put their own houses in order. This public demand for accountability is likely to increase markedly in the 1980s and 1990s.

The fourth and fifth tendencies intermesh closely. For almost two decades the processes of planning and developing university facilities in Australia have been moving away from the state to the national arena. For the last decade or so this has been true of other forms of tertiary education as well and the decision of the Australian government, accepted by the states in mid-1973, to accept full financial responsibility for all tertiary education has *de facto* if not *de jure* placed the whole future development and rationalisation of education at this level squarely in Canberra's lap. The Australian government has announced the establishment, in addition to the existing universities and advanced education commissions, of a Sub-Tertiary Technical and Further Education Commission. The existence of these three bodies in company with the Schools Commission and the Pre-Schools Commission virtually ensures the appointment of a 'Commission of Commissions' to plan and supervise Australian education generally during the two decades under discussion.

THE UNIVERSITIES IN THE 1970s

All of the tendencies referred to above date from World War II. Before the war the universities, all state institutions, were distinctly provincial in character. The entry of Japan into the war in 1941 rapidly stimulated the interest of the Australian government in the work of the universities and this interest grew further under pressure from the demands of post-war reconstruction. In 1957 the Menzies Government appointed a committee under the chairmanship of Sir Keith Murray, (significantly) chairman of the University Grants Committee of the United Kingdom, to inquire into the role of the university, the extension and co-ordination of university facilities, technological education at university level and the financial needs of universities. The Murray Report[15] was sympathetically received by the government which not only made large sums of money available to the universities in order to rehabilitate them, but also undertook to set up an Australian Universities Commission

(AUC) with functions not unlike those of the United Kingdom body.

During the 1950s the government of the United Kingdom, facing problems of postwar construction even more daunting than those facing Australia, had expanded higher-education opportunities through the establishment of colleges of advanced technology (CATs) which were to provide advanced technical education in parallel with the universities. The 'binary' system so established aroused considerable interest in Australia; the Australian government's later acceptance of something like the British binary-type model (but with 'parity of esteem'), and its apparent rejection of the Californian three-step hierarchical model, have presented Australia with a major educational problem for the next two decades for the role of the university, once so clear-cut, is to many shrouded with uncertainty.

Until the 1960s 'higher education' in Australia had referred only to university education. The courses offered in teachers' colleges, agricultural colleges and technical colleges, the great majority of which were controlled by state-government departments, were not generally recognised by universities as being of tertiary quality. However, demand for university places and a considerable criticism of university teaching standards and failure rates, coupled with state interest in future tertiary developments, led the Commonwealth Government in 1961 to establish the Committee on the Future of Tertiary Education in Australia under the chairmanship of Sir Leslie Martin.[16] The committee's charge was rather like that presented to the Robbins Committee in the United Kingdom. It was asked to report not only upon universities, but upon technological institutions, technical and other colleges and teachers' colleges.

The committee made recommendations for the relief and expansion of universities, but also called for the large-scale development of colleges of advanced education (CAEs) with 'parity of esteem', some to be based on single existing technical, agricultural or teacher-education institutions, some to grow out of combinations of such institutions and others to be established *de novo*. Each state was to set up autonomous 'institutes of colleges' to plan, co-ordinate and accredit the non-university sector, and the AUC was to be expanded to become a tertiary education commission which would ensure 'a balanced development of all forms of tertiary education in Australia'.

Any understanding of the role of the university in the future must be based on the developments which have followed the Martin Report. Several of the report's recommendations have been adopted by the Australian government; others have not. For example, the proposal for a national tertiary-education commission was rejected: the AUC was retained and a new body, the Commonwealth Advisory Committee on Advanced Education (CACAE) was established to serve the non-university sector. Again, although the report recommended against the expansion of external teaching in universities, this has in fact been expanded.

None the less, the main thrust of the Martin Report has found expression in government policy, though in very different ways in each state. In New South Wales, the oldest and most populous state, a Universities Board co-ordinates the activities of the universities and an Advanced Education Board those of the colleges of advanced education, while a Higher Education Board, in turn, co-ordinates both of these. The state teachers' colleges which have not become CAEs were until recently under the control of the Department of Education, but have all become single-purpose or multipurpose CAEs or lost their existence through formal linkage with an adjoining university or CAE. It is important to notice that all of the CAEs, including the NSW Institute of Technology, are to become degree-granting, following accreditation by state bodies and the Australian Council on Awards in Advanced Education. Thus, the scene in New South Wales is one of a wide spectrum of tertiary-level institutions, all granting degrees, and all operating under a loose but effective co-ordinating ministry.

Another state, thinly populated Western Australia, has provided a model for all others with its Tertiary Education Commission which co-ordinates all forms of higher education and is concerned with long-term planning in the field. At the other extreme is the small but thickly populated state of Victoria. Three universities serve the vast metropolis of Melbourne, and as far as the Australian Universities Commission is concerned, a fourth metropolitan university is mooted. The state government, however, apparently without consultation with the AUC, has promised a new tri-campus rural university. The state has established an Institute of Colleges, which co-ordinates the work of the fourteen institutes of technology, and a separate State College Board which co-ordinates the many institutions which were until recently teachers' colleges.

The agricultural colleges meanwhile remain under the control of the Victorian Department of Agriculture.[17] There is no co-ordinating ministry as in New South Wales, though there is an advisory Council on Tertiary Education with a full-time chairman.

Obviously, largely unco-ordinated developments like this, within even one state, cannot be permitted to go on if the nation's resources are to be expended efficiently and economically.

The election of a Labour government in Canberra in December 1972 after more than twenty years of Liberal rule set the scene for a national co-ordination and rationalisation of higher education. The new government made a considerable impact on higher education in Australia for at least the next two decades, for the policies espoused are exceedingly difficult for any following governments to reverse. The major policies adopted are basically concerned with *access* to higher education. They include:

(1) The acceptance by the Australian government of responsibility for all costs associated with tertiary education. This policy replaces the previous policy of 'matching grants' under which the state governments paid $1.85 for every $1 of recurrent expenditure and $1 for every $1 of capital expenditure paid to the state universities by the Australian government.

(2) The acceptance by the Australian government of responsibility for the payment of all tuition fees and other compulsory fees (except union, sports union and student representative council fees) for full-time, part-time and external students accepted by institutions of higher education. Individual students are to be paid a living allowance and an incidental expenses allowance on the basis of a means test; unlike previous Australian government scholarships and allowances, these are restricted to no age limit.

(3) The establishment by the AUC at the request of the Australian government of a committee to enquire into extra-mural teaching at university level.

A development of considerable importance for certain Australian universities during the last twenty years was the development of teaching by external studies. This approach was pioneered by the University of Queensland and was later required of the University of New England in terms of its charter.[18] Since that time Macquarie University in Sydney, which specialises in teaching science subjects externally, has entered the field. However, teaching by external studies is envisaged for the new university to be established at Albury-Wodonga. In addition to universities, some institutes of technology and colleges of advanced education also offer external programmes.

Whatever type of 'open university' approach the government's committee recommends, whether it be the establishment of a single, central open university on the British model or the development of several integrated 'internal-external' universities like New England, it is certain that the tradition of external teaching will be encouraged and developed in Australia during the next two decades.

THE ENIGMA OF THE 1970s: THE COLLEGES OF ADVANCED EDUCATION

As has been shown, the most notable development following the publication of the Martin Report was the development of a system of higher education which in some senses paralleled that of the universities. A crucial 1965 decision to design these colleges for 'those students who, though qualified, do not wish to undertake a full university course' and a later decision to equate salaries in CAEs with those in universities have given them a particular shape. The new institutions, variously termed colleges of advanced education, institutes of technology, institutes of advanced education and state colleges (but all referred to in this chapter as CAEs) have aroused a great deal of discussion in Australian academic circles. These institutions will enrol an increasing proportion of students in tertiary education, so their influence on the future role of the university is likely to be considerable. As Barbara Burn perceptively describes their role:

> In effect, they are providing studies which are offered at universities in such countries as Canada and the United States but which have not yet been judged compatible with the academic emphasis of Australian universities.[19]

By the early 1970s the nature of the differentiation between the roles of the two institutions was a recurring theme. The Australian Universities Committee wrote in its Fifth Report:

> Many people in universities appear to be troubled about the confusion which they believe exists in the relative roles of universities and colleges. In the Commission's view the only situation in which confusion would be likely to arise would be if the colleges were to become more like universities than they are at present . . . this Commission would not regard the Australian arrange-

ment as constituting a binary system of tertiary education, rather it believes that the proper way of viewing it is as a continuum of educational opportunities.

The Commonwealth Advisory Committee on Advanced Education (later the Australian Commission on Advanced Education) pointed out in its Third Report that it was concerned to note signs that the basic purpose of the colleges, which was to increase the range of opportunities for tertiary education having a strong practical application, was tending to be changed by academic pressures and a demand for courses leading to senior degrees. None the less, the commission did not feel that overall the colleges were failing in their commitment to essentially vocational and community orientation. However, a sober warning was given:

> If colleges should ever emphasize research at the expense of undergraduate teaching, or concentrate on full-time students to the exclusion of part-time students, or give priority to degree courses while diploma courses are allowed to languish, or accept students and appoint staff solely on the grounds that they have obtained certain traditional academic qualifications, or divert their attentions away from the technological and social needs of the community, then the college system will have failed.

Somewhat smugly (and, as it turned out, inaccurately) the commissioners commented that it was encouraging to find that the uncertainties about the role of colleges were not found within the colleges themselves!

The AUC, apparently speaking on behalf of those who *were* uncertain about the roles of the two institutions, went to a great deal of trouble in this Third Report to spell out the basic differences. These were:

(1) The vocational emphasis is greater in the courses offered by colleges.
(2) The academic staffs of universities have a commitment to research . . . Although some research activities will occur in colleges, the staffs' commitment is essentially to teaching.
(3) The universities offer higher degrees by research work. The colleges do not offer such degrees.
(4) Some colleges offer some courses of a lower level than university courses.

Further, the commission pointed out, the colleges usually have lower entry standards in terms of academic qualifications, they have a greater commitment to part-time studies than have universities, they have a more direct relationship with the future employers of their graduates, they employ relatively fewer staff of the equivalent of professorial rank and they attract students whose interests are more vocational than abstract.

To even the most casual observer with recent experience in Britain or North America, the 'official' distinctions between the institutions read like Canute's commands to the waves. They seem to represent a desperate effort to avoid facing up to the realities of the blurring of roles and to the realities of status differentiation.

Already the lines between the universities and colleges with regard to territorial imperatives are sometimes blurred.[20] A good example of the blurring of roles is seen in the field of agriculture. As Lazenby described the situation in 1972,

> Present relationships between Universities and Colleges of Advanced Education are . . . at best ill-defined or fluid and often non-existent . . . it is unlikely in the foreseeable future that the responsibilities between the two types of tertiary institutions will be able to be clearly drawn. After all, both give courses suitable for training for employment as extension and advisory officers, farm management consultants and secondary school teachers; even some of the farmers and farm managers are trained in universities.[21]

But if lines are blurred, statuses are not, as perceptive observers from abroad have been quick to see. Eric Robinson, then of North-West London Polytechnic, a strong-minded product of what Trow[22] calls the 'managed' or 'controlled' binary system, gave a clear indication of battles to come when he spoke in 'non-binary' Australia in 1970:

> Most of the discussion I have heard [in Australia] presumes a 'steady state' situation in higher education . . . We read, for example, that the CAEs are to be complementary to the universities, to do the work that the universities are not doing, to apply the knowledge that universities are discovering. I find this type of analysis unsatisfactory because it presumes that the universities have a fixed, clearly-defined role and I do not think this can be so . . . What we have to look for is a dynamic model . . . The role of the colleges is to set the pattern of the university of the future, not to help preserve the university of the past.[23]

LOOKING TOWARDS 1999

The political tendencies referred to earlier in this chapter point to significant developments in the 1980s and 1990s.

The decline of the historic cultural, economic and military links with Britain and the strengthening of links with North America, coupled with the rapidly increasing demand for higher education in Australia in the mid-1970s, suggests a swing in Australian thinking towards the adoption of North American models for mass higher education. It is doubtful whether under such circumstances the university-CAE 'parity of esteem' system can survive.

The most likely emergent model is that apparently rejected by the Martin Committee in 1964 – the Californian model of junior (or community) college, state college and university. Interest in junior colleges has been growing rapidly and the country's first community college had, at the time of writing, just been established at Darwin in the Northern Territory. By the 1990s the nation's twenty-five or so universities established before 1980 (there are eighteen in 1975) are likely to remain at the apex of the educational pyramid, together with five or six of the major institutes of technology. All of these will award the doctor's degree. *Below* them (despite all protestations of 'parity of esteem') will lie the nation's many multipurpose and single-purpose tertiary institutes of technology and colleges of advanced education, all of which will award bachelor's and master's degrees. *Below* them again will lie the community colleges and, where they have survived, the technical colleges. The universities will be more concerned with preparation for the 'high' professions and the emerging 'high' professions, the colleges with the 'low' professions and the emerging 'low' professions, the universities more with pure research, the colleges more with applied research, the universities with high-level community service, the colleges with that of a lower level. Of course, these lines will be by no means clearly drawn, but the universities, to assert their seniority, will deliberately have set out to develop research institutes, graduate schools and 'think tanks'. They will thus tend to be more elitist in academic and professional standards, though less elitist in social-class membership than is the case in the 1970s.

As one sardonic prophet put the case, as early as 1969:

In the very dim future the university as an institution may come into its own again. That will happen when it is realised that, although almost every mother's son and daughter in this age of universal literacy, automation and upward social mobility needs a tertiary education, comparatively few need, want or are fitted for a university. Then enough splendidly equipped, staffed and administered institutions of tertiary education will perhaps be founded to satisfy everybody. The university can then perhaps be left to those who are actually interested and who are not really looking for something else in disguise.[24]

The need to find a *modus vivendi* for providing almost universal higher education in a population of less than 20,000,000, does seem to point to a rationalisation on the North American model, with the university, indeed, 'coming into its own again'.

The third tendency suggests that irrespective of what educational structure emerges, the question of accountability will greatly concern tertiary institutions.

Universities can be expected to react by setting up education research and development units to inquire into failure rates and quality of teaching as well as to train and retrain university teachers. Indeed, by the 1990s university teachers might perhaps be required to have undertaken courses in teaching as well as demonstrating competence in research. The lonely post-graduate diplomas in tertiary education offered in the 1970s by such universities as Monash and New England are likely to become much more common and much more sought-after during the 1980s.

But accountability will not be limited to the area of teaching. Questions will be asked about quality of administration and the expenditure of the managerial dollar. The decline of the myth of education and the wider introduction of formula financing and systems analysis will produce demands for institutional research which no Australian university has, at least at time of writing, had seriously to face up to.

The fourth and fifth tendencies refer to national planning and the growing power of the Australian, as opposed to the state, governments. The Martin Committee had called unsuccessfully for a single higher-education authority. By 1973 the chaotic and uneconomic competition which marked some areas of Australian higher education made the demand for a given national approach all the more obvious.

As shown earlier, a number of developments in 1973 suggested the growing importance of firm national planning and rationalisation of higher education. These developments include the offer of the Australian government, accepted by the state governments, to meet all costs of higher education and to pay the fees of all students (except those enrolled in adult education courses) accepted for entrance to institutions of higher education.

At an address in Armidale on 6 July 1973, the Federal Minister for Education, the Hon Kim Beazley, stressed his government's concern for *access* to higher education. He pointed out that the decision to pay fees and, in certain cases, living allowances, will undoubtedly encourage a wider spectrum of society to attend university. It would be naïve to expect a sudden 'democratisation of higher education'. None the less, it would be reasonable to look for a considerably greater proportion of Australian aborigines, migrants to Australia and children from poorer urban and rural areas in higher-education institutions by the beginning of the 1990s.

Yet much of the effort of the Australian government will be wasted if universities and colleges do not introduce more flexible entry requirements. Clearly, if universities continue to restrict entry to students whose backgrounds are overwhelmingly educated middle-to-upper class, then the effect of free tuition will be merely to make it even easier for such students to enrol.

An important implication of full federal funding is the likely increased geographical mobility of students. Even as late as the 1970s the Australian universities, with the possible exception of the Institute of Advanced Studies in the Australian National University, are largely provincial in their patterns of student attendance. While a few departments or faculties attract students across state borders, the vast majority attend a university within their own state. This is a function partly of tradition, partly of economics, partly of state control and allocation of state bursaries and scholarships of various kinds. Again, the state universities, mostly overcrowded and unable to accept all qualified students seeking admission, have applied quotas for entry to most faculties and have necessarily given preference to in-state applicants.

Under the new pattern of funding, some major changes in 'catchment areas' can be expected. Even if the shortage of university places continues, the universities can be expected to select from the best students from all over Australia rather than from a given state. The insidious US practice of state universities having differential fee structures for in-state and out-of-state students will be avoided.

Such mobility, coupled with the tendencies referred to earlier, will hasten the demand for an overriding co-ordinating body, referred to above in order, either to advise on all funding matters or at least to rationalise the recommendations of the three commissions concerned with higher education.

THE UNIVERSITY OF THE 1980s AND 1990s

What, then, will be the role of the university in the 1980s and 1990s? It will be essentially the same as it was in the 1940s, or, indeed, the 1890s, namely:

(1) the preparation of professionals and quasi-professionals;
(2) research and scholarship;
(3) service to society.

The only real difference will be that the university (including the new technological universities) will be at the apex of a pyramid which will include near its base institutions much more like universities than was the case in the 1940s.

So far as role 1 is concerned, the university will continue to train for the high professions and some of the emerging high professions. The colleges of advanced education or 'state' colleges will tend to cater for the low professions, and the low emerging professions, the junior colleges for the skilled and semi-skilled occupations. All will have a major role to play in recurrent education, each tending to specialise in the level of it most appropriate to the internal preparation it offers.

In performing these tasks each institution will, as in the past, be contributing to upward social mobility. There will however be a marked increase in the proportion of students from disadvantaged groups in society attending such institutions, and especially, *pro rata*, the universities.

The chief difference in the role of universities by comparison with the 1970s will be the emphasis on postgraduate studies. Postgraduate students are likely to make up a much greater proportion of all students enrolling in universities, especially in faculties whose areas of interest with CAEs are blurred as the colleges provide a large pool of candidates with first degrees.

In role 2, one of the chief characteristics to mark off the university from other tertiary institutions will be its emphasis on research and scholarship. This does not mean that colleges of advanced education will ignore research, but merely that it will play a smaller part in their activities. The emphasis in the CAEs, as in the US state colleges, will be on teaching and course-type degrees at bachelor's and master's level. The universities will tend to stress research-oriented thesis-type honours degrees and study at the doctoral level.

In role 3, all the tertiary institutions will play some part in service to society. As Fitzgerald points out, the universities will continue to provide high-level consultancy services and will take a new interest in recurrent education for graduates.[25] The CAEs, on the other hand, will take over service of the extension-type activities which in the past have been the domain of the universities in some states. They will devote special attention to the needs of industry and commerce for the upgrading of middle-level personnel. The junior colleges will offer a wide range of upgrading courses and activities for most non-professional occupations.

Thus the myth of 'parity of esteem', so simply and egregiously unreal in spite of its apparent appeal to those who met in Armidale in 1969 and who issued the statement quoted at the beginning of this chapter, will die a predestined if lingering death. The universities (including, it must be emphasised, the new technological universities) will perform their role at one level of the pyramid, the colleges at another, the junior colleges at yet another.

The position will be no different if all the institutions are termed 'universities'. Should that happen, then as in the USA and Canada there will develop a hierarchy of universities with the newly established teaching and vocationally oriented ex-colleges near the base of the pyramid and the long-established research and professionally oriented metropolitan universities at the apex. Thus the role of the university will not change so long as the university is defined as the institution at the apex of the pyramid. There may be differences of emphasis within roles, and different means of playing them, but the roles themselves will stand.

Earlier in this chapter Clark Kerr's six discontinuities were listed. The battles implied in those discontinuities were: between universality of access and excellence, the public will and academic autonomy, society and the intellectuals, representative and 'participatory' democracy, the needs of production and the interest in consumption, the older methods and the newer electronics.

As this discussion has implied, these discontinuities are clearly on the Australian horizon. As suggested earlier, such discontinuities will affect emphases in roles and the way in which roles are played but they are unlikely in the 1980s and 1990s to change the roles themselves. Moreover, the adoption of the hierarchical structure university–college–junior college will assist universities in meeting and coming to terms with these discontinuities.

Kerr looks for the elusive 'golden mean' solutions to each of these conflicts. Whether the 'golden means' are achieved or not, there can be no question of the greater involvement of Australian universities in the life of society and no question of a return to Veblen's isolation of academe.[26] The 'golden means' are, however, achievable by AD 2000. In a hierarchical structure, with universities sufficiently responsive to societal needs, the universities, as Kerr puts it so well, will provide the cathedrals of the twenty-first century, serving as great centres of inspiration and aspiration.

4
The University in India

AMRIK SINGH

While it cannot be claimed with any certainty that a particular country has stability in terms of its social and economic structure which will endure for the next twenty to thirty years, such a statement can be made more easily about certain countries than about others. For India, any claim of stability would be untrue and even misleading. This is because her situation is very dissimilar from countries like the USA and the USSR, for instance. In these two countries, though different systems of government prevail, there is a kind of stability and, to that extent, predictability in regard to what can happen tomorrow. This, in turn, depends upon a certain relationship of productive forces, class structure and all the other jargon that economists and sociologists use all the time. It would be wrong to say that no changes in such matters are likely in these countries in the next few decades. But it is reasonable to affirm that the parameters of these changes are to a considerable extent already defined. Any changes outside those parameters are on the whole unlikely. This cannot, however, be said about India.

In a sense, India is ready for a change. But how long it will take before such a change can come is unknown. In terms of history even half a century is not too long for a thrust in the direction that a country is likely to take. Those of us who are alive at this moment feel impatient with the pace of change. Maybe this was also the feeling of people who, for instance, lived through pre-revolutionary France or pre-revolutionary China. Pressures for change, as one can see in retrospect, were building up in these countries over a long period of time. Sometimes these were perceptible, sometimes not. But building up they were, slowly, gradually and inexorably. Something of the same kind is happening in India today, though the direction of the change is uncertain, if not also unpredictable. Only two things can be said with certainty. One, some kind of a change will take place; two, how late or soon it takes place is a matter which cannot be determined with any accuracy.

The first of these two statements, however, needs to be qualified somewhat. Change in the Indian situation may not prove to be particularly radical or thoroughgoing. There is not much in the recent past of India to suggest a tradition of violent or drastic change. For centuries a kind of passivity has characterised the Indian scene which it is possible to explain but not easy to justify. A number of elaborate attempts have been made to explain the cause and nature of this passivity, its existence is not disputed. What is questioned is its source and character.

Several thinkers have argued that passivity in the past need not mean passivity in the future. What needs to be specified here, however, is the span of the future that one is referring to. If one talks of the next five or ten years, it is possible to talk in somewhat precise terms. What happens after that is highly uncertain. This is because of the basic instability of the system that prevails in India today. There is discontent and frustration all around but it is not assuming the dimensions (or direction) of a movement. In the absence of a clearly identifiable movement pressing for a change in a certain direction, the only reasonable inference is that while there will be shifts and compromises, the basic character of the system stays unchanged.

The case for a change is however overwhelming. Not only is the basic social and economic structure stagnant, but demographic pressure is intense and unremitting. In other words, were it a static situation things could have continued as they are for a long, long time. But here is a situation where if nothing at all happens except that more time passes, things will automatically get worse. There will be more people to feed, to clothe, to educate, to look after and this, in turn, would generate pressures that would not permit the polity to remain stable. The pressures for change are thus irresistible; only the will and the means seem to be faltering.

In this highly unstable situation it becomes difficult to speculate about the near future in a meaningful manner. Not to do so, however, would be as unrewarding an exercise as to build a whole structure of speculations in regard to the shape of things to come. To speculate about the future of the Indian university is particularly difficult. This is mainly for two reasons. The Indian university today is very much a part of that unstable, uncertain social and economic situation. Secondly, despite a tradition of more than a century, the Indian university has not become stabilised as a social institution. Nor has it become indigenised in any meaningful way.

THE STATUS OF THE UNIVERSITIES

Developments since 1947 have served to underline two features of the Indian university which make its continued survival in its present form somewhat doubtful. One is largely a matter of definition. What is it that constitutes a university? On what level of performance does it function? What category of students does it seek to serve? All these matters are defined somewhat differently in India as compared to other countries.

In countries where the university tradition is strong, the average age of entry is eighteen plus. In certain countries it is even nineteen or twenty. Students joining the university have usually had good schooling and are, on the whole, mature in their thinking. In India, however, the average age of entry is fifteen or so. Only one-third of Indian universities insist upon a student being sixteen years old on entry. So the average age of entry in an Indian university is fifteen. Not only have these students not had good and sufficient schooling, they are most decidedly immature in their thinking and outlook. Consequently, the kind of work that they do in the first two years or so at college is the kind of work that students in other countries finish at school.

Because of this looseness of definition of what constitutes university education, the Indian situation is somewhat disconcerting in some respects. In the year 1973–4 something like 3·5 million students were enrolled in the universities but only 6 or 7 per cent of them were pursuing a postgraduate course. Generally speaking, Indian students do at the postgraduate level what is usually done at the undergraduate level in advanced countries. From one point of view, therefore, the university system has 3·5 million students. From another point of view it has only 0·2 million students. Which of these two figures should be regarded as relevant to the argument under discussion depends upon the yardstick that one chooses to apply.

The problem is not one of looseness of definition, however. The real problem is why hordes of students enter college knowing full well that a college degree is not going to get them a job. The rate of expansion over the last decade or so has been about 12–13 per cent per year. There is hardly a year when it is less than 10 per cent. No other country in the world has had a rate of expansion higher than 5–6 per cent per year. Because of the extraordinarily rapid rate of expansion in India, academic standards could not but get diluted. Even when financial resources for this rate of expansion are available – and they are not – the scarcity of the right kind of teachers is a severe constraint. Consequently the quality of teachers has been declining sharply over the years. With every year that passes the bottom of the academic barrel is scraped more and more desperately and teachers who were regarded as ineligible yesterday are not only declared eligible but are found to be competent and even satisfactory. The country is fast approaching a situation when, on the analogy of a concept in economics, bad teachers will outnumber good teachers.

This process is to be seen at work already in certain institutions, and before long even the so-called good institutions will feel devitalised and empty of academic content. This is as true of postgraduate education as of undergraduate education. Indeed, in certain universities even the PhD degree has been devalued to an unpardonable extent.

To draw a line of distinction between undergraduate education and postgraduate education is not simply a matter of having the right kind of definition. The issue is much more complicated and has unmistakable social and economic dimensions to it. It is also linked with the social and academic status of university teachers. With wages being generally low and scarcity of jobs being a chronic feature of the social scene, teachers more than anyone else have developed a vested interest in favour of the existing system. Whether this is academically sound or not is beside the point. Had the economy not been stagnant, one could have criticised the role of the teachers in this situation. But as the economy has not been growing, as prices have been rising for several years, and as the entire direction of social change has had the effect of widening the economic gulf rather than narrowing it, an average teacher has no choice except to do his strenuous best to stay in the ranks of the middle class. Despite the teachers' best endeavours, and despite the fact that the investment on higher education has been growing much more steeply than could have been anticipated a few years ago, not even 33 per cent of the teachers manage to do so.

A majority of them have good reasons to be frustrated with their lot. Whether frustrated or otherwise, in their collective thinking and orientation, they are in favour of the status quo, but this is becoming more and more untenable. At the present rate of expansion, the university enrolment which today stands at 3·5 million is likely to touch 5·5 million in another five years. With resources already overstretched it would become almost impossible to sustain such a heavy superstructure. But on when or how soon it gets modified one cannot speculate too precisely. In any case this is a matter which is also partly linked up with the other feature of the university system – the place of the university in Indian life.

India's failure to integrate her universities with her process of economic development has parallels and implications beyond her own frontiers. To have a situation where those passing out from the universities cannot find employment is as much a comment upon the strategy of growth that the country has adopted for itself as upon the irrelevance, to put it no more strongly, of the universities to the growth of the country. Whether universities are relevant to a country like India or not is an issue that has to be faced. It is central to what is under discussion. Unless it can be established in terms of theory as well as practice that universities are important, both as institutions and as contributors to the growth of economy, questions are bound to be raised. That such questions are not being raised in India today is not because they are not pertinent or urgent but because those who can raise them, teachers as well as other intellectuals, do not do so. They are so passive in their responses and so lacking in perception in regard to the emergent trends that they themselves have become a part of the crisis of irrelevance. But more of that later.

THE EFFECTS OF SOCIAL INJUSTICE

Whatever might have been the situation earlier, in the modern world no country can have stability without growth as well as social justice. Both these requirements must be met, more or less simultaneously. If there is growth of national income but its distribution is defective and lopsided, it leads to social tensions. In certain situations, and this is particularly true of contemporary India, growth cannot take place unless it is accompanied by distributive justice. In fact the absence of distributive justice hurts the process of growth. This is precisely what is happening in India today.

Both in absolute and relative terms there has been considerable growth of national income in the last quarter-century. The distribution of it, however, has been so uneven and so biased in favour of certain sections of the population that the country's economy has now entered upon a period of prolonged stagnation. There are other economic and institutional reasons for this situation. The sense of social injustice is, however, so acute and so widespread that it is impeding the very process of growth. To the extent that growth can take place with the help of increased resources, new and improved technology and other such adventitious factors, it is taking place. But to the extent that growth is dependent upon good motivation and good performance, it is being thwarted.

It is astonishing how throughout history, for centuries together, men have accepted poverty as a way of life. What awakens the feeling of protest in them is either the glimpse of a better life which seems to be within their reach or a feeling of oppression and injustice. In other words, men accept poverty but not injustice. To argue that seldom has there existed a completely just society is not relevant here. Somehow or other, when men are persuaded into believing that the order of things in which they live is just, or that it cannot be otherwise, most of them do not protest. Even if it means stark and unrelieved poverty, they still accept it. How they are deluded into believing such a falsehood is beside the point. What is important is the fact that they are led to believe that, all said and done, most people are getting their desserts.

Indian polity is unstable today because more and more people are coming to believe that they are not getting their desserts and, secondly, they see some others enjoying a much better life than they feel they are entitled to. These two factors are creating all manner of tensions in the social sphere and gross distortions in the economic sphere. Higher education, by its very nature, cannot remain unaffected by these pulls and pressures. So much of what is wrong with higher education today arises from the mismatch between the imperatives of growth with social justice and growth organised in the interest of certain sections of the society.

One particular aspect of the mismatch might be referred to in some detail. About two decades ago when the total outlay on education was 15 to 20 per cent of what it is today, the investment on higher education was about 15–16 per cent of that. Today higher education's share has risen to something like one-third of the total outlay on education. That this has been at the cost of other sectors, particularly elementary education, is explicitly recognised by the proposal to allocate something like half of the total outlay on education in the Fifth Plan to elementary education. Expenditure on higher education will continue to be considerable; only in terms of its proportionate share will it come down.

The question to ask here is how this came about and what were the pressures – social, political and economic – behind the increased emphasis on higher education? Were the pressures economic in character or social and political? Or to put it another way, was higher education being treated as an agent of growth or was it looked upon as a facility for which there was extensive social demand which had to be met somehow or other even if it meant neglect of some other important sectors of education?

Some years ago one could have taken more than one position in answering these questions. For the last half-decade, however, unemployment amongst engineers has been so acute (currently in the neighbourhood of 50,000) that no one can any longer pretend that the demand for higher and professional education has to be met in the interests of the growth of the country. Today it is clear that the demand for higher education is social rather than economic. It is also clear from the fact that any attempt to recover the cost of education, even partially, from the students is met with resistance. What the state spends per student is much higher than what the individual student is required to spend. In consequence, the share of government expenditure on higher education has been increasing steeply as compared to support from any other source. Today approximately two-thirds of the total expenditure on education is met from government funds.

A number of factors have thus combined to underline the class character of higher education. The rate of literacy is so low (it does not exceed 30 per cent even after a quarter-century of independence) that even in statistical terms the chances of poor students entering institutions of higher learning are very low. Secondly, since the bulk of enrolment at the higher-education level comes from the middle class or the upper-middle class, it is they who stand to benefit from the increased facilities for higher education. Thirdly, tuition fees are kept at a low level so that the element of state subsidy is remarkably high. And, finally, higher education has been allowed to grow at the expense of elementary and other levels of education, a distortion of planning and investment for which correction is now being sought in a fairly drastic manner.

This emphasis on higher education is an aspect of the strategy of growth which has been followed by the country for a quarter-century now. Whatever the merits of this strategy may otherwise be, it has failed to ensure social justice. If anything, it has perpetuated and strengthened privilege and injustice. Not only do people feel that they are not getting what they deserve, they also feel that a substantial majority of those who are doing well for themselves do not deserve to do so. The social and economic implications of this state of mind are so far-reaching that what is at stake today is not only the future of the Indian university but also the future of the Indian polity.

Whether the Indian university can survive the impending crisis – or a series of them – of the Indian polity is not a very legitimate question to raise, for the simple reason that in India as elsewhere the university has no autonomous existence outside the polity. How the problems of growth and of social justice are resolved does not have to be discussed here. In what manner the Indian university will have to be restructured and given a new focus in the changed circumstances is, however, very much a part of the argument under discussion. Three issues have already been identified, two of them directly and one by implication. These may now be taken for further analysis.

One was described as a matter of definition. In specific terms, however, it refers to the question of drawing a line of distinction between undergraduate and postgraduate education. As long as this distinction cannot be clearly established, it is obvious that the Indian university will continue to be clogged with numbers. And let it be added that as long as the present strategy of growth is not changed, the Indian university will never be able to discover its identity, nor indeed its parameters of functioning.

Today the Indian university is being made to perform tasks which are clearly beyond its range of responsibilities and therefore beyond its capacity also. A university can train people for jobs that are either available or are expected to be shortly available. It can do nothing to create jobs. Nor can it be one of its responsibilities to pacify those within its portals and keep them occupied till jobs become available. The universities, however, are being obliged to discharge these responsibilities today even though they are not competent to discharge them. One could even say that the universities are being treated as safety mechanisms for the mounting anger and frustration of students who are unable to get jobs. Could there be a cheaper and socially more acceptable way of looking after 3 million young men and women than to enrol them in the universities? To have them let loose in the streets would start a conflagration which might be difficult to contain.

Evidently, the universities are waiting-rooms for those young men and women who are preparing to enter life. They are not necessarily anxious to have university education. Quite often they are neither well-motivated nor well-equipped for the purpose. They need a degree so that they can get a white-collar job. But jobs are scarce and too many people are chasing them. Under the strain of impossible expectations and intolerable pressures, the university system is breaking down. What is worse, it is difficult to see how the universities, acting on their own, can do much to rescue themselves.

The basic issue confronting the Indian polity today is how to ensure a rate of growth which is high enough not only to neutralise the growing pressure of population but also to enable the teeming millions to get out of the morass of starvation and squalor. These twin objectives, however, cannot be accomplished without most people being made to believe – rightly or wrongly – that the system in which they are living is basically just. Yet in contemporary India the situation is exactly the contrary. The feeling of being discriminated against is so all-pervasive that the legitimacy of the system is being called into question almost all the time. As most people perceive it, there is a vast loot in progress. Whoever can help himself to whatever is available gets away with it. There is no question of what belongs to whom and whether he has a right to have what he has. Any question of what is right or wrong is a marginal issue in such a situation, therefore.

To some people this may appear to be an attempt to caricature what is happening: the system is not that erratic or corrupt, it will be said. This would be to ignore one basic law of social change: look at what is emerging, not at what is decaying. The general thrust is in the direction of grab-whatever-you-can. The number of people who still do their job honestly and with some sense of satisfaction is fairly substantial. But the number has been declining steeply and the decline is likely to be still steeper. This is leading to two devastating consequences. One is the undisguised increase of corruption at almost every level. The second is the impact on the general level of productivity.

High productivity is the end-product of a combination of several factors, one of the more important being people's attitude to work and performance. In India, over the years a kind of cult of nonperformance has grown up, with the result that while the number of jobs has been proliferating there has been a marked decline in the output and quality of work done. Excluding the armed forces, the central and the state governments have more than 10 million employees, and their total wage bill is more than the tax revenue collected by the central government in a particular year. For the last decade or so this expenditure has been mounting at the rate of 10–12 per cent every year. Today a very substantial part of the increase of the national income goes to meet the costs of this bloated bureaucracy. In a sense, therefore, the country is caught in a vicious circle. National income is not increasing because productivity is low, and productivity is low because whatever the increase, most of it is appropriated by the bureaucracy. In fact the bureaucracy has become so enormous and so well entrenched that it constitutes the largest pressure group in the country. In certain parts of the country the whole administrative machinery has been known to be held to ransom in pursuit of parochial interests.

To some extent university and college teachers too belong to this pressure group. Their number is not very large, being in the neighbourhood of 1,300,000. Nor do they constitute by any means a particularly vociferous group. In their social outlook and attitude towards performance, however, they are not at all different from others who are part of the general bureaucratic structure. Were the teachers aware of their professional obligations, the situation could have been saved to some extent. As it is, professional awareness is absent and in addition teachers suffer from the same universal sense of dissatisfaction.

The academic situation will continue to be difficult for some time. Two important pre-conditions for a real change are a sharp decline in numbers and a total re-orientation of the outlook of teachers. To some extent the two are inter-related and even interdependent. Pressure on the university will be eased only when the school system is strengthened as well as diversified and, secondly, new avenues of employment are opened up for the young people. These steps involve such far-reaching social and economic changes that without a basic shift in the strategy of growth being followed by the country today, no moves in the new direction can be taken. Once these steps are taken, the Indian university will be free to discharge its basic functions. These are not particularly different from the functions discharged by universities in other countries, only that in a country like India their role of training skilled manpower in relation to the manpower requirements of the economy would receive somewhat greater attention.

What would happen to the teachers manning the university system would continue to be a problem. Their quality has declined so steeply in recent years that even to hope that things will not deteriorate further looks like an exercise in optimism. No university system in any country is known to have regulated the affairs of the academic community only through bureaucratic means. These means might be somewhat relevant in other situations; in the academic situation they only make things more complicated. Teaching at the higher level is different from any other kind of work. Nothing is more crucial to a teaching situation than the ability of the teacher to teach and the willingness of the student to learn. On both these requirements there are strong reasons to feel concerned and indeed frustrated.

If the Indian university is to survive as a meaningful institution this situation will have to change. Professional awareness will have to grow. No one today knows how it will do so, only that it cannot be imposed from without. Outside influences will help, but they cannot be a substitute for attempts at self-regulation and self-regeneration. In specific terms, reduced pressure on universities would create the conditions for the liberation of the Indian university from its present crisis. But by itself this will not accomplish everything. The battle for professional standards will ultimately have to be fought within the universities and by the academics who constitute them.

Today the university is virtually indistinguishable from the market place. In the changed circumstances it will have to evolve an ethic of its own. So depressing is the situation today that such a hope may be regarded as utopian. This would be taking a somewhat static view of the situation. The Indian university has to evolve if it is to survive. The only way it can survive today is to preserve its identity as an institution against the pressures of the market place. That these are too many and too oppressive is not reason enough for the university to abdicate its responsibility to think. What is undermining both its integrity and its vitality is the reluctance of academics to involve themselves in the problems facing the polity. To be rendered irrelevant in any situation is a misfortune. But to become irrelevant, when the choice to be relevant is available, is both a misfortune and a folly. No one other than the academics can be blamed for it.

5
The University in the Caribbean

ERIC WILLIAMS

The Caribbean area – defined to include with the archipelago the main-land territories of Guyana and Belize – is geographically an expression, politically and constitutionally a confused patchwork reflecting the metropolitan imperialist rivalries of previous centuries, and socially a melting pot of a variety of ethnic groups and their inevitable permuta-tions and combinations. Cuba's 9 million people are counterbalanced by the few thousand in the British Virgin Islands. Spanish, English and French rub shoulders with creole, talky-talky and papiamento. Only a few miles of sea separate the arrowroot of one island or nutmeg of another from the offshore oil deposits of a third. Between the allegedly pure descendants of Dutch settlers in Saba and St Eustatius and the black state of Haiti, there is the mulatto Dominican Republic and the so-called 'whiter' societies of Cuba and Puerto Rico; while there are large Asian groups – Indians and Pakistanis in Guyana, Surinam and Trinidad, Indonesians in Surinam, Chinese and Arabs in all countries, with the Chinese element particularly large in Cuba. There are also original Amerindians in Guyana.

Constitutional patterns run the whole gamut from British colonialism (Montserrat, British Virgin Islands and Anguilla) through Associated States (Puerto Rico, Leeward and Windward Islands) to assimilated Overseas Departments (French and Dutch), to Independent countries of both Latin and British background, these varying from Haiti's *caudillo* to Marxist Cuba.

The first colonial countries historically in the modern world, these variegated territories have certain things in common:

(1) The slave plantation economy based on sugar, the latifundia, African slave or Asian indentured labour, foreign white capital.

(2) A common struggle against colonialism.

(3) A common fear of American neo-colonialism since 1898, when the Americans took over Puerto Rico from Spain, later established protectorates over Haiti and the Dominican Republic, purchased the Danish Virgin Islands in 1917, transformed Cuba which had won its independence from Spain into a vast American sugar colony, and in 1941 extracted from Britain leased naval bases in the British West Indies, the chief of which was Chaguaramas in Trinidad.

(4) A predisposition to emigration patterned on the absentee sugar planters of the seventeenth and eighteenth centuries; hence the large British West Indian communities in the United Kingdom, Canada, the United States of America, Panama, Venezuela and Costa Rica, the large French West Indian community in France, the large Dutch West Indian community in the Netherlands, the large Puerto Rican community in the United States, the large numbers of Cuban, Haitian and Dominican political exiles in the United States; as well as the steady migration between the islands themselves, for example the 'swallow' immigrations of Haitians and Jamaicans to Cuba sixty years ago, the regular Haitian movement across the border to the Dominican Republic, until interrupted by the 1937 massacre, the constant movement from the British Virgin Islands to the American Virgin Islands, the virtual takeover of St Croix in the American Virgin Islands by the Puerto Ricans, the large-scale movement from Trinidad to the oil refineries of Curacao and Aruba, and the long and steady migration from the smaller British islands and Guyana to Trinidad.

In this setting there are three key issues for the future:

(1) The independence of the entire region and its economic integration – the elimination of direct colonialism where it still exists, the resistance of any tendencies to become or to be regarded as banana republics, economic independence with greater national control of natural resources.

(2) The search for a Caribbean identity and the struggle against metropolitan cultural domination, whether in the form of the American consumer society, or the domination of the metropolitan mass media, or the control of the education system still exercised in large part by the churches, and evidenced today by the international lending agencies

84

whose loans influence and determine the pattern and direction of development.

(3) The fundamental improvement of race relations.

With the Caribbean territories in 1973 politically in a state of flux and constitutionally so diversified, any analysis of the Caribbean university in the last two decades of this century must, therefore, start with certain precisely stated assumptions. The assumptions on which this present analysis is based are as follows:

(1) Cuba will not again become America's sugar colony – no matter what happens to Castro, or however much he himself may depart, as he seems to have done, from the strict communist ideology to which he has subscribed.

(2) Puerto Rico will opt for independence, which was the first goal of Munoz Marin and his Populares, rather than statehood, a state of the United States of America – notwithstanding the substantial economic success of Munoz Marin's compromise since 1940 in taking advantage of the fact that Puerto Rico in 1898 became a part of the United States customs and monetary union, with Puerto Ricans as American citizens enjoying freedom of movement to the mainland.

(3) The Netherlands territories in the Caribbean – Surinam and the Netherlands Antilles – will achieve their independence, remaining associated with the European Economic Community.

(4) The French Overseas Departments will remain a part of France, associated with the European Economic Community, despite the pledge of the French Left to accord independence to them if they should achieve power in France.

(5) The present movement towards the establishment of a Caribbean Community in the Commonwealth Caribbean will be expanded and accelerated; the prospect of a new Caribbean Federation, whilst it poses difficulties, is not to be excluded as, at least, the path prescribed both by political logic and external realities. The present structure of the regional University of the West Indies, serving the entire Commonwealth Caribbean, is assumed to continue (it is now guaranteed to 1981), despite stresses and strains, but with greater autonomy on individual campuses.

(6) Some progress will be made towards the larger goal of the economic integration of the entire Caribbean area, where possibly even Puerto Rico, if it should become a state of the United States, may be accommodated; at the present time, the Dominican Republic, Haiti and

Surinam have all expressed their wish to be associated with the Caribbean Community which came into being on 1 August 1973, as a substantial expansion of the existing Caribbean Free Trade Association.

THE CARIBBEAN UNIVERSITIES TODAY

The Caribbean universities reflect their political heritage with its cultural dependence on the one hand and nature's dispensation on the other. University developments in the area are shown in the table.

Two points may be noted about these Caribbean university developments. The first is the cultural domination of the metropolitan countries to which they were attached, reflecting the basic metropolitan philosophy of colonialism as serving primarily for the transmission of Western culture and learning and the subordination of indigenous values, customs and languages. This was the essence of the infamous minute of Lord Macaulay in respect of India and dominated the Indian universities subsequently established by the British. From India the British exported the same policy to Australia, New Zealand, Northern Ireland and colonial Africa. Almost incredibly, notwithstanding the voluminous evidence of the lack of wisdom of this policy, especially in India, the Asquith Commission and its West African and West Indian subsidiaries, appointed after World War II to consider the question of university developments in those colonial areas, opted for the imitation of British residential universities affiliated to London University for examination purposes, and therefore cribb'd, cabin'd and confin'd within the London curriculum – that is to say, compulsory Latin, and Anglo-Saxon and Middle English in the English literature curriculum.[2] A mere fourteen years after the inauguration of the University of the West Indies in 1948, independence came to the Commonwealth Caribbean in Jamaica and Trinidad and Tobago. The absurdity of the non-independent colonial university tied to the apronstrings of a metropolitan mother was apparent even to the most dyed-in-the-wool imperialist, and the Trinidad and Tobago five-year-old campaign against affiliation resulted in the independence of the University of the West Indies in 1962.

In similar fashion, the establishment of the University of Puerto Rico in 1903 was an integral part of the policy of Americanisation which the first commissioner of education (American) thus expressed in his first annual report in 1901: 'The spirit of American institutions and the ideals

Country		University	Date	Enrolment	Remarks
1 Dominican Republic (1970–1)(a)	1	Santo Domingo*	1538	23,028	With 3 regional centres
	2	Madre y Maestra Catolica	1962	2,153	With 2 regional centres
	3	Pedro Henriques Urena	1966	3,874	
	4	Eastern Central	1970	692	
2 Cuba (1972–3)(b)	1	Havana	1721	32,060	Of which 3,778 part-time
	2	Oriente	1949	6,760	Of which 1,212 part-time
	3	Las Villas	1952	4,340	Of which 1,352 part-time
3 Puerto Rico (1972–3)(c)	1	University of Puerto Rico	1903	47,533	3 campuses, 5 regional colleges, 12,041 part-time
	2	Inter-American	1912	15,354	2 campuses, 10 regional colleges, 4,713 part-time
	3	College of the Sacred Heart	1938	1,946	Of which 668 part-time
	4	Catholic University	1948	6,930	6 regional colleges, 1,915 part-time
	5	Puerto Rico Junior College	1949	5,592	1,202 part-time
4 Haiti (1972–3)(d)	1	University of Haiti	1944	2,000	
5 Commonwealth Caribbean (1971–2)(e)	1	University of the West Indies	1948	5,678	Also 7 university centres in smaller islands
		(a) Mona (Jamaica) Campus	1948	3,376	Includes faculty of medicine
		(b) St Augustine (Trinidad) campus	1960	1,737	Includes faculties of engineering and agriculture
		(c) Cave Hill (Barbados) campus	1963	565	Includes faculty of law
6 Virgin Islands (1972–3)(f)	1	College of the Virgin Islands	1970	576	Separate campus in St Croix Also 1,200 part-time
7 Guyana (1972–3)(g)	1	University of Guyana	1963	1,303	Includes 31 special students
8 Netherlands Territories (1972)(h)	1	University of Surinam	1968	301	Law faculty 1968; Medical Scientific Institute 1970 (formally opened 30 June 1973); technical institute planned for October 1973
	2	Netherlands Antilles	1970	85	Law school
9 French Overseas Departments (1970)(i)	1	University now being established. At present there is a Centre Universitaire Antilles-Guyana	1970	1,750	Law and science; Institute of Technology at Space Centre at Kourou, Cayenne, affiliated to University of Bordeaux

* The oldest university in the Americas

of the American people, strange as they seem to some in Porto Rico, must be the only spirit and the only ideals incorporated in the school system of Porto Rico.' This meant, first and foremost, the compulsory study of English and the teaching of Spanish as a special subject – it took the Puerto Ricans several years to remove this millstone from around their necks.[3] The Puerto Ricans themselves, however, under the stimulus of Munoz Marin's Commonwealth of Puerto Rico as a free state in association with the United States of America, have expanded the State University of Puerto Rico into a typical American 'multiversity'.

It is pertinent here to recall also the attempt of the United States government, when it established a protectorate over Haiti in 1915, to abolish the French literary structure and system of education and substitute the American pattern, with its emphasis on agriculture. The attempt was a total failure and contributed powerfully to the confusion then prevailing in Haiti.

The French, as is well known, have been even more anxious to assimilate in their colonial policy than the Americans or the British. They showed this particularly in Senegal in respect of the University of Dakar before Senegal achieved its independence. If Senegal, on independence, officially requested that Dakar be regarded as the eighteenth university of France, to the point of having a French rector and many expatriates on its staff, it is unlikely that one will see in the university developments now under way in the assimilated Overseas Departments of the Caribbean any deviation from French centralisation and French uniformity.

The second important characteristic of these Caribbean university developments is the sharp divergence, in respect of financing, between the American model in Puerto Rico on the one hand and the British model in the University of the West Indies on the other. Federal funds on a large scale have been and continue to be available to the University of Puerto Rico. This began in 1908 when the University of Puerto Rico became a land grant college – which meant not only the traditional American intellectual emphasis on agriculture, engineering, home economics, adult education and the variety of utilitarian subjects despised (until recently) by the British tradition, but even the inclusion of military barracks and training in the core of the campus. In 1931, with the application to Puerto Rico of pertinent American laws, federal funds became available for the development of agricultural extension services and the agricultural experiment station. In 1935, under the auspices of another American law, federal funds were made available for research at the University of Puerto Rico – with priority to research in tropical medicine and sanitation as well as agriculture. Federal assistance can also be discerned in such new programmes as nuclear technology, radio- logical physics and advanced science training. And, of course, the American financing of veteran programmes applies to Puerto Rico, whose population, as American citizens, are subject to the American draft. The purely Puerto Rican contributions to university expansion cannot be divorced from the political relationship with the United States developed by Munoz Marin, under which Puerto Rico (not being a state) was exempt from federal income tax but entitled to the return of federal excise taxes on its rum, while its inclusion in the American customs and monetary union enabled it to attract an enormous number of industries, under special incentives, to Puerto Rico, whose surplus population can migrate without hindrance to the United States.[4]

As a land grant college, the College of the Virgin Islands is also eligible for federal funds. Its endowment as a land grant college was US$3 million, equalling in 1971–2 an operating budget provided from legislative appropriation in the Virgin Islands, and the sums raised by donations from major firms operating in the islands and the Rockefeller family. Its St Thomas campus is composed in part of the former United States Marine Corps Air facility transferred to the college by the United States Government in 1964. The college conducts marine research pro- jects for the United States Bureau of Sports, Fisheries and Wild Life and the United States Bureau of Commercial Fisheries.

By way of contrast the independent University of the West Indies is today financed almost entirely by the Caribbean governments, on the basis of contributions to capital costs made by the British government. The West Indian investment in its university through governments is shown in the following figures (in West Indian dollars) for the period 1947–72:

Capital cost: $56·9m of which $30m from the British government and $20m from West Indian governments.

Recurrent cost: $184m of which $167m from West Indian govern- ments and $12m from British government.

Total cost: $241m of which $197m from West Indian governments (over 80 per cent) and $42m from British government (less than 20 per cent).

West Indian contributions are dominated by Jamaica and Trinidad and Tobago. Jamaica has contributed $68·6 million recurrent and $2·3 million capital – a total of $71 million or nearly 30 per cent of the total. Trinidad and Tobago has contributed $59·7 million recurrent and $12·7 million capital – a total of $72·4 million or 30 per cent. In respect of recurrent contributions alone, Jamaica has contributed nearly two-fifths and Trinidad and Tobago nearly one-third.

Contributions from other governments (Canada), foundations (such as Rockefeller, Ford, Nuffield), oil companies, Friends of the University and other donors totalled £600,000 to 1969 in capital funds, and less than £5 million in recurrent contributions.[5]

The University of Guyana started functioning from its own campus in 1969. Capital grants from the government of Guyana between 1968 and 1972 were approximately $1 million; British technical assistance contributed £90,000, Canadian technical assistance $100,000 (Can), and the University of Guyana Appeal Fund brought in $250,000. With respect to the recurrent expenditures during this period, the government's subvention amounted to $4·35 million as compared with $250,000 from 'external aid' and $170,000 from the Carnegie Foundation.

It is reasonable to assume that French and Dutch contributions to university developments in their own spheres of influence in the Caribbean form a part of the assistance made available to those territories under the European Development Fund of the European Economic Community, also that the considerable financial assistance reported as having been made available to Cuba from the Soviet Union has facilitated university expansion in Cuba. By way of contrast, university developments in the Dominican Republic and Haiti seem to depend on contributions from those governments.

Thus the main line that university development in the Caribbean will probably take in the last two decades of the century is clear: the governments, paying the piper, will more and more call the tune. French and Dutch developments will be subject to considerable metropolitan influence.

UNIVERSITY AUTONOMY

This raises the whole question of 'university autonomy'. This must be seen in its proper international perspective. The state controls the state university in the United States; one need only point to Governor Reagan in the University of California. In France and Holland the university is almost an arm of the civil service in the European tradition; the French university professor is appointed by the Ministry of Education from a list of candidates in the ministry's files. Universities are subject to increasing direction from provincial governments in Canada. There is increasing direct control by the University Grants Committee in Britain; as well, the comptroller-general has power to inspect university accounts. The British government consistently interfered in the most intimate university matters in colonial India and Africa, and this tradition has been handed down to the state governments in India and to the independent governments in Africa.

The British did not include university autonomy when they exported their universities to India and Africa. The essence of the university system developed by the British in India was that the governor-general, or in the provinces the governor, was *ex officio* chancellor, who appointed the vice-chancellor and most of the professors, and who reserved the right to approve university byelaws and regulations. Whether local colleges were to be affiliated to the universities or not was a matter for the government of India to decide. In one extreme case the government of India sought to write into the constitution of a state university a provision for the government's right to suspend the university's constitution. As stated by one of the governors-general, the government was to have the power of direct control and interference in all the affairs of the university with reference to the University of Calcutta. In respect of proposals for the establishment of the communal universities at Aligarth and Benares, the secretary of state insisted not only on approval by the governor-general of changes in the statutes, but that grants-in-aid were conditional upon government inspection and the submission of annual accounts to the Department of Education. The 1919 Commission on the University of Calcutta described Indian universities as 'among the most completely governmental universities in the world'.

This was not, as it may seem, vulgar racialism, but simply more vulgar colonialism. Britain did not lay the foundations for a tradition of

academic autonomy in its colonies. The government was free to interfere in the University of Sydney; half the council of the University of
the Cape of Good Hope was perpetually nominated by the government;
in the Queen's University in Ireland the vast majority of the members of
the senate were appointed for life by the crown, and in 1851 a professor
was formally dismissed by the crown for absenteeism. The colonial
tradition was transplanted to colonial Africa. As late as 1958 the British
government in Tanganyika tried to dictate to Makerere who should
speak and on what topic at a seminar organised by the university which
included American participants.[6]

Thus was the stage set for conflicts between foreign-inspired universities and nationalist governments. When Nkrumah interfered with
university autonomy in Ghana, going so far as to abolish the constitution
of the University of Ghana and substitute one dictated by the government (but he sought also to remove the right to leave passages to the
United Kingdom), there was an outcry against him. In fact, in transferring agriculture and education to other colleges, in appointing himself chancellor, in seeking to abolish English as a compulsory subject in a
West African School Certificate, in making personal appointments to
so-called 'special professorships', and in prescribing that the goal of the
university should be the furtherance of African unity, Nkrumah was
merely treading in the footsteps of British governors-general in India.
In Nigeria, the council of Ibadan University makes an annual report to
the prime minister which is laid before parliament, while at Nsukka five
of the seven council members in 1961 were *ex officio* members appointed
by the government of the then Eastern Region of Nigeria on the ground
clearly stated by Azikiwe, that power should reside with a body the
majority of whose members are appointed by the state which is responsible to the electorate. As one of Nigeria's leading educators put the issue
in the immediate past colonial setting: 'It is not easy to argue that academic freedom is necessary in order to train the professional manpower
required by Nigerian society . . . at present it is merely one of the em-
bellishments attached in its country of origin to an imported
product.'[7]

Dr Corry, for so long principal of Queen's University in Ontario,
Canada, in his presidential address on 'The University and the Canadian
Community' to the Association of Universities and Colleges of Canada
in Vancouver, October 1965, warned that the university no longer

belonged to the private sector and was no longer a matter of private enterprise, and should come to terms with the governments which financed it; 'votes will tell in the long run; if not with present governments, then with those that succeed them'.[8] A commission appointed by the Canadian Association of University Teachers is even more specific: 'the financial accounts of universities should be made public, and the provincial governments should have the right of post-audit inspection . . . they should be submitted to the legislature and made subject to potential examination by its committee on public accounts'.[9]

In the Caribbean, as far as Cuba is concerned, Castro's government has already laid down the law. Education in general, and the university in particular, is to be used to build the new society, to develop the 'socialist man', without racial prejudices, doing away with money, correcting the aversions to manual labour and the relegation of women to the home. The old liberal arts university was to be transformed into a technologically oriented institution. The great obstacle was university autonomy. This, therefore, was abolished. As a former rector of the University of Havana stated in 1966: 'In countries like Cuba, where the people are running the country through their government machine, university autonomy is really something that is quite inconsistent. The university is a part of the State . . . it is under the Ministry of Education, which determines its general policy and which correctly fits the university into overall educational plans.'[10]

The University of the West Indies has generally had to cut its cloth to conform with the priorities of its contributing governments, and this can confidently be expected to be intensified in the last two decades of this century. The newly independent governments, or the governments moving towards independence, have inherited educational deficiencies which have been most pronounced at the primary and secondary school level, with a tradition of state contribution to an effort left in large part to the churches. In Trinidad and Tobago, for example, first priority was given to the secondary school, and secondary education was declared free in 1960 (Jamaica has recently followed suit). As there were only two government secondary schools then in existence, together with about one dozen denominational schools, mostly Catholic, the first emphasis necessarily had to be placed on the construction of secondary schools and the introduction of the much maligned Common Entrance Examination to provide at least a more objective test of eligibility on grounds of merit rather than on grounds of colour, or race, or parental influence, or religious affiliation.

With the diversification of the secondary school system now in full swing to include the junior secondary school and the vocational school as well as the comprehensive school, attention is being given on a fundamental scale to the primary school as the most urgent educational priority in Trinidad and Tobago, repeatedly indicated over the past year by parental protests and demonstrations. Where Trinidad and Tobago contributed $83·9 million to the university between 1947 and 1973, it spent $431 million on primary schools, of which $18 million was capital expenditure, and $168·2 million on secondary, of which $48·1 million was capital expenditure. The primary school population in 1973 was 226,675, and the public secondary school population 30,989, as compared with the total Caribbean university enrolment of 5,678. Any proposal, therefore, to expand the university or to increase staff emoluments must necessarily be rigidly scrutinised by the government in a situation where of the 471 primary schools, 18 need to be demolished and 141 need urgent major repairs, the estimated cost of each new 400-place school being $200,000.

It is against this background that the heads of governments of the Caribbean territories in 1972 agreed to collaborate with the university in a manpower survey of the area and to re-appraise the residential system. The West Indian territories cannot call on wealthy foundations for assistance, and the entire tradition of Caribbean history has been an anti-intellectual one almost entirely devoid of the philanthropic donations which built up the University of Chicago, for example (including a $2 million Rockefeller chapel in 1920 money), or, with the powerful assistance of Lord Rootes, the University of Warwick, or which provided a £7 million grant to Balliol from its alumni (it is said that 70 per cent of the alumni contributed) in its 700th Birthday Appeal. The University of the West Indies has to depend on government contributions, and if Dr Corry could reiterate over and over again that universities in Canada, in depending on government funds, had 'joined the scramble at the public trough' with 'other ravenous feeders there: health, welfare, highways, and so on, rousing envy, irritation and opposition',[11] the dilemma is still more critical for West Indian governments with their limited financial resources, endemic unemployment, especially among the youth, and rising populations.

The university population explosion has already reached the Caribbean. For example in Puerto Rico total university enrolment increased from 41,216 in 1965-6 to 80,395 in 1972-3. At the University of the West Indies the enrolment increased from 2,187 in 1963-4 to 5,698 in 1971-2.

Two planning estimates for the current decade are available. For Puerto Rico the estimated cost of increased physical facilities varies from $61 million at the lowest to $108 million at the highest for the year 1975, and from $156 million at the lowest to $340 million at the highest for the year 1980. For the University of the West Indies, which by governmental arrangement operates on triennial estimates and which obviously cannot command the resources or methods of financing available to the Puerto Rican institutions, the planning projected last year for the current triennium envisaged an increase of 1,570 students, or a little more than one-quarter of the enrolment in 1972, at a capital cost reaching $47 million in 1975.[12]

LEVEL OF ENTRY

In such a situation the governments contributing to the University of the West Indies have much to say about 1975, and will say still more about the period 1980-99. Their first concern has been and will be the level of entry. For the past three years in particular, the university, in co-operation with some of the governments, has called for the reduction of A level entry to O level, that is to say for the wider recognition of the O level entry which has for several years been permitted especially in the natural sciences, on the basis of an additional preparatory year of study at the university itself. This was strongly resisted by the government of Trinidad and Tobago which produced in 1971, with less than one-quarter of the Caribbean population, over half the A level successes of the entire Caribbean combined (2,931 out of 5,756) and nearly half the O level successes (19,593 out of 44,571).

The situation, as is well known, is not peculiar to the West Indies. In India, where in 1901 the curious proposal was advanced that, as a memorial to Queen Victoria, the standard of examination at the University of Calcutta, already deplorably low, should be lowered, the BA failure rate was 40 to 60 per cent up to 1890 and over 75 per cent in the next decade. In Africa the general trend has been, especially in Nigeria, to insist on the retention of A levels, thus requiring the improvement of secondary education; the result was seen in Ibadan, where in 1957 there were 11,000 applicants for 300 places. Apart from Nkrumah who, with his American heritage, plumped for O level entry, from Malawi with its totally inadequate secondary school system, and Rhodesia where A level entry was in fact a discrimination against Africans afflicted with an inferior primary education, the consensus appears to be the maintenance of the sixth form,[13] if only because, as Trinidad and Tobago effectively argued with the full support of its secondary school principals and students, sixth-form education with a three-year university course was much cheaper than to add a fourth year, subject to university rates of pay, to the university curriculum.

A more important consideration, however, is the question of numbers that would qualify for admission if O level entry was accepted. There seems no obvious reason why the West Indies should be attracted by the 40,000 student enrolment familiar in Japanese universities or the 110,000 enrolment on nine campuses at the University of California, with Berkeley alone accounting for 28,500. The O level entry advocates claim that it is possible for the O level West Indian student to get admitted to a foreign university. The large numbers of Trinidad and Tobago students now studying abroad (in 1970-1, in the United States of America 944, Canada 681, United Kingdom 187), find it difficult enough to get admitted when they have two A levels, whilst the government of Trinidad and Tobago pays very special attention in its recruitment practices to the foreign universities from which its students have graduated. The controversy has been for the moment resolved on the basis that there should be no change in the existing pattern for five years. At the moment of writing, it is difficult to envisage any situation in which, with the democratisation of secondary education and the steady improvement in quality that is certain to take place, at least some of the governments would not continue to resist any tendency towards the lowering of entry requirements.

As it is, whilst the University of the West Indies allows O level entry, especially in the sciences, a large number of students admitted are A level students and the percentage has been increasing in recent years with the improvements in secondary school teaching. For example, university statistics[14] show that O level admissions declined from 33 per cent of the total in 1968 and 1969 to 25 per cent in 1970. In Trinidad and Tobago the proportionate percentage of O level admissions was as low as 15 in 1969. O level admissions to arts-based courses declined from 27 per cent in 1968 to 19 per cent in 1970, when for Trinidad and Tobago they were as low as 4 per cent. On the other hand, the percentage of students admitted from those who had the qualifying A levels averaged 73 in the three years 1968–70, the percentage in arts-based courses increasing from 68 to 78.

The following figures indicate the difference in performance between A level and O level entry in respect of admissions 1963–6:

	A level	O level
Preliminary science		
Did not qualify after 1–2 years	13%	36%
Graduated in 4 years after admission	45%	16%
Arts, evening students		
Did not qualify after 1–2 years	22%	45%
Graduated in 4 years after admission	35%	21%

This would be a particularly retrograde step at a time when in other parts of the world the question has already been raised, and in some areas is being actively considered, as to whether one does not need to re-appraise existing practice of an automatic transfer from the high school to the university – that is to say, as the director of the OECD Centre for Educational Research inquired in 1969, drawing attention to the war veterans who enrolled in universities after World War II: 'What would be the effect on the labour market of school-leaving at, say, 16–18, followed by access to higher education between the ages of 22–30 and even later?'[15]

Driver himself, in considering the possibility of 'diluting the pre-dominantly adolescent culture' of the university as one way of dealing with the problem of 'generational inequality', suggests credits towards university admission for post-secondary school continuation courses, and emphasises the possible reduction in university costs through recruit-ing a larger number of students with family obligations who will not want to live in high-cost university halls of residence.

A variant is the worker-farmer faculty, inspired by the Soviet *rabfac*, introduced by Castro into the Cuban universities, beginning with Havana in 1963. The aim is to train workers in technical and scientific studies on a level higher than or equal to that of secondary education. The nucleus of the curriculum is physical sciences. Admission is limited to organised workers or peasants and to personnel of the ministries of industries and the armed forces. For classes, school buildings and factories are utilised. The problems encountered have been principally shortage of qualified teachers, absenteeism and transportation.[16]

This is an innovation which the University of the West Indies, with its limited financial resources, will have to consider; if not, the contributing governments will do it for the university. The university's estimates of needs for the current triennium to 1975 include nearly $8 million for new student residences to accommodate 1,100 students – despite the fact that in 1971–2 the halls of residence, which are expected to break even over periods of three years, experienced a deficit of $366,338.[17]

There are other basic considerations on the future of their university which Caribbean governments will have to face:

(1) With expanding secondary education, both in quantity and in quality, can some additional form of post-secondary education be devised to take care of the larger numbers? One example would be the junior college, affiliated to the university but financed by individual governments and using university teachers as far as possible.

(2) Would that proposal solve the present enormous wastage at secondary school level? In Trinidad and Tobago, notwithstanding the superiority to other territories indicated above, the 1972 GCE O-level results indicated 1,565 passes with five or more O levels in 11,272 entrants – wastage of some 86 per cent. The situation will not improve, and may be worsened, with the country's present programme for a 90 per cent enrolment in the junior secondary school for ages twelve to fourteen, with a 40 per cent intake in the secondary schools taking GCE.

(3) Would the Caribbean Examinations Council, created after several years of argument among the governments, succeed in producing a superior, and publicly accepted, test of aptitude as a substitute for GCE?

(4) Can a university whose faculty and students talk glibly about 'involvement' and 'relevance' and 'responsibility to the community' continue to operate on a philosophy imposed by a British commission a quarter of a century ago, anticipating large numbers of expatriate staff in a colonial university? For example, a teaching load of twelve hours a week – a contributing government would collapse if that was the responsibility of its senior civil servants. As another example, a staff-student ratio imitating the British, as follows:[18]

	1971–2	*UWI* *Target 1974–5*	*British ratio* *(UGC 1966–7)*
Arts and social science	13·2	12·7	11·3
Education	11·9	9·3	13·4
Science	10·8	11·2	10·5
Agriculture	6·4	7·3	8·2
Engineering	10·3	10·2	11·0
Medicine, pre-clinical	10·1	8·4	8·1
clinical	8·7	8·4	7·1

As a third example, there is the cost per place, again taking the United Kingdom as the frame of reference for the Caribbean. The following picture, in Jamaica dollars, emerges, in respect of the University of the West Indies' claim for greater government subventions:[19]

	1971–2 *UWI*	*1966–7* *UK*	*1974–5 (projected)* *UWI*	*UK*
Natural sciences	1,434	1,589	1,710	1,907
Arts and social sciences	1,141	1,218	1,399	1,462
Education	1,320	1,254	1,795	1,505
Medicine, pre-clinical	1,861	2,106	2,117	2,539
clinical	1,234	2,184	3,756	2,621
Engineering	1,635	1,626	1,911	1,951
Agriculture	2,711	1,782	2,551	2,078
Law	1,591	1,218	1,625	1,462

As a further example, there are staff perquisites – housing allowance, children's allowance, incentive housing plans.

(5) Can the university, following overseas patterns, afford to think in terms of expanding graduate facilities when more and more potential undergraduates are knocking at the door? The graduate emphasis is increasingly being criticised overseas, by undergraduates (the neglect of undergraduate teaching for graduate students is identified as one major cause of student dissent), and by the public generally.

To the extent that the younger student, immediately after high-school graduation, continues to be enrolled, the governments contributing to the University of the West Indies are almost certain to pay attention in future years to emphasising the relationship between study and work – not in the sense of the American student working at a job after university hours, on weekends and in vacations to earn money to finance his studies, but in the direct association of the university studies with some form of community activity and responsibility during the period of study itself – possibly as a fourth year. They will have before them two Third World examples: Castro's Cuba and Nyerere's Tanzania.

Castro, in his attempt to break down Caribbean elitist tendencies among university students, emphasises the close relationship between study and work and compels his university students to spend, at some cost to their study requirements, a part of their time in voluntary work cutting sugar cane or eliminating illiteracy. This is particularly important where at student level the modern cliché 'involvement' is perhaps more honoured in the breach than the observance; one recalls the student confrontation in Tanzania with Nyerere in 1966, before the Arusha Declaration, when students supported by the state bluntly refused to accept the state's prescription for National Service, and Nyerere personally had to deal severely with the ringleaders, rusticating some and expelling others.

They could also consider the recommendation recently made in respect of one of Venezuela's newest universities, Oriente, established in 1959 in the most underdeveloped section of the country and drawing particularly on students from working-class and lower-middle-class families. It is to the effect that, as an aid to development of the region, the university should work out 'internship experiences with regional planning offices, community development organisations, and literacy and public health campaigns [which] could be included in the curriculum as an integral component of degree programs'.[20]

Most of all, the Caribbean governments in future are certain to pay greater attention to the university curriculum in relation to their manpower needs and to their nationalist perspectives. The situation in respect of major fields of study in the Caribbean universities is brought out in the table on page 101.[21]

Very valuable conclusions can be drawn from the table:

(1) Cuba is in the lead in the Caribbean in respect of the relevance of the university to Caribbean needs and conditions, especially so far as technological and agricultural emphases are concerned, while its universities pay considerable attention to education, medicine and natural sciences. Four students in technology are shown at Oriente to every one at the University of the West Indies, where enrolment is approximately

UNIVERSITY ENROLMENT BY COURSES OF STUDY (CARIBBEAN)

	Total	Technology (eng and arch)	Education	Medicine	Agriculture (vet science)	Natural sciences	Economics	Social sciences	Humanities	Law	Remarks
Havana (1972–3)	28,282	7,115	4,979	6,008	2,008	3,352	1,749	—	3,071	—	
Oriente (1972–3)	5,548	1,573	1,191	1,632	519	280	141	—	212	—	
Las Villas (1972–3)	2,988	970	844	437	369	273	53	—	42	—	
Santo Domingo (1970–1)	23,028	2,971	698	4,028	765	440	——2,601——		1,395	260	
Madre y Maestra (1970–1)	2,153	752	359	—	—	86*	523	—	—	147	* Incl humanities
East Central (1970–1)	602	33	25	137	—	—	65	—	—	26	
Haiti (1972–3)	1,741	—	92	832*	59	160	332†	—	—	—	* Incl pharmacy † Economic science and law. Also ethnology, 121; international studies, 79
University of the West Indies (1972–3)	5,678	360	166	844	180	1,544	—	——2,400——		183*	* Recently started
Guyana (1972–3)	1,309	243	86	—	—	265	—	345	364 (arts)	—	
University of Puerto Rico (1972–3)	35,492	3,551	5,517	411	450	3,807	—	2,869	3,779	559	Business administration, 3,839; dentistry, 169; pharmacy, 729

the same, seven to every one in education, two to one in medicine, three to one in agriculture; while in arts and science, for every student at Oriente there are thirteen at the University of the West Indies. The University of the West Indies is superior only in the natural sciences, where the ratio is more than five to one in its favour.

The position in the University of the West Indies is even worse than the table indicates. Between 1963 and 1971, with an increase in total enrolment of 130 per cent, the increase in social sciences was 267 per cent and in arts and general studies 77 per cent, as compared with 111 per cent for medicine and 81 per cent for agriculture. If the increase registered in engineering was 200 per cent, the fact of the matter is that in 1963 there were 114 engineering registrations as compared with 216 for social sciences and 840 for arts and general studies, whilst in 1971 the number of registrations was 343 in engineering, 794 in social sciences, and 1,484 in arts and general studies. New admissions into first-year medicine, engineering and agriculture were 10 per cent of all new admissions to first-degree courses in 1963 and less than 20 per cent in 1970 – the figures being 120 out of 1,052 in 1963 and 262 out of 1,421 in 1970.[22]

(2) The University of Puerto Rico at Rio Piedras is also in a commanding position in its emphasis on technology, education, business administration and natural sciences. The emphasis on social sciences and humanities – when combined, nearly 20 per cent of the enrolment – seems a little strange. The under-representations of agriculture emphasises the increasing urbanisation of the country, where 40 per cent of the 2·7 million population are concentrated in the metropolitan area of the capital. In American supermarket pattern, the university now has a School of Social Work, an Institute of Tropical Meteorology, a School of Public Administration, a School of Dentistry, a College of Business Administration, a School of Architecture, a graduate programme in library science, a graduate programme in psychology, a graduate School in Public Communications, and present plans include emphasis on the study of urbanisation, a computer centre, action programmes in respect of drug addiction, intensification of criminological research and stimulation of penal reform, consumer education, and training of community recreation workers.[23]

(3) The Haitian statistics, with the prominence of ethnology and international studies as compared with the under-representation of agriculture, education and technology, must be seen in the general con-

text of economic underdevelopment. The per-capita gross domestic product in 1970 was $72; less than one-fifth of the population is literate; less than one in four of the population between the ages of five and fourteen attends primary school; in life expectancy, infant mortality rate, ratio of hospital beds and doctors to population, calorie intake, index of agricultural productivity, output of electric power, Haiti ranks lowest among the Latin American republics.[24]

BRAIN DRAIN

This brings us, therefore, to the question of the brain drain. Castro, who allowed the bourgeois professors and technicians that he inherited to emigrate, once bluntly put it: 'to train a university-educated technician costs thousands upon thousands of pesos . . . should we train technicians who are later going to leave to work in the United States? I don't believe that's right.'[25]

The critical situation can be seen in the realities facing two Caribbean areas. First, Haiti: Haitian professionals can be found everywhere in Africa – judges, teachers, engineers, doctors, even in the foreign service (eg Guinea) or in the official establishment and the security forces (Congo). A mission from the Congo sought to secure teachers in Haiti; half the graduating class at the teachers' training school at the University of Haiti applied. Only three of 264 medical graduates in the past decade remained in Haiti. There are more Haitian doctors in Canada than in Haiti.[26]

The second area is Trinidad and Tobago. From the Commonwealth Caribbean as a whole, between 1962 and 1967, the United States of America received 1,127 engineers, 388 natural scientists, 1,184 physicians, and 1,733 nurses; of the nurses 269 were supplied by Trinidad and Tobago.[27] Of the 425 doctors who graduated from the University of the West Indies between 1954 and 1968, 133 – three out of ten – emigrated.[28] For the years 1968 to 1971, professional emigration has been: architects, engineers and surveyors, 80 to the USA, 30 to Canada; nurses and midwives, 450 to USA, 70 to Canada; teachers, 180 to the USA, 270 to Canada; draughtsmen and science and engineering technicians, 80 to the USA, 50 to Canada; administrative, executive and managerial workers, 50 to the USA, 50 to Canada; other professional, technical and related workers, 90 to the USA, 70 to Canada.[29]

DISSENT

In the question of university dissent, involving both staff and students, relations between governments and the universities are involved.

'Involvement' has become one of the fashionable university clichés. At the level of the faculty, it involves more or less a direct incursion into politics – as made by professors in Italy, or in pre-Castro Cuba, where at least two became presidents of the republic. At the University of the West Indies political parties have emerged on the campus in open opposition to governments, and faculty members hold office in trade unions. At the time of writing, in Puerto Rico a critical situation has emerged between the chancellor, the nominee of one political party, and the supreme council on which the alternative party, rejected in a recent election, had nominated a certain number of members. Again, at the University of the West Indies, essentially political newspapers are produced, one being notorious for its scurrility.

Caribbean governments have already begun to challenge this conception of academic freedom; it is obvious that no such claims could be advanced in Castro's Cuba. At a recent heads of government meeting of the Commonwealth Caribbean, many of the author's colleagues denounced the social science faculty of the University of the West Indies, more than one suggesting that it should be closed; the author, who was chairman of the meeting, as a product himself of a social science faculty opposed these proposals and indicated that he could not agree to throwing out the baby with the bathwater. The recent court decision upholding the dismissal at the London School of Economics of a faculty member who incited students to break down the gates, on the ground that such action was not consistent with academic freedom, seems to point a likely road to the future for many governments, including Caribbean governments. The most obvious step seems to be a commission of inquiry to delimit academic freedom. More than one Caribbean government has already denied work permits to West Indians who are non-nationals on the ground that they compromise their university responsibilities and abuse their academic freedom by indulging in activities inimical to national security. By the same token, Caribbean governments, both on grounds of national security and of their obligations to other states, have been forced to scrutinise more closely expatriates selected by the university for appointment.

Student dissent has since 1964 become a familiar pattern in almost all countries, with 1968 as the year of student revolution. Mathew Arnold's scholar-gypsy of a hundred years ago has become the itinerant student agitator of the last decade.

Major world problems have been one of the principal factors in student revolt – Vietnam in the United States, nuclear disarmament in the United Kingdom, Algeria in France, the American occupation in Japan. But whilst opposing war, nuclear holocaust and the draft, students have been rebelling in connection with more personal domestic grievances – for 'participatory democracy' in relation to vital areas of university life affecting students, especially curriculum, library facilities, discipline, and even the evaluation of teaching and appointment of staff. Among some of the students, conventionally regarded as a minority, a highly political element seeks to use the university as a base from which to confront the entire society and reorganise it in its own image and likeness, whatever that may be. This has been particularly so in Mexico and Venezuela, with students in Puerto Rico opposing the ROTC programme for training of officers,[30] and with students in the University of Havana before Castro, who treated the university as a virtual fortress for the storing of arms and ammunition and for the concoction of plans aimed at the overthrow of the government.[31]

Student power is nothing new in university history. The fourteenth-century university of Bologna in Italy was organised, run and managed by students who appointed their rector, disciplined their professors, and imposed regulations against the introduction of women into the dormitory. The rector in Scottish universities was elected by the students; no appointment made by professors could have been as bad as the election as rector by the students of Edinburgh of Thomas Carlyle, the notorious neo-fascist, opponent of democracy and universal suffrage, regimenter of the working classes, hater of black people. Even at the older British universities of Oxford and Cambridge, students have from time to time manifested their power – whether at Oxford by refusing to vote for king and country or, at a later date, refusing to allow the foreign secretary to speak, or the vicious demonstration at Cambridge against the admission of women to higher degrees.

But there is no apparent reason why students should not have a major say in their own discipline, in the organisation of library or cafeteria, or in co-operating in the improvement of teaching, especially at undergraduate level. Vast changes would result, not altogether bad, if students participated in the evaluation of their teachers; in Italy the effect on professorial absenteeism would be felt immediately. There is also every reason to encourage student involvement in community problems, subject always to their effective performance of their primary responsibility, which is study.

The limited number of studies analysing student revolt has so far brought out the following points:

(1) It is only a minority, seldom exceeding 5 per cent, who have actively participated in protests.

(2) Organised protests in America in 1967–8 indicated that, for the institutions involved, 38 per cent were against the Vietnam war, 29 per cent concerned civil rights, 25 per cent the draft, 25 per cent military recruitment, 34 per cent living group regulations, 27 per cent student participation in campus policy-making, and 15 per cent curriculum inflexibility.

(3) American student activists are usually those with above-average grades and incomes (80 per cent of the students at Berkeley came from families earning more than $8,000 annually).

(4) The boycott and sit-in at the London School of Economics in 1967 showed that a high proportion of the activists were studying sociology (it is reported that 75 per cent of the protesters at American universities are reading social science).

(5) The London School of Economics disturbances of 1967 showed a lower proportion of activists among graduate students than among undergraduate, with a tendency for the undergraduate proportion to fall among third-year students compared with first-year students.[32]

However, the Venezuelan study referred to above, of Oriente University, suggests that 'the higher the prestige of a field, the higher is the level of political participation and interest'. Medical students – perhaps conforming to the Latin American tradition – as well as those in engineering are more activist than students in sociology, biology and animal husbandry.[33]

With the 'international identity' claimed by university students, and the pronounced tendency in the Caribbean to imitate the metropolitan countries, the unrest in the Caribbean can be expected to develop, possibly as the wave recedes in metropolitan countries. Both the Berkeley demonstrations of 1970 and the CND marches in Britain seemed to suggest that the infection is spreading more to children as opposed to undergraduates. Governments, as well as adult electorates, are not likely to look kindly on such developments among the privileged classes where, in the international context, universities draw only 6 per cent of their enrolment from working-class families in Germany and under 4 per cent from farm families, in Italy effectively discriminate against the underdeveloped South, and in Japan still subordinate the education of women in accordance with the Japanese 'code of morals' that 'the minds of women generally are as dark as the night'.

There remains the larger question, which dominates universities the world over today, of making university studies more 'relevant' to the students.

CARIBBEAN STUDIES

The first and most important requirement in this field for the Caribbean is the development of Caribbean studies. This would be an absolute prerequisite to the integration of the Caribbean area which has been foreshadowed above as one of the primary needs for the rest of the century. The sad fact is that, with the unprecedented attention paid to the Caribbean area in the past fifteen years, most of the work has come from outside sources, principally the United States and Britain. A surprisingly insignificant amount of work has so far been done on the Asian populations of the Caribbean – basically the Indians in Guyana, Surinam and Trinidad, but also the Chinese in Cuba, Guyana and Trinidad. Very little has been done on the Indonesian element in Surinam. Much more remains to be done on the Bush Negroes of Surinam and the Maroons of Jamaica, as well as on the Amerindians of the Guyanas. Greater emphasis on Caribbean studies will include not only history and the social sciences but the continuation of agricultural research initiated at the former Imperial College of Tropical Agriculture in Trinidad which is now the Faculty of Agriculture of the University of the West Indies, as well as in Cuba with its new Institute of Economics at the University of Havana, the emphasis on political science, and the quite important work in agriculture and livestock research which has already begun.

One particular aspect of this new emphasis on Caribbean studies requires special mention: that is, in the field of literature. The Commonwealth Caribbean behaves as if Caribbean literature is embraced only by novelists they have produced.[34] It is true that, thanks largely to publishing houses in England, some important names have appeared – Naipaul,

Lamming, Selvon, Salkey, Mittelholzer, James (with particular reference to his superlative book on cricket, *Beyond a Boundary*); some attention has been paid to Claude McKay with his Jamaican origins in the United States. But this excludes Cuban literature, Haitian literature, Puerto Rican literature, and above all the literature of the French Caribbean Departments. The outstanding name in the history of Caribbean literature is that of Aimé Césaire of Martinique, Deputy in the French Parliament in Paris, of whom it has been said that he handles the French language better than any living Frenchman. Césaire, with Leon Damas of Guyana (who has a very valuable anthology of black poetry) and President Senghor of Senegal, is one of the original and principal exponents of the concept of *Négritude*. There is no more decisive document in the humanities in the Caribbean than Césaire's 'Cahier d'un retour au pays natal', whilst his study on Toussaint l'Ouverture in the field of history, and his pamphlet *Discourse on Colonialism* in the field of politics, constitute him one of the greatest literary figures that the Caribbean has ever produced.

The Cuban poets and novelists, especially Nicolas Guillen and Regino Pedroso (of Chinese ancestry), cannot possibly be excluded in any consideration of the Caribbean humanities. Nor can the Haitian poets and novelists, especially Jacques Roumain and Jean Brierre; on the social side, the work of Price Mars, sociologist, *Ainsi parla l'oncle* – a former president of the Societé Africaine de Culture – is also decisive. In Puerto Rico, the poet Luis Pales Matos has his place in Caribbean letters. All this will involve much more serious emphasis on the three basic languages of the Caribbean: English, French and Spanish.

Caribbean studies would necessarily emphasise the whole question of race relations, defined as relations between all ethnic groups, with the Western hemisphere involving contacts between Europeans, Africans, Asians and Amerindians. Emphasis would be placed on the Caribbean family, and the Caribbean economic system as it has evolved and is evolving. A note of warning, however, is here appropriate.

Among the most militant of the student activists in the past decade have been the blacks of America, whose disabilities and concerns go much beyond the international malaise and the particular grievances of white students. They have brought to the front the question, in relation to the curriculum, of black studies, as programmes more relevant to black experience in the ghetto. This student criticism of curricula is not limited to black American students. The Italian university allows the student a large freedom of choice on the ground that he should be free to select any course in accordance with his cultural and professional needs. It has been pointed out that on this basis an engineering student could leave out hydraulics and a medical student anatomy, and instead opt for sociology and fine arts. But it is in America that the system of student electives has made greatest headway, to the point where some 12,500 different courses are offered at Cornell, and even in the early twenties the University of Chicago was described, after one of its principal architects, as Harper's Bazaar. It is usual to speak of Berkeley as typical of the American supermarket pattern in university education. The black studies programmes now being developed on many American campuses are in line with this general tradition.

More and more criticisms, from both black and white scholars, are being made of these programmes. As a protest against white racism in both the selection and content of university courses, the black protest is one of the decisive contributions to university education in the twentieth century. But as John Blassingame, assistant editor of the Booker T. Washington papers, has protested, it appears difficult to justify, on intellectual grounds, such courses in black-studies programmes as 'the sociology of black sport', 'relevant recreation in the ghetto', 'the selection and preparation of soul food', and even possibly 'the black family in the rural environment'. Another critic, Andrew F. Brimmer, in pointing to belated steps made to assist black families to catch up in terms of family income with white families, questions the advisability of so segregating black studies as in the long run to deny blacks the opportunity to assume a more meaningful and superior position in the American economy as a whole. Many have stressed the danger that these black-studies programmes could be, on the one hand, 'deliberately organised ill-conceived programmes (by predominantly white schools) because they are intended solely for Negro students', whilst, on the other hand, when supported by white intellectuals, they 'are really supporting a recrudescence of "separate but equal" facilities', and introducing apartheid, segregated halls and residences on white campuses; in between they involve a serious disruption of black colleges by raids on faculty and students, whilst exposing the black students on white campuses in their black-studies programmes to poorly prepared teachers, mostly black.[35]

Already the black revolt in America has had its influence on the Caribbean (dashikis, Afro hair-dos, soul music, clichés), especially with the West Indian origins of such leaders of the American black protest as Marcus Garvey from Jamaica, Stokeley Carmichael, born in Trinidad, and Roy Inniss, born in the United States Virgin Islands. In so far as the black protest movement, in the context of the large number of independent African states, rescues Africa from the intellectual opprobrium and disdain to which it has been consigned by the white developed countries and their intellectuals, and in so far as the black protest movement introduces a new element into the world racial situation of conscious pride in blackness and the African cultural heritage, then the movement has come to stay and will make an enormous intellectual contribution to the world by its correction of historical distortions and repudiation of the great lie of history, that Africa had no history before the contact with Europe in the slave trade period. To the extent that this movement will provide an opportunity for black scholars and researchers to write and publish without the conventional prejudices to which many are subjected by white publishing houses, then this is a great step forward in the history of academic freedom as it relates to the prosecution of research.

To the extent that the current American emphasis on black studies will encourage further research in the Caribbean on black influences – one thinks of the work of Fernando Ortiz, a white man in pre-Castro Cuba, on African influences on the Spanish spoken in Cuba and in the music of Cuba, then this should be an encouragement to the researcher in Caribbean universities who, outside of a limited amount of work in Puerto Rico, Jamaica and Trinidad, has not done much intellectually to explore the African heritage to the Caribbean. On this point, however, one cannot be too sure. To a group of Afro-American students visiting Cuba in 1963 and their comments that school textbooks had no reference to Africa and its peoples in a country with a large population of African descent, Che Guevara replied as follows: 'African history does not exist . . . I see no more purpose in black people studying African history in Cuba than in my children studying Argentina . . . black people in Cuba need to study Marxist-Leninism, not African history.'[36]

The second emphasis for the Caribbean universities for the future is a matter of concern to universities all over the world, which are becoming more and more conscious about what Edgar Faure, formerly a minister of education in France, described as 'balkanising higher education' four years ago. The problem, as Faure saw it, was 'une somme monstrueuse de connaissances disparates' – a monstrous sum of specialised knowledge, with its tendency, as he put it, to 'de-alienate man'. This has been the background to all sorts of experiments in various countries in inter-disciplinary contacts and area studies, but it appears at least from the student disturbances, that they have so far not succeeded in achieving a synthesis of knowledge, which each scientific and technological advance makes more difficult: the universities in the Caribbean have an opportunity to experiment in this field and to make an enduring contribution to university education the world over. This would be particularly necessary in the current mood of cultural xenophobia in some areas where – perhaps influenced by Leroi Jones with his dismissal of Shakespeare as irrelevant because of his use of 'thee' and 'thou' – one has heard young secondary school students in Trinidad at a national forum criticising the importation of pianos and violins and advocating exclusive emphasis on the steel band instrument.

A new line of development might be to take a number of key themes and issues which are of concern to students, relevant, to use the modern jargon, and of deep abiding personal interest, and explore these in their historical, interdisciplinary and international context. A few suggestions might serve to illustrate the basic proposal. One such major field of student concern, very relevant to the modern world, would be the subject of women's liberation or, to be more blunt, sex. Concern of students with sex is now an accepted fact; even Berkeley's president and California's board of regents would probably not react today as they did in 1956 to the famous panty raid on a sorority which is reported to have netted 1,006 panties for which appropriate compensation was paid (with the spread of women's liberation and the form it is supposed to take, the number might be much less in a similar raid in 1975), though one is a little disturbed at the reaction of the city council in withdrawing its subvention from the University of Keele because some male students stripped in a heat-wave. A discussion of women's liberation in its historical and international context would go right down from Aristotle and the Greek society, as well as early non-Western societies, to the contemporary period, taking the study through relevant texts in the humanities – for example, Ovid, St Augustine, Chaucer, Dante, Shakespeare, Goldsmith and T. S. Eliot – right down to contemporary pornography and the illustrated report to President Nixon of the Commission on Pornography and Obscenity.

Another subject of great concern to students and very suitable for elaboration and presentation in its historical and international context is religion and religious beliefs. The University of Lancaster makes provision for a professor of religious studies, the course including modern religions and atheistic thought, modern scientific prejudices to religion, New Testament studies and history of Indian religions. The scope here proposed is even more comprehensive. It would include all religions, not only Christian, Hindu and Islam, but also African – and Caribbean variants of African religion as in Haiti. The subject would take the student through, for example, the power of the Roman Catholic church in the medieval period – including economic power and its attitude to science and academic freedom, the Protestant Reformation emphasising religion and the rise of capitalism, Voltaire and the Enlightenment, the doctrine of evolution, the spread of atheism, right down to the contemporary revolt against papal authority on the pill, abortion and the celibacy of the clergy.

As a third theme, special attention could be paid to the subject of the university and society, showing the relationship in different countries and in various periods, and correcting so many of the misconceptions of so many students about the irrelevance of the modern university. Another useful theme could be work and leisure, which would involve not only the system of slavery, pre-classical, classical and modern, including slavery in Africa itself, semi-free or free agricultural labour, factory labour including the labour of women and children in the nineteenth century, but also the development of science and technology in relation to the organisation of work and the increase of production; and the development of mass sports, especially football.

Such exploration will call for an intercourse and a dialogue between Caribbean universities and their competent authorities that does not exist today. The government of Trinidad and Tobago is to establish a Gallery of Caribbean Emancipators and to sponsor a Caribbean Youth Expression bringing the young people together in sport, art, culture, handicraft and dialogue. The Caribbean universities in the year 2000 will be merely items in the island budgets of the next quarter of a century, mere excrescences on the body of universities in affluent countries, unless they take as their goal, consciously and deliberately, the production of citizens of an area which is *sui generis*, completely different from that great Trinidad novelist, Vidia Naipaul, apostle of Caribbean nihilism and escapism, who has publicly confessed that he would have been a more important writer if he came from a more developed country, instead of from 'a fairly simple, barbarous and limited background' (far less simple, barbarous and limited than Césaire's Martinique), and of whom his biographer has said, in what would be praise abroad but condemnation at home, that 'no country can claim him'.[37]

6

The University in
South Africa

STANLEY P. JACKSON

University education in the Republic of South Africa is under critical scrutiny at the present time, for, whatever justification there may be for a slow retreat from 'apartheid' or separate development of racial groups in some levels of social and economic life, at the level of university education and in the social and intellectual intercourse between the country's advanced thinkers racial separation is neither attainable nor desirable. The universities are producing the most significant opposition to apartheid and any attempt to look ahead into the next twenty years must take into account the changing views of the young intellectuals in all South African universities and especially the growing reluctance of black students to co-operate with the system for much longer.

There will be extensive changes in the next two decades, but it is difficult to predict what they will be. The most likely changes and those that are needed most are the extension of the facilities for black and coloured students, especially in professional fields, and the encouragement of free movement of students from one university to another, at least at postgraduate level. This latter is possible at present only in limited circumstances and is discouraged under the apartheid policy of the present government of the Republic of South Africa.

The population of the Republic of South Africa is at present 21,423,000.[1] Of these roughly 3,779,000 are European with English or Afrikaans as their mother tongue; 2,036,000 are of mixed race and in South Africa are classed as coloured; their language may be either English or Afrikaans. South African Indians living mainly in Natal account for about half a million. The remaining 14,975,000 are Africans speaking a variety of Bantu languages. The policy of the present South African government is to provide separate university facilities for Afrikaans and English sections of the white population and also to provide separately for the coloured, Indian and Bantu sections of the non-white community. Separate universities for the latter groups have been established only recently, following the passing of the Extension of University Education Act in 1959. The Act provided for the establishment, management and control of separate university colleges for Bantus and for other non-white persons.

It is interesting to note how university education developed in South Africa. Like many other cultural activities it started in the south-western Cape Province. The South African College was founded in 1829, by churches and private persons. It developed into a school with a university section at the top – arts and science to begin with and, later on, law. Stellenbosch, now the premier Afrikaans-language university centre in the country, came on the scene with the foundation of Victoria College in 1887, the jubilee year of Queen Victoria. The establishment of Elsenburg School of Agriculture, soon to be formally attached to the college, started technological education in South Africa. The degree-granting body was the University of the Cape of Good Hope. Founded in 1873 it remained the parent university of these colleges till 1916, when the Universities of Cape Town and Stellenbosch received their own charters. The functions of the University of the Cape of Good Hope were transferred to the new University of South Africa which took under its wing the institutions for university education which by that time had grown up in other provinces of South Africa. Regional centres for higher education were established as the need was felt. Rhodes University, in the eastern Cape Province, began like the University of Cape Town – in the upper levels of a school, by preparing students for degree examinations of the University of the Cape of Good Hope. A separate college was founded in 1904, principally to provide courses in the humanities and basic natural sciences. In the Transvaal a technical institute, founded in 1904, continued the training of mining engineers that had been started in Kimberley in 1896. In 1905 classes in arts, science and commerce were introduced and the Transvaal University College, ultimately to become the University of the Witwatersrand, was founded. The new university college opened a branch in Pretoria in 1907. The division of functions between the two branches of the college

– humanities in Pretoria and technology in Johannesburg – was a disappointment to the Johannesburg community and indeed it was on account of this that university education was not established on the Witwatersrand until 1916 when the Johannesburg branch of the college was renamed the South African School of Mines and Technology, with status of a separate constituent college of the University of South Africa. The University of the Witwatersrand received a separate charter in 1922. The province of Natal began with technical education in Durban in 1907, and in 1910 a university college was founded in Pietermaritzburg. The present University of Natal has retained these two local branches, the less expensive faculties being duplicated but the expensive professional faculties confined to one centre only. The Universities of Potchefstroom and of the Orange Free State in Bloemfontein began as colleges for the study of humanities and pure science and they have played important roles in the training of teachers. More recently their expansion into the technological field has met a demand for training in the sciences of agriculture from the rural communities which these institutions have served.

These university centres had this in common. They provided for the regional needs of higher education up to about the level of a general degree in a British university. They were expanded on the assumption that they should supply most of the needs of the provincial communities in which they were situated – that is train the teachers, lawyers, business executives and, so far as their resources allowed, pure and applied scientists. They aimed to be self-sufficient and tried to expand in order to meet new regional demands as they came along, recognising that they had been strategically placed to draw students from natural catchments.

This regional distribution of university centres for the white population of South Africa encouraged the choice of the local centre but did nothing to compel it. Cape Town, Rhodes and Stellenbosch have always attracted many students from far afield. Pretoria, Potchefstroom and Bloemfontein – Afrikaans-language universities – serve extensive rural populations in the central and northern parts of the country and consequently have a large proportion of students in residence. Witwatersrand University has retained its metropolitan regional character since it was founded. At present it serves mainly the metropolitan Witwatersrand and the southern Transvaal. Less than 5 per cent of the students come from farther afield and less than 10 per cent are in residence. And so it has a greater proportion of home-based students than any other South African university. The case for the home-based student is often understated. In an area which is culturally and socially active – like the industrial Witwatersrand – there is a kind of exposure to social and intellectual stimuli in the homes of the students themselves and those which they visit which may be harder to find in university residences where students have not been subject to rigorous selection. There is also the point that, just as in the early stages of child education parents and homes must play their parts, so the moral and social development that goes along with university work needs the support of homes and the social institutions to which students and their parents have access. Perhaps some of the less attractive postures of youthful communities today may be attributable to leaving the whole job of education to educational institutions. Education may be too serious a task to be left entirely to teachers.

The present university system in South Africa which provides for the white community has developed from the colleges described above. After World War II university centres were expanded greatly, and at the same time their scope was extended. Within a short time the University Colleges of Natal, Rhodes, Potchefstroom and the Orange Free State attained independent status and their parent institution, the University of South Africa, became a university for external students. In the twenty-five years since then it has grown into one of the largest correspondence institutions in the world.

UNIVERSITY STRUCTURE AND GOVERNMENT

The universities of South Africa owe their origin not to state initiative, but to the efforts of private persons. They are not state institutions but they are aided by the state. Regrettably, perhaps, the measure of state aid has grown with the rising costs of development and recurrent expenditure, and the early desire to create university institutions which could operate more or less independently of the exercise of state authority has been recognised to be impracticable. Nevertheless, despite increasing dependence upon state financial support and the virtual supervision exercised by the state over such items as expenditure of capital for development and the salaries of academic staff, there is a substantial measure of university freedom. Each university is a corporate body established by an Act of Parliament. The powers of general control of university affairs are vested in the council while the senate has the usual powers in academic matters. The councils of South African universities are composed predominantly of laymen, including a minority of government nominees. The senates are represented, and provision is made for local authorities, financial benefactors and past students to participate in university government. The universities are free to decide the courses they will offer, within the limits of the financial resources available; they are free to select and appoint their own staff and their own students from those who are legally and academically qualified for selection. In terms of the Universities Act of 1955 there are common requirements for admission to degree courses, prescribed by a Joint Matriculation Board of the Universities of South Africa.

The university structure was built up essentially to meet the needs of white students. In 1916 the University College of Fort Hare was opened after a long endeavour in the field of Bantu education by the United Free Church of Scotland. A guarantee fund had been started in 1907. A grant of R20,000 was made by the Transkeian Territories and the United Free Church of Scotland contributed R10,000 and promises of further support were received. A constitution was adopted in 1914 and the college was opened in 1916 by the prime minister with a promise of an annual grant from the government. The College of Fort Hare's first five years were devoted to preparing a few students for university entrance, and assisting a much greater number to make up for deficiencies of their secondary education or to study for diplomas in commerce and agriculture. Incorporated as an institution for higher education under the Act of 1923, the college prepared students for external degrees of the University of South Africa, eventually being granted some of the privileges of the constituent colleges. In 1950, when constituent colleges of the University of South Africa were granted independent university status, the University College of Fort Hare was affiliated to Rhodes University, its nearest neighbour, which supervised its academic standards till 1960 when it became a university college under the government's Department of Bantu Education, catering for the Xhosa-speaking group of Africans.

At the time of this latter transfer there were approximately 400 students in the University College of Fort Hare. While it was the only institution catering exclusively for the education of non-white persons, other universities in the country were making a contribution. Out of a total of approximately 22,000 university students in the country 1,300 were non-white, about 500 of these attending the Universities of Cape Town and Witwatersrand. Admitted on the basis of their academic qualifications, in all academic matters they received the same treatment as the white students. However, in social matters these universities conformed to the prevailing South African practice of separation. The University of Natal admitted non-white students but at undergraduate level they were required to attend separate classes which were offered in Durban only. Rhodes University did not admit non-white students to undergraduate courses in view of the facilities nearby at Fort Hare; nor did the Afrikaans-medium universities admit non-white students. The English-medium universities which did so came to be known as the 'open' universities.

In 1959 the passing of the Extension of Universities Act imposed upon all South African universities a uniform policy in accordance with the doctrine of 'apartheid'. Separate university institutions were established for the non-white groups – two for Africans, one for Asians and one for Coloured persons – and the 'open' universities were prohibited from admitting non-white students, by law becoming segregated institutions. They protested vigorously and bitterly but with no effect. In the University of the Witwatersrand a bronze plaque at the entrance to the Great Hall bears the inscription:

> We affirm in the name of the University of the Witwatersrand that it is our duty to uphold the principle that a university is a place where men and women, without regard to race or colour, are welcome to join in the acquisition and advancement of knowledge; and to continue faithfully to defend this ideal against all those who have sought by legislative enactment to curtail the autonomy of the University. Now therefore we dedicate ourselves to this ideal and to the restoration of the autonomy of our university.

And in the University of Cape Town a bronze plaque in the lobby of the main library bears this inscription:

> MONUMENTUM HOC AENEUM
> DEDICAVIT CANCELLARIUS
> ERAPTAE LIBERTATIS ACADEMICAE
> QUAE DEFECIT ANNO MCMLX
> REDIT ANNO ———.

Feelings in the open universities still run high on the issue of their loss of freedom to admit non-white students and there are annual mass meetings to reaffirm their position.

At present there are nine residential universities for the white population and four for the non-white. In addition there is the University of South Africa, at which both white and non-white students may register for external study. Approximately 50,000 students are in attendance at the white universities, about 3,500 at the non-white, ie roughly 1·25 per cent of the total white population and 0·03 per cent of the non-white population.

THE NON-WHITE UNIVERSITIES

There are thus two more or less distinct university systems or streams. The non-white stream, being the more recent, has not yet attained anything like the stature or stability of the former, and it is difficult to predict which way it will go. Will it work out its own future in an apartheid society or is apartheid a temporary phase, in higher education at least, destined to break down under the mounting social and political pressures upon South African society? A single university system would serve the country best. The financial strains of apartheid can be borne by a buoyant economy more easily than the strains upon the resources of educated manpower. The literacy level of the white population is fairly high – though not as high as in Britain, Germany or Holland; that of the non-whites is very low indeed. Education for all is a long way off and the country is far from producing enough university graduates for the professions such as law, medicine and engineering and also the vast numbers of teachers required in schools, colleges and universities. Till it does the educated minority must do the best it can.

At the level of university education, apartheid almost certainly hinders progress; the educational opportunity of association in an academic community of people varying in age and experience from young students, lively, eager and fresh from the constraints of school discipline, to mature professors, whose scholarly works have earned them recognition as public figures in their own countries at least, is less easily achieved in isolated institutions created for ethnic groups with low standards of education and of living. In order to flourish, young universities need enormous freedom – freedom that leads to the development of individual qualities of teaching and research – of areas of excellence perhaps encouraged by environmental advantages for certain fields of study – reputations for the production of scholars notable in various fields which can be turned to community service. Grouped together these qualities make up what may be called the personality of the university. The personalities of the great universities can be attributed to a variety of factors, many of which go back a long way in history. But somehow they managed to gather inside their walls the brightest young people of the country and also to receive contributions of talent in students and staff from the world outside who, attracted by the academic lustre of the place, came along to complete their university education. The non-white universities of South Africa, good as they are as centres of post-school instruction, will be many decades achieving that kind of standing.

The system of non-white university education in South Africa as it is structured at present seems destined to develop slowly. It suffers from lack of significant contact with the academic communities of the older universities in the country and with the world community of universities. Nevertheless, as undergraduate-training institutions, the non-white universities have done well and they deserve respect and encouragement. The professors and lecturers are an unusual group of men – mostly Afrikaans-speaking – with an admirable dedication to the cause of African education. Their notable service in the cause of African development is not acknowledged as generously as it deserves to be. It is to be expected that university institutions in developing communities will grow slowly and indeed may take most of a century to attain the standards of the universities of Europe and America. But the process will be all the more difficult if it has to take place without the sort of aid and encouragement that new universities all over the world have received from their older neighbours and from the international community of universities.

Today the development of universities is the business of the world. International exchange and co-operation in the circulation of students in the interests of wider intellectual and recreational experience, specialist gatherings for research, inter-university and international programmes and the social and organisational activities that go with them are all part of the commerce of university education. It is inevitable that the ethnic universities of South Africa and the successful students within them will wish to see these institutions grow to the stature of other new universities in Africa, and to enjoy similar freedoms to associate with the universities of the world. The quality of university education in South Africa in the next twenty years will depend very much upon the encouragement which the South African government gives to these institutions. They need the freedom for their teachers and students to associate with other universities inside and outside the country, to control their external relations and to choose and develop for themselves those fields of academic study for which they have environmental advantages. Fortunately recent events in South Africa indicate that official thinking is turning in this direction.

THE WHITE UNIVERSITIES

The reasons for establishing regional centres for university education in South Africa were good at the time: distances are great, travel was difficult and expensive and the regional higher-education needs were more or less similar. After World War II facilities for undergraduate university study were expanded rapidly. The established universities – Cape Town, Stellenbosch, Witwatersrand and Pretoria – grew rapidly, and at the same time university colleges in Natal, Potchefstroom, Grahamstown and Bloemfontein were granted full university status and developed more or less on similar lines. The country did not at the same time create an infrastructure between the schools and the universities which would provide for the substantial body of students with a need for post-school education, but not necessarily of the kind that leads to a university degree. Most of the effort went into providing for school-leavers proceeding to university. As the years have gone on, conditions have changed and the universities themselves have improved; they are demanding more of their undergraduates and not all are intellectually equipped for this. In addition there is now a considerable section of the student community in South Africa that needs facilities for advanced work – viable centres for advanced study at which there are enough students and teachers working together with modern facilities to create the kind of stimulating atmosphere in which research can prosper. And, of course, this need applies to all the common fields of university study. In the present situation, with non-white students, with few exceptions, restricted to their own institutions, there are too many universities competing for the students that come from a white population of about 4 million. The need for regional centres, more or less alike, has passed. Fewer centres would serve the country better, but each centre should strive to acquire its own special character by devoting special attention to fields of study especially appropriate to its own location. At this stage South African universities should strive to become national centres with differences rather than regional centres that are similar. Inter-university movement needs encouraging, more especially for work at advanced level.

Although the total number of white students in South African universities is impressively large for the size of the population, postgraduate numbers are small. Research groups are difficult to build up and sustain. The country is not turning out enough people of the right intellectual quality to meet the demands for university teachers. The English-language universities still rely heavily upon immigrant teachers, the non-white universities on the Afrikaans-speaking section of the community. In addition to this the universities have not enough money to provide both the teaching services and the opportunities for following careers in research and scholarship expected by people who enter university life. The struggle to keep the best South African scholars for our own country is one that we are not really winning.

Yet in spite of these difficulties the country has accomplished a great deal. South Africa's degrees compare well with degrees of a similar structure awarded in Europe and America. In a recent address to the congregation of the University of the Witwatersrand the writer said: '. . . of Witwatersrand University it can be said that our good students hold their own wherever they go; our advanced degrees are held in high esteem. The research record of our staff commands international respect.' No doubt comparable claims could be made on behalf of the other well-established South African universities, all of which are jealous of the standing of their degrees.

Unfortunately the South African school system has not kept up with the increasing demands imposed upon university students. Formal requirements for entering the university have not been raised for a long time and it is not easy for the universities to select their students, in any but the severely restricted faculties, as rigorously as they would like. South African universities have in fact widened the gap between acceptable school pupils who may pass a school-leaving examination and young students well-enough educated to accept the responsibility of learning by reading and discussion, essential processes of learning in a university.

QUALITY AND SCOPE OF UNIVERSITY TEACHING

University failure rate is a matter of considerable public interest. The schools claim that they send good pupils to the universities and they fail. The teaching must be bad, they assert. There should be no gap between school and university; it is the universities' job to take over where the schools leave off. To this the universities reply that if they were given more time – five years instead of three – more plant and more staff, they would bridge the gap. The non-white universities, which draw their students from schools inferior to those for white pupils, have accepted the situation and are prepared to give university time to making up for deficiencies in school education. A lower standard in some universities may be preferable to a high failure rate for a short time, but the problem of the poorly prepared student is a serious one for all the South African universities, and if the state is serious in its endeavours to provide high-quality university education for students of all races, the situation should not be allowed to last longer than is necessary. The students are interested in this question. Their demands are insistent for more skilful presentation of lecture material, summary notes, exercises and tutorial facilities, in short for all the skills and procedures of schoolroom teaching to be applied in the universities. Now and then there are signs of public pressure with some official support to make life easier in universities for, it is argued, the state spends a lot of money on universities and they mustn't be allowed to waste it by failing too many students.

The universities may soon have to decide how far they can go to meet these pressures. Their own houses are not entirely tidy. Their teaching is not always good, and insufficient thought has been given to the efficiency of various teaching practices. We can admit straight away that lucid communication in speech and writing is essential for any kind of fruitful relationship between university scholars at all levels. Of that there can be no doubt. But if the universities are to be persuaded to adopt the best of schoolroom teaching methods and conduct their courses in rooms adorned with all the teaching devices of modern technology, some estimate must be made of the consequences. You may do two things. First you may, at the cost of slowing the pace of some courses, prolong the academic lives of some students who find it hard to get along by themselves. And second you may increase the capacity of the university for undertaking vocational courses which are intellectually undemanding and which may do no more than pass on knowledge and skills required immediately in the pursuit of certain careers. But you may do something else too. You may delay the time when the best young students learn to teach themselves. And you may drive them away to places where the pace is faster and suits their talents better. In short, you may drive away your good students in an effort to ensure the success of the mediocre ones.

There are signs that the South African universities are being pressed towards providing most of the higher education beyond the school stage required for careers. It is thought to be good training for students to spend some time in a university, even if they are not capable of staying the course for a degree. Courses in secretarial practice, pharmacy, domestic science, physical education, business practice and some para-medical skills are being offered already, and requests are coming in for more of a similar kind. The main difficulty confronting the universities is not that these disciplines are unworthy of serious study or that they do not demand diligent attention from the students. It is that the body of knowledge that makes up the curricula is not yet of a kind that can be preserved, communicated and developed by the ordinary procedures of a university institution. The research that advances the knowledge is not normally done by those who teach it. Consequently a different kind of university staff is required which cannot be selected, employed and assessed for advancement on the basis of the criteria applied to conventional university teachers.

It is realised that there is a need for well-organised and well-presented vocational instruction for students who are about to enter a variety of occupations important to the nation's economy. The argument is advanced that the universities are there already; they are organised to teach students and will probably do so better than vocational colleges. Moreover, the incentive of an award that bears the seal of a university will encourage many school-leavers of the right calibre to offer themselves for vocational training. The economy has expanded fast and demands are insistent for young men and women with a much higher standard of education than the schools can provide and with some evidence of the intellectual capacity to succeed and progress in the employment they enter.

The South African universities have not gone so far along the road to comprehensive university education that they cannot retreat. But before the dawn of the 1980s decisions must be taken that will determine the university pattern of the future. The decisions will be taken partly in the light of political policy and partly to serve the urgent educational needs of the country. Within the last year or two in South Africa the public has become aware of the need to educate and train the African population. Higher wages, better housing, retirement benefits and medical aid are accepted as necessary in the interests of economic prosperity and social and political harmony. But along with these must go a greater capacity to serve, to initiate change, to accept responsibility and so on. To achieve these changes and the most efficient use of the country's population resources, a vastly improved system of education is needed and one which moves as speedily as possible towards compulsory education of equal quality for all sections of the population. The removal of apartheid in university education could hasten the attainment of this objective.

It is important to realise that South Africa's supply of men who are intellectually good enough and suitably trained to serve as university teachers is small, too small for our needs. These scarce resources must be used carefully. For a start let us distinguish between the kinds of higher education that demand a high level of scholarship and those that do not. For the less demanding courses we can establish separate institutions, call them colleges for further education, in which the career opportunities for the teachers are not necessarily linked with achievement in research and originality in scholarship. Then the universities can be preserved for what they are intended to do, the vocational and technical colleges catering for the large number of students who want post-school education but who are unlikely to be interested in, or to succeed at, university work. A properly structured system in which colleges were developed into institutions of high quality offering carefully planned curricula under the guidance of dedicated college teachers would soon gain public respect.

The universities in South Africa at present reserved for white students should not develop differently from those reserved for the non-white groups. In time – and hopefully a short time – all universities will be free again to admit students of any colour who will pass freely from one university to another in order to work in those most suitable for their special fields of interest. This change will certainly come, even under the present government some relaxation of university apartheid for advanced students does not seem unattainable. The demand for university education from the non-white population of South Africa is going to increase slowly, because of the poor quality of the schools and the low level of literacy. If the students of the ethnic universities were to go to the white universities some would do well, and of these a reasonable proportion would find their way into the top academic strata of the country, competing successfully for overseas scholarships and eventually taking honoured places amongst the distinguished intellectuals of the country. Others would find the transition too difficult and fail. The existing universities for whites and non-whites could, between them, without seriously straining their resources, cope with the present university-going population. By the late 1980s the total population may reach 30 million. There is plenty of room for imaginative expansion of university education as the whole educational system improves.

It is difficult to think with any conviction of an educational system which educates a large African population through the language medium of English or Afrikaans and passes the more able students into universities which contribute nothing to the quality of life of the African communities. In time the universities must surely direct themselves to African culture under the leadership of new generations of African scholars. How this is going to work it is difficult to tell but obviously there are very different problems in developing a system of university education suitable for the population of Southern Africa, where there is a substantial European community, than there are in, say, Zambia or East Africa where a move towards an African-oriented education system seems logical and feasible. For the time being in South Africa it might be wisest to leave the ethnic universities to develop in their own way, encouraging them with legal and financial freedoms to take the lead in all aspects of educational development in the communities which they are specially qualified to serve.

Changes will come about partly as a result of modification of the government policy of apartheid and partly from economic and social pressures to involve the black people of the country in the economic development and to enable them to share in its prosperity. The most urgent change in the university pattern is likely to come from a move to grant more autonomy to the non-white universities and to draw them into closer association with the white universities. Already the government has approved the inclusion of black people on the governing councils and their appointment to the highest academic and administrative posts. There are signs of the relaxation of university apartheid in moves to encourage black students to enter white universities for advanced work. Almost surely will follow the admission of white students to non-white universities which can offer superior facilities in certain fields of study for which they have natural advantages, eg African languages, social anthropology, African history, and so on. Moves such as these will bring about a closer integration of all the universities of South Africa into a single community and promote better relationships with other universities in Africa and elsewhere. In addition the resources of intellectually able men for work in all the universities of the country will be increased substantially.

It is doubtful whether the existing universities for white people will change their character much in the next twenty years. Non-white students will be admitted in increasing numbers as they become qualified to pursue advanced courses; and without much doubt the need to provide for advanced study in many fields important to the economic growth of the country will lead to the formation of special centres for advanced work in appropriate parts of the country. The establishment of new multi-faculty universities seems unlikely for many years to come. More probable is the creation of new colleges with university affiliations, partly for the training of teachers and for instruction in the common subjects of arts and science and commerce, and partly for providing career training, not up to degree level, for entrants to commerce, industry and administration. It is to be hoped that new institutions of this kind might relieve the burden of unfruitful work undertaken by the present-day universities in which about 40 per cent of all new students fail in their first year.

For a country where only a small proportion of the population receives school education to university-entrance standard, the South African universities are remarkably good. It is to be hoped that the system can be improved rapidly and that in the 1980s the university education that is now readily available for a privileged minority will be within easier reach of the rest of the population.

7

The University in Latin America

SYLVIA HEWLETT

Latin America is a large and extremely diverse area of the world. Extending between the Rio Grande and Tierra del Fuego, it covers 8,250,000 square miles, something like 15 per cent of the world's land surface. Geographically, Latin America is easily defined, but in the political, social and economic spheres its unity is only superficial.

The sub-continent was originally colonised some four centuries ago by the Spaniards and the Portuguese, but at the beginning of the nineteenth century, at the time of independence, it fragmented into nineteen different countries. These range in size from Brazil, which is four times as big as India and has a current population of over 90 million, to El Salvador with a mere 8,000 square kilometres and a population of just over 3 million. The governments of the various countries of Latin America have very little in common: they have ranged from the late Allende's left-wing brand of democratic socialism in Chile to the repressive military autocracy characteristic of present-day Brazil. However, it is probably true to say that the latter is more typical of Latin America than the former.

In terms of social variables, the ethnic, linguistic, educational and religious structures vary considerably from country to country. In Argentina, Uruguay, Chile, Brazil, Venezuela, Colombia, Panama and Costa Rica, the great majority of the population come from Europe, or in some cases from Africa. In Mexico, on the other hand, and the rest of Central America, in Ecuador, Peru, Bolivia and Paraguay, the vast mass of the people are of Amerindian origin. The two major languages there are Spanish and Portuguese and the ruling classes, who rightly lay claim to a Western culture, are proud of their European origins. Yet in fact nearly 30 million Indians still use languages or dialects which go back to long before the conquest. In the educational sphere, the attainments of governments in Latin America differ widely. Argentina can boast a 91 per cent literacy rate while in Bolivia only 32 per cent of the population are literate. Chile spends 5·4 per cent of GNP on education (equivalent to US$49 per capita in 1968) while Brazil spends a mere 3·4 per cent (equivalent to US$10 per capita in 1969). Throughout the subcontinent poor educational facilities and low teaching standards tend to be closely correlated with the backward rural areas, ie precisely those regions that are most in need of education. The superficial nature of the cultural hegemony in Latin America is particularly pronounced in the field of religion. In theory, Catholicism is the official faith of all Latin Americans, but there is a desperate shortage of priests (one per 5,600 people in 1965) and in many cases – particularly in Central America, the Andean areas and Brazil – Catholic beliefs have been superimposed on old Indian ones, or on the fetishism of the former Negro slaves. Furthermore the de-Christianisation of the urban masses has been extremely rapid.

LATIN AMERICA: SOME BASIC STATISTICS

Country	Area (in thousands of km²)	Population (1969 in thousands)	Annual rate of population increase %	Per capita income (1968 US$)
Argentina	2,776	22,876	1·5	657
Bolivia	1,098	4,804	2·6	171
Brazil	8,511	90,840	3·0	283
British Honduras	43	2,500	3·3	242
Chile	756	8,231	2·4	518
Colombia	1,138	20,463	3·2	338
Costa Rica	19	1,514	2·1	423
Ecuador	283	5,890	3·4	214
El Salvador	8	3,100	3·1	262
French Guiana	91	48	na	na
Guatemala	42	4,717	2·9	297
Guyana	214	742	3·1	283
Mexico	1,972	47,236	3·5	553

Country	Area (in thousands of km^2)	Population (1969 in thousands)	Annual rate of popula- tion increase %	Per capita income (1968 US$)
Nicaragua	57	1,685	3·4	357
Panama	29	1,329	3·0	583
Paraguay	406	2,314	3·3	214
Peru	1,285	13,172	3·1	268
Uruguay	177	2,852	1·2	584
Venezuela	1,972	10,035	3·5	977

Source: *United Nations Statistical Yearbook.*

It has been said that the only real unifying factor in Latin America is underdevelopment. But, as can be seen from the table (pages 130–1), poverty is not uniform: in 1968 the gross national product per head was 977 dollars in Venezuela and 171 dollars in Bolivia. Between the two extremes were Chile (518) and Brazil (283). National averages are, however, extremely deceptive in the Latin American context, as structural dualism is characteristic of many economies, ie areas of rapid expansion exist alongside and in interaction with areas that are grossly under-developed. To take an example, Piaui, a state in north-east Brazil, had a per capita income of only US$84 in 1970 while São Paulo state had a per capita income of US$840. In summary, Argentina and parts of other Latin American countries are, in economic terms, part of the developed league, but the remainder of the sub-continent shows most of the signs of underdevelopment: inadequate diet; wastage or under-use of natural resources; poor returns from agriculture; insufficient or incomplete industrialisation; dependence of national economies on foreign powers; archaic social and economic structures; generalised under-utilisation of available labour; and high levels of both illiteracy and population increase.

Generalisations in the context of Latin America are obviously extremely difficult. This is particularly true in the sphere of education due to the way in which educational structures both reflect and influence the social, political and economic dynamics of nations. However, with careful regard to qualifications, I would like to outline those features which in a broad way do serve to distinguish university education in Latin America.

HISTORICAL DEVELOPMENT

More than 150 universities exist at present in the nineteen Latin American countries. Some of them are old-established institutions with a continuous tradition at least as long as that of many European foundations. The National University in Mexico and the University of San Marcos in Peru opened their doors in 1551, and during the following two centuries more appeared in Colombia (Javeriana), Argentina, Venezuela, Ecuador and Bolivia (Chuquisaca). The early universities in Spanish Latin America were mainly religious foundations, the Jesuit order being prominent in the initial phase of development. The rectors were priests and the function of the institutions was to train priests to carry out the civilising work that the church had set itself in the Americas.

A second wave of university expansion occurred in the 1810-25 period as a byproduct of the nationalistic atmosphere accompanying the attainment of independence. Bolivar himself decreed the foundation of universities at Cartagena in Colombia and Trujillo and Arequipa in Peru. Among others were the Venezuelan University of the Andes (1810) and the University of Buenos Aires (1821). These universities, unlike the original establishments, were secular, even anti-clerical in nature, reflecting the republican political attitudes of the time.

Throughout this early period Brazil constitutes an anomaly. Spanish Latin America has a historical record in the sphere of university education at least as good as that of North America and Europe, but the Portuguese legacy in this field is distinctive if not distinguished. Higher education was forbidden in the colonial period (a peculiar component of Portugal's strict mercantilist policies, Brazil was not supposed to compete in any way with the mother country). One or two isolated professional schools emerged in the nineteenth century, but Brazil could not boast a university until the 1920s.

To sum up, by the end of the nineteenth century a pattern of Latin American university education had emerged. The background was provided by the religious foundations, but superimposed upon this were the secular institutions. Law, the most useful professional qualification for the sons of the oligarchs, had ousted theology as the main subject of study. Service to the community had ceased to be a conscious objective of either teachers or taught, and scientific research, which had been a feature of the previous century, had no chance to evolve as a university function given the lack of emphasis on scholarship and the turbulent political conditions of the age. It was generally accepted that the main purpose of higher education was to prepare students for the professions, as a means of inculcating the values and standards proper to their class and to the positions of authority they expected to inherit – to 'train practitioners of the liberal professions, especially law and medicine; and to enable sons of high-status families to maintain their status'.[1]

With the onset of the twentieth century, the modern world with its sophisticated and fast-evolving technological attributes began to encroach on the elitist social structure of Latin America, and university education was reshaped under new pressures and influences.

FORM AND FUNCTION OF UNIVERSITY EDUCATION

The socio-economic make-up of most Latin American countries has changed drastically during this century. Significant increases in the importance of the industrial and service sectors, a transformation of occupational structures, and a resultant shift in the population from the countryside to the towns, are some of the more obvious changes. Some economies have experienced rapid rates of economic growth, eg the GNP of Brazil grew at a rate of 9 per cent pa between 1969 and 1972, but the general picture is that of erratic progress with average rates of growth for all Latin American countries being in the region of 2 per cent pa for the postwar period.

Partly as a reflection of the changing economic complexion of these countries, and partly as a result of policy measures designed to promote the development process, the form and function of university education has changed dramatically in recent years. In particular, the last two decades have witnessed the emergence of higher education as a self-conscious instrument of governmental planning and a topic of considerable official concern. As stated in the Brazilian ten-year development plan: 'Exceptional importance ought to be given to the problem of Brazilian university education, which is already acting as an obstacle to economic development and as a bottleneck to the aspirations for progress.'[2] Similarly: 'The declared aim of the Colombian government in the last decade has been the transformation of the higher educational system to make it a more responsive instrument of economic and social development policies.'[3]

Generally speaking, university education is thought to have two broad aims. On the social front it is meant to contribute to the achievement of equality of opportunity by acting as a vehicle of social mobility. Its economic function is to impart the attitudes and skills required in the developing economies, and in this context particular emphasis is placed on meeting the manpower needs of industry.

Needless to say, as a result of this new appreciation of the 'worth' of higher education, public financing of universities has increased substantially throughout the sub-continent and enrolments have escalated in recent years. In Colombia enrolments in higher education increased 14·2 per cent pa between 1960 and 1968 (from 1·6 to 3·0 per cent of the school-age population). In Mexico, national enrolment increased by 282 per cent between 1940 and 1960, an average annual rate of 14·1 per cent. All but five of Brazil's thirty-two universities have been created since 1946 and enrolment has grown at an average rate of 8 per cent pa since 1940. In the late 1960s almost 300,000 Brazilians were enrolled in higher education and this represented 2·4 per cent of the school-age population.

Despite the impressive increases in the numbers involved in higher education (and the rates quoted above are representative of Latin America as a whole), one should not forget that Latin American universities are still reserved for an elite. A bare 3 per cent of the school-age population receive higher education. In Britain – which is often labelled as being elitist – three times this proportion attend university, while in the USA well over 30 per cent of the relevant age cohort, or ten times the Latin American rate, receive higher education. So despite recent increases in university enrolments, the current record of the sub-continent is not impressive even in crude quantitative terms.

It is now necessary to probe rather more deeply into the functioning of the modern university structure of Latin America in order to answer the rather more important questions of how the institutions are faring in qualitative terms, and whether they are fulfilling the social and economic developmental aims that have been generally ascribed to them.

The bulk of university students in Latin America attend large, non-residential universities, normally located in the largest cities and staffed by part-time faculties. The University of Chile, centred in Santiago, enrolled 13,000 students in 1963, more than half of the total Chilean university population, while in Mexico the National University and the University of Nueva Leon had approximately 60 per cent of the total enrolment in higher education in 1960 (45,000 students). The advantages of this type of institution for a nation with limited resources are numerous and obvious. Two of the usual constraints on university expansion, shortage of dormitory space and scarcity of qualified teachers, are avoided. Money for student residence and maintenance of full-time faculty can be used to increase the number of classrooms and enlarge the size of the part-time faculty.

The scheduling of classes early in the morning and in the evenings and the absence of rigid chronological requirements for the various degrees allow students to hold jobs while they are studying. In 1961 at the National University (Mexico), 16,958 students, 39 per cent of the total enrolment in higher education, were doing outside work, and over half of these were working six hours or more per day. Unlike the summer jobs of most British or American university students, the jobs held by Mexican students are more commensurate with their level of education: data on the National University show that in 1961 almost all working students were employed in white-collar positions, most of them in government offices, banks, insurance companies and other commercial establishments.

The money from this employment and the very low cost of enrolling in non-residential universities theoretically allow students from poorer families to attend but as we shall see later, this does not work out in practice. An additional advantage of this system is that the work experience of students in non-residential universities has educational as well as economic value. In many cases it provides supplementary in-service training in the same field and even the same institution that the student will enter upon graduation. The final advantage is that highly qualified men in other occupations are willing to teach part-time. With their limited financial resources, it would be difficult for the universities to compete for these men on a full-time basis; many economically (and politically) more desirable opportunities are available to them elsewhere. 'When offices close in the Federal District, some of the high-level *technicos* in the government go by taxi to the National University, and students, many of whom work in the same offices, go by bus.'[4]

In short, the positive attributes of the large, urban, part-time Latin American university are that they cut the costs per student to a bare minimum and bring the universities closer to the institutions and establishments which have always employed the majority of graduates.

The disadvantages of the system are fairly serious. The flexible time requirements for the various degrees often permit students to remain at the universities for an inordinate number of years, crowding the facilities for new entrants. The dependence on part-time professors has severely limited university research and has constrained the development of effective courses at the graduate level. The low salary scale[5] has forced men who would prefer full-time employment at the universities to seek supplementary income elsewhere, and the outside commitments of most faculty members have greatly reduced contact between professors and students. Naturally, such a system has militated against the emergence of high-calibre departments which are, the world over, heavily dependent on original research.

Although the large non-residential university dominates the Latin American scene, one should not forget that small residential universities (normally private foundations) do exist. The Monterrey Institute of Technology and Advanced Studies (Mexico) and the Technological Institute of Aeronautics (São Paulo, Brazil) are examples. These particular institutions are run on American lines and are academically excellent; however, in numerical terms this type of higher education is insignificant.

The main organisational features held in common by Latin American universities are undoubtedly the large, urban, non-residential and part-time characteristics already described. However, similarities also exist in the academic structure, the emphasis of the curricula, the mode of entry, the system of financial support, and the social-class composition of the student body.

The early format of the university in Latin America was that of a loose federation of professional schools and this academic structure has persisted to the present day. In Chile the university has been described as 'a loose collection of quasi-independent professional schools'[6] and in the huge National University of Mexico faculties and schools have remained separate to such an extent that even buildings and library facilities of one department cannot be used by students from another department. Both facilities and personnel are often wastefully duplicated, and of course 'cross-fertilisation' between disciplines is practically impossible. Various attempts at co-ordination have met little success. To take just one example, in the spring of 1968 it was still impossible for a basic chemistry course taken by a first-year pharmacy student to be accepted for credit in the medical school of the Federal University of Rio de Janeiro, should that student transfer into medicine. This was true despite the fact that faculty members in both schools agreed that the basic chemistry courses offered by the two schools were essentially the same.

The changing functions of universities, particularly their new role of training people for technical work in industry and business, is reflected in the evolution of enrolments in the various disciplines, and in the emergence of new curricula to serve modern needs. In Brazil, the percentage of students enrolled in medicine and law, the traditional prestige subjects, dropped from 70 per cent in 1940 to 43 per cent in 1964; while the economic sciences, engineering and the faculty of philosophy, science and letters (which primarily trains secondary-school teachers) increased their share of enrolment from 15 to 47 per cent. In Colombia until recently the favourite fields were medicine, civil engineering and law, but since 1955 the traditional studies have given way before a rising tide of interest in the pure and applied sciences, the social sciences, education and in the various branches of engineering other than civil. These trends are typical of Latin America as a whole.

Methods of selection for university education conform to a similar pattern throughout Latin America. The system in Chile illustrates the problems attached to current procedures throughout the sub-continent. To enter university in Chile, a student must have completed the general secondary-school programme and the requirements for a *bacillerato* (a certificate or diploma) in humanities. Examinations leading to this degree are administered by teachers appointed by the Facultad of Philosophy and Education of the University of Chile. Fulfilling these requirements does not guarantee admission to university schools, because each school may impose additional requirements, including its own entrance examinations. The *bacillerato* examination includes a comprehension and composition test for all students, a test of reading in a foreign language, and three tests in the field of specialisation. The special entrance examinations of the individual schools of the universities also focus on the candidate's chosen field of studies. So a student who wishes to study at a university must take three sets of examinations within a short space of time: those of his secondary school, of the university administering the *bacillerato*, and of the particular university school which he plans to enter. Failure to pass any one of the three can block his pursuit of higher education.

The admissions system has come under severe attack from many quarters. Critics point to the undesirable influence that university entrance examinations, which emphasise mainly factual knowledge, have on the secondary schools, where the upper grades of the *liceo* concentrate on preparing students for the *bacillerato* to the neglect of other objectives. This is particularly serious in view of the large percentage who fail to qualify for university admission and who must then seek employment without any specialised training. Studies of scores on the *bacillerato* examination and university marks have shown a positive but low correlation, raising a serious question about the validity of this examination as a predictor of university success; the high rate of failure in the first two years of university work adds further doubt.

As long as university facilities are limited, admissions will necessarily continue to be selective and competitive, but the search for more objective and reliable admission criteria seems to be a worthwhile exercise. The current drop-out rate amongst university students in Latin America is around 50 per cent, a wastage that the sub-continent can ill afford. Many factors contribute to this attrition, eg part-time study and a high student to staff ratio, but it seems that the admissions procedure is a contributory cause.

A further organisational feature held in common by Latin American universities is their subsidisation by public funds; that is to say, there are few direct costs associated with attending university and even indirect costs (in the form of foregone earnings) are low, given the common practice of holding full-time and part-time jobs during the course of study. In Brazil 57 per cent of total enrolment was in the federal universities in 1964; the remainder was concentrated in private institutions heavily dependent on federal subsidies where fees were low. In Colombia the same situation prevails. Approximately 60 per cent of enrolment is in public universities but even in the private sector fees are a mere US$20–US$100 pa. This subsidisation of university education does not however allow the poorer elements in the population the equal access to higher education that might be expected: the structure of financial support at the lower rungs of the educational ladder precludes this possibility. In the majority of Latin American countries, secondary education is extremely selective and predominantly private. There is a scarcity of places, so that the private institutions are able to charge excessive fees and make large profits. Consequently, only the privileged are able to attend secondary school. In Brazil only 7 per cent of the relevant age cohort enter secondary school and these pupils are exclusively from the middle and upper classes. As Higgins has put it, 'the traditional system of providing free elementary and university education while secondary education remains very expensive is a recipe for preserving higher education as a device whereby the privileged classes protect their privileges'.[7] This statement applies equally well to the rest of Latin America. Free (or at least heavily subsidised) university education, is, in this context, merely a cover for subsidising the elite.

It seems to be amply evident that university education is not fulfilling the explicit social role assigned to it by governments in Latin America, ie it does not encourage equality of opportunity or act as a vehicle of social mobility; in fact it reinforces and perpetuates the hegemony of the elite. It now remains to decide whether higher education in Latin America is any more successfully fulfilling its economic role; we should consider the relevance of university education as an investment, in the Latin American context.

EDUCATION AS AN INVESTMENT

Economists started to show concern for education in the late 1950s, when empirical investigations in the United States revealed that output was growing much faster than inputs as conventionally measured. The part of the growth of output unaccounted for by conventional inputs came to be known as the 'residual'. Original explanations of the residual such as 'technical change' or 'shifts in the production functions' were of little analytical help. They simply led to the question of how a country could shift its production function or induce technical change so as to achieve a higher level of output. The initial attempt to explain the residual in a more profound fashion involved mainly the quantification of the increase in the quality of labour inputs, and this led to the creation of a new field in economics known as the 'economics of human capital', or more narrowly, the 'economics of education'. Since then there has been a huge shift in emphasis in development planning, from physical to human capital as the major source of growth.

Once education had been seen as an investment, the next logical question was: what is the monetary pay-off from this investment? For, if the objective is an efficient allocation of resources between different uses, the yield of investment in human beings has to be compared to that on investment in other forms of capital. At the centre of any discussion of optimal resource allocation lies the concept of a profitability measure of investment in education.

Casual observation and statistical data indicate that people with more education earn higher wages than people with less education. For example, the average earnings of a male college graduate in the United States in 1959 was US$9,255 and the corresponding earnings of a high-school graduate US$6,132. Therefore, a college graduate would expect to earn annually, over his working life, a net US$3,123 over what he would be earning as a secondary-school graduate. But in order to enjoy this extra benefit he would have to invest a certain amount of money in higher education. The total private cost of four years of college education was estimated to be US$14,768 in 1959, which includes direct expenses such as tuition fees and books, as well as indirect costs in the form of foregone earnings while studying. The investment equivalent of the above venture is that of buying a promise to receive annually US$3,123 at a cost of US$14,768 now. A simple calculation shows that the annual yield of this particular investment is about 20 per cent, and this is known as the internal rate of return to investment in higher education. Rates of return to investment in other levels of schooling can be computed in a similar fashion.

In the last decade, rate of return analysis has been extensively applied to evaluating educational systems in developing countries as it is particularly useful in planning decisions.

> The simple truth is . . . that there is no way of avoiding a cost-benefit approach to the planning and programming of education or of any other aspect of 'social development'. An implicit cost-benefit comparison is always involved whenever the cut-off point is determined. Deciding not to spend another million *esperitos* on education means deciding that for the same cost, higher returns—in whatever form or however measured—can be obtained in some other way. Much confusion has been introduced into the discussion by presenting the manpower approach or the residual factor approach . . . as an alternative to cost-benefit analysis . . . Since an implicit cost-benefit analysis is always involved there is much to be said for making it explicit and as accurately quantified as possible.[8]

Ideally, a calculation of the social rate of return on the various levels and types of education should allow the optimal distribution of resources both within the educational sphere and between this and other sectors of the economy. The table following contains a summary of the rates of return that have been calculated from Latin America. Several conclusions can be drawn. Firstly, the social rate of return to investment in university education is high; with the exception of Colombia, the rates are in excess of the chosen opportunity cost for social capital (calculated by the authors to be in the region of 12 per cent). Secondly, in the case of Mexico and Venezuela the social rate of return to university education is higher than the return to secondary schooling but lower than the return to primary schooling. The reverse is true in the Brazilian calculations, while in the Chilean case higher education seems to be less profitable than either of the other levels. A final point to emerge is a pronounced discrepancy between the social and the private rates of return at the university level (confirming our earlier discussion of the implications of the cost structure of university education).

RATES OF RETURN TO EDUCATION IN FIVE LATIN AMERICAN COUNTRIES
BY LEVEL OF EDUCATION (%)

| Country | Author | Date | Social | | | Private | | |
			Primary	Secondary	University	Primary	Secondary	University
Brazil	Hewlett	1962	10·7	17·2	14·5	11·3	21·4	33·2
Chile	Harberger and	1959						
	Selowsky	1959	24·0	16·9	12·2	—	—	—
Colombia	Selowsky	1966	40·0	24·0	8·0	50·0	32·0	15·5
Mexico	Carnoy	1963	25·0	17·0	23·0	32·0	23·0	29·0
Venezuela	Shoup	1957	82·0	17·0	23·0	—	18·0	27·0

Compiled from G. Psacharopoulos, *The Economic Returns to Investment in Education in the Process of Growth and Development* (Amsterdam: 1973), Appendix C.

There has been considerable discussion in Latin America as to the scarcity of high-level manpower,[9] and as we saw earlier this concern has permeated official thinking. Despite recent dramatic increases in university enrolments, only a tiny proportion of the relevant age cohort receive the benefits of higher education. The rate of return calculations tend to confirm a picture of substantial under-investment in university education, ie it would be profitable (as well as socially desirable) for governments in Latin America to increase the amount of public investment in this level of education, not at the expense of secondary and primary schooling, which also receive high rates of return, but by a transference of resources from other sectors (perhaps defence!). The rate of return calculations also have equity implications, as it seems that some of the costs of university education could be borne by the recipients. The money saved by such a scheme could perhaps be used to extend public secondary education to the poorer elements in the population.

The university system in Latin America does not seem to be fulfilling its economic or social roles with any degree of success. The problems are both quantitative and qualitative. In the first instance there seems to be ample scope for further increases in enrolment. There is a demonstrable need for more highly qualified people in the economies of these countries, and certainly the social objectives of higher education will never be achieved with a mere 3 per cent of the school-age population attending university. However, careful attention should be paid to the structure of educational financing, so that increased public expenditure on higher education does not accrue solely to the privileged. In qualitative terms the room for improvement is enormous; the student-staff ratio, the lack of co-ordination between the various component faculties of a university, the admissions procedure, all can and should be improved.

Needless to say quantitative and qualitative considerations are intimately interlinked, as reducing the drop-out rate in higher education (a result of qualitative improvements) would automatically expand the capacity of the system to produce additional graduates at no extra cost. As a final note, I should like to add that several distinctive features of university education in Latin America are highly admirable and are capable of providing object lessons for systems elsewhere. In particular, the urban, non-residential, part-time university can, at its best, provide a unique combination of relevant work experience with higher education at a cost per student that is amongst the lowest in the world.

8

The University in West Germany

JOACHIM H. KNOLL

(trans KLAUS KÜNZEL)

Discussions about university reform have been going on in Germany for over fifty years now. Shortly after World War I, at a time when cherished traditions collapsed, voices were first raised to urge the necessity for university reform. The university, it was maintained, which in the past had so often uncritically adopted the Wilhelmian philosophy of life, should henceforth breathe a republican spirit. During the first tentative steps on republican ground, the educational system was to become a guarantee for political and social stability. The road backwards was to be closed for all time, the past overcome by constitutional directives. As it turned out, this phase of naïve perfectionistic belief passed fairly quickly, and contemporary discussions about educational reform are characterised by greater circumspection and objectivity.

Carl Heinrich Becker, at one time minister for culture in Prussia, to whose cautious progressiveness the educational system of Weimar Germany owed a lot, submitted his *Thoughts on University Reform* as early as 1919, maintaining that 'the roots of our universities are healthy'.[1] It was this kind of attitude which lent character and direction to the prevailing reform conceptions. There could be no question of abandoning the idea of a university as it had been moulded at the beginning of the nineteenth century, or even of partially modifying and weakening it. Rather it was a change in the university's relationship with the existing political and social realities which its reform was to achieve.[2] The university of the 1920s was felt to lack the essential open-mindedness and flexibility which the novel phenomena of twentieth-century reality demanded. Current criticisms of our universities tend to point in the same direction.

UNIVERSITY REFORM IN GENERAL

However, Becker's considerations and proposals met stiff opposition. In those days, as in our own time, even otherwise knowledgeable observers might accept loose and hasty judgements. Admittedly, discussions of this kind have of late increasingly been superseded by progressive reform intentions of a more explicit nature. Where reforms have been implemented between 1965 and 1970, the general consensus seems to have been that the idea of a university, adequately defined by 'unity of research and instruction', is still valid and applicable. Occasionally, sceptical voices have been raised during the first phase of university reform as to whether unity of research and instruction could possibly be maintained in the face of continuous university expansion, and whether the university was still equipped to help the student to come into fruitful contact with research at all.

To those acquainted with organised research it is an open secret that, due to its ever-increasing specialisation and differentiation, some branches of it simply cannot be communicated to the ordinary student. West Germany's Max Planck Institutes are so highly specialised that they should not be burdened with tasks arising from a largely practically oriented professional training. Connections with higher education are usually established through their directors, who frequently occupy chairs in university departments. As a rule, the number of research institutes of this type depends upon the quantity of working areas a university cannot administer. These establishments allow the universities to retain adequate space for the preservation of the traditional concept of unified research and instruction.

Some current reform proposals, however, resemble American models, according to which the university is divided into two main 'levels', the level of preparatory professional training and that of research.[3] The American institutes for advanced studies, entirely focusing on specialised research, are distinctly separated from the ordinary university establishments which, in turn, equip students for their occupations and enable them to make an initial 'amateurish' contact with research. The sociologist Helmut Schelsky, whose support for this type of structural differentiation is shared in a particular recommendation of the *Wissenschaftsrat* (Science Council) writes: 'Within the context of such [a] differentiated tertiary system there should exist a form of university establishment' – he calls it a 'theoretical university' – 'which avails itself entirely to the theoretical aspects of modern knowledge. By abstaining from a direct involvement in professional training tasks and due to a lack of a highly sophisticated research organisation, such an institution will be in a better position than the universities to reach some of the targets envisaged by current science and higher-education reform plans.'[4] And yet, rather than following the suggestions expressed in this model, the post-1965 universities (Bremen, Regensburg, Bochum, Konstanz and Augsburg, for instance) have structured their reform concepts in accordance with the specific needs arising from the academic status quo.

One thing, I believe, has been made clear so far, that the present university reform is firmly rooted in the traditional idea of a university. It is therefore fair to say that the reform of tertiary education unites elements of tradition and progressiveness. To what extent the internal and external structures call for reform will be shown later on. If we intend to examine the relationship between university and society, we should first consider what we mean by 'society'. Obviously in our context it does not stand for the entirety of adult citizens, many of whom are indifferent to or untouched by the university's peculiar problems. Here, 'society' would mean those organisations, associations and groups which have a more or less substantial interest in the university. Naturally, the motives of their interest are multifarious and subject to constant revision; they may reflect group egoism or a highly developed sense of collective concern, they can express themselves in realistic judgement or fancy ideas. In principle, there are two different motives of university reform: first, the reforming zeal from within, an impulse which is carried by the notion that the university has to adapt to the changed realities of life, and second, those forces which spell out their wishes and claims to the education authorities and universities from outside.

It would be wrong to assume that our society tends to approach only the newer universities for the realisation of its claims. It is indeed with them that most new 'adventures' are likely to find an open ear; they can operate on a more flexible basis than the traditional universities feel able to. But the latter, too, are prepared to accept their share, even if the process of reform is likely to be slower there, established institutions having a tendency towards retention of their status quo.

PROFESSIONAL PREPARATION

Looking at those reform impulses which originate from inside the university, both old and new universities undoubtedly hold on to their traditional task of providing preparatory professional education.[5] As early as the time of Wilhelm von Humboldt, one specific branch of professional education was made the sole responsibility of the university. Together with the foundation of the Friedrich-Wilhelm University of Berlin, the *examen pro facultate docendi* – ie the proficiency test for teaching in a higher secondary school – was introduced. As the late Hans Wenke, educationist and foundation rector of Bochum University, has pointed out, this was evidently proof of a conspicuous demonstration of trust on the part of the state.[6] It should be stressed, furthermore, that we are here dealing with a legitimate, genuine state interest. One should not succumb to taboos on talking about finances in university circles. Is it altogether unreasonable if the state, in return for its substantial material investments, expects some assistance and co-operation from the universities in matters of professional training? Naturally, the autonomy of the university should remain unchallenged.

No sensible person, however, would expect a university to orient its teaching and research primarily towards practical vocational requirements, and indeed only a small part of its activities can legitimately be called 'vocational training'. Not training, but professional preparation in a wider educational sense is the university's main concern. Hermann Heimpel occasionally spoke of a 'stream of wrong opinions according to which one had to learn everything in the university which one would need in later life',[7] adding that only 'preliminary professional preparation could be the task of universities'.[8] Although this sounds convincing, it remains to be seen whether the students are of similar opinion or whether they would not expect clear, straightforward professional training courses. Currently, students attend the university not mainly in order to acquaint themselves with rigorous intellectual activity and structured modes of thought, but because they hanker after the final certification which guarantees them, amongst other things, high social prestige. Among the most common demands expressed in this context are: reduction of course duration, restructuring of study courses, protection of study careers by means of intermediate examinations, regulations for study, etc. The second reform phase—from 1970 onwards—has however brought some counter-current tendencies.

Such demands have their justification, but only if they are separated from a utilitarian certificate mentality; moreover, they have to be differentiated according to each individual university discipline. The natural sciences will be better equipped to meet these requirements than arts subjects where a school-type study course is, generally speaking, neither possible nor desirable. In public, the demands are frequently disguised in terms such as 'topical', 'modern', 'appropriate' or 'of contemporary appeal'. More than anything else, these notions demonstrate a lack of understanding for the intrinsic nature of the university – which after all is not a vocational school of higher rank.

Thus one frequently finds in universities a blatant materialism, a utilitarianism and, above all, a growing ignorance as to what *universitas litterarum* is all about. A multitude of particular group interests all too often expect the university to provide an entirely pragmatic training for their designated employees.

Much as the university has to care about professional preparation – stimulating for both student and teacher – under no circumstances can it allow pressure from so many students to turn it into a school, to dictate the course of development. Academic freedom will not, on the other hand, be renounced by the universities. In this freedom – the precondition of all forms of mental activity – lies the opportunity for self-education; to make sensible use of it requires discipline and some mental maturity. One often comes across public complaints about the university's tendency to grow into a body of increasingly anonymous character and hence to become unable to contribute substantially to the education of its students. And, indeed, there are no direct educational measures for the university to undertake, although its indirect educational influence is positively present in the contact between student and organised knowledge.[9] Hans Wenke has characterised this situation:

> Nowadays the university is often challenged to fulfil its educational duties by preventing the student from failure—that is, by offering study aids and counselling instead of leaving him to his own destiny. In this obligation to provide human assistance, which I accept in principle, we have to recognise a symptom for the fact that the encounter between knowledge and man as an intrinsic formative element has ceased to be a generally accepted proposition. This does not imply a lack of confidence in the formative power of organised

knowledge but rather a legitimate doubt as to whether the university in its present state is able to realise this potential fully. Above all, this sceptical attitude stems from the conviction that there are a great many students for whom the impulse towards self-education through academic pursuits cannot be presupposed or expected. In addition to this, one has to take into account the influence of some modern social thought according to which the university would neglect its students in certain essential respects if it relied solely on the formative power of academic self-education and otherwise left them to the free play of success and failure without provision for stronger guidance... In these opinions right and wrong are so intimately tied up that in the everyday work of universities they can hardly be distinguished. It is therefore all the more necessary to attempt a distinction and clarification.

My first respective preposition runs: the conviction that intercourse with organised knowledge (*Wissenschaft*), with its content, questions and order of ideas, directly affects the spiritual and intellectual structure of the individual and must remain the starting point and basis of our university . . . I am fully aware, though, that knowledge should always keep in mind the radius of its own sphere just as it is always prepared to realise and acknowledge its limits of understanding.[10]

THE PROBLEMS OF MASS EDUCATION

Public opinion is concerned that the universities are becoming increasingly mass-oriented. Statistics do show that in terms of student number some have already exceeded their maximum size. Munich lodges over 25,000 students, Hamburg 20,000, and a few other universities which originally offered places for some 4,000–5,000 students have left the 10,000 mark far behind. According to the estimates of the Ministry for Science the student population will be over a million by the end of this century.[11] Is it realistic to hope for a personal tutor-student relationship under these circumstances? Will not the state of frightening anonymity be intensified rather than diminished?

First of all, it is my conviction that only a tiny minority of professors build a 'wall of assistants' around themselves to keep students away. Secondly, there exists a kind of 'moulding at a distance'; one can be 'impressed' by an academic personality amongst an audience of some 1,500. Dialogues are not restricted to the sphere of personal communication. This is an experience which students of so many former generations have already had. And finally, certain kinds of students do not seek personal contact with the professor at all. They choose a form of intellectual solitude which makes them by no means inferior to other students. All these arguments lack, however, sensational appeal and are therefore not likely to evoke public appreciation; also they only touch the fringe of our problem.

THE NEW UNIVERSITIES

One way of dealing with the enormous numbers of students is the foundation of new universities – or the expansion of existing ones. Years ago the Federation of German Students (VDS) called for no less than ten new universities.[12] The fact that the financing of such a programme is simply not possible is casually brushed aside, as is the problem of where the additional teaching staff are to come from. Personally, I think it is naïve to suggest that present priorities within the budget should be rearranged. In fact, current expenditure on culture and education is already very considerable. North Rhine Westphalia's budget, for instance, shows that more than a third is spent on education and general cultural activities. That, clearly, is no fact to keep silent about.[13]

We are still talking about the first phase of reform: some years ago the *Wissenschaftsrat* published its views on the general expansion of university establishments[14] in which apart from the problems of numerical and geographical extension, new university models were being put forward. These new universities were not envisaged solely in terms of sheer numbers, just as they were not intended as sort of 'relief' institutions for overcrowded universities. If Regensburg, as an example, were to be developed on these lines – say as a relief university for Munich – it would most probably fail to fulfil its function. Which student would voluntarily renounce Munich in favour of settling down on the fringe of the Bavarian Forest? Alternatively, if these new institutions decided on a different form of teaching and study organisation, or on intensified research facilities, smaller numbers, etc, they would exercise some attraction.[15]

The chances of securing new alternatives and progressive formulas are evidently realised in the universities most recently founded.[16] The teachers on whom their development was bestowed are firmly rooted in the traditional university, so one need not fear that an extravagant passion for originality will force on the reform of the university for its own sake.

Every single concept developed during this first reform phase appears to have its own distinctive characteristics. There are those which resemble the Anglo-American pattern of a campus university, a model, however, which was not naïvely copied but adjusted to German conditions: there are others – Bochum in particular – where the principle of co-operation between related disciplines is realised; and, lastly, there are universities still in their planning stages which will orient their teaching and study activities towards the pursuit of specific selected disciplines.[17]

Of all recent foundations, Bochum University, which took up its teaching duties in 1965, has developed most dramatically. Its structural set-up indicated strikingly to what extent it is indebted to the traditional universities and where and how modifications are being carried out. The foundation committee has neither yielded to external social pressures nor simply hankered after pleasing solutions; its prime objective has been to create efficient, functional forms of university organisation. The faculties of traditional universities have been turned into large boards dealing with specific subject-related questions which can only be judged and properly decided by a small circle of its members, ie those who just happen to be concerned. Hence it seems sensible to start structural reforms at this point and to develop organisational models which allow for a greater degree of subject correlation. These new models have been realised in so-called departments (*Abteilungen*) of which there are nineteen in the whole university. Apart from aiming at a more efficient organisational scheme, the foundation committee paid greatest attention to the question of co-operation, faculties being split up in units consisting of related disciplines or working areas. Nobody can seriously be under the illusion today that the unity of knowledge can still be re-established. The optimistic attempts in early postwar Germany to design and offer a *studium generale* have by and large been unsuccessful. Co-operation as conceived in Bochum is something different.

It could be argued that this co-operation can only be achieved in an ideal situation. Indeed, ultimately this principle greatly depends upon whether enough professors can be found who agree to exercise co-operative wisdom and to show concern for neighbouring areas within their own fields of interest. The specialist who treats related disciplines – outside his own territory – with contemptuous indifference is certainly out of place. To overstress the importance of co-operation, suggesting that only research topics which provide a basis for co-operative efforts are being selected, would be wrong. But there are a great many problems which call for this type of co-operation.

The University of Bochum has also broken new ground by including engineering sciences in its spectrum. As early as 1946, Karl Jaspers[18] advocated some form of co-ordination between philosophical disciplines (*Geisteswissenschaften*) and engineering sciences. Sternly opposed to such notions, Helmut Schelsky replied: 'Reading Jaspers' interpretation of the "idea of a technical faculty" one unfortunately gets the impression that technicians, once admitted to the university, were expected to philosophise about technology and its implications. In actual fact, however, the addition of an engineering faculty to the present university structure would result solely in new, eminently pragmatic study courses and specialised research institutes in applied science.'[19] Yet there are alternative views worth mentioning, some of which imply that philosophical disciplines should not be allowed to retain their complacent existence as if the phenomenon 'technology' did not exist. Philosophy, if it pretends to be open to the questions of our age, cannot talk its way round technical issues; if it wants to make relevant propositions it must join in a dialogue with the engineering sciences.

SOCIETY'S DEMANDS ON THE UNIVERSITIES

The demands which society imposes on the universities are not aimed at structural details – these are of secondary importance. Basically, these demands are directed towards the integration of new disciplines which have hitherto not been represented in the university. Here claims are quite massive, and it seems to me frequently not substantiated, other than by a desire for increased social prestige. This must be due to the fact that in Germany the educational system is primarily conceived as a pyramid, the university resting on its top: upon her all eyes are fixed in devoted ecstasy. Thus, whenever West Germany's present educational set-up attracts the attention of critical voices, discussions will focus on upper secondary-school leavers (*Abiturienten*) and students. The fact that in future an increasingly wide reservoir of technical intelligence at an intermediate level will be required has obviously not yet been fully realised in this country. Both America and the USSR are far more realistic. Also, their educational systems appear to be viewed more or less as platforms from which many opportunities for advancement are initiated, those which do not necessarily lead to the university not automatically carrying inferior status.

In the Federal Republic of Germany an inappropriate desire for social prestige and a false concept of educational feasibility, a lack of self-confidence as well as naïve aspirations, are responsible for a widely shared belief that professional preparation confers less status if carried out elsewhere than at university. One should in fact bear in mind that some issues and problems can be and, indeed, must be dealt with at university level. Universities have not, in general, refused to adopt a kindred view. One has only to consider which disciplines, 150 years ago, were dominantly in vogue and which were regarded as being unworthy for university treatment. Social sciences, for instance, managed to break through the wall of ill-founded prejudices only under enormously trying conditions. In nineteenth-century Germany, neither sociology and economics nor political science was recognised in an institutional sense. The same applies to education (*Pädagogik*) which was only conceived in conjunction with philosophy or theology. In the 1920s education, like economics and social sciences, received the official recognition it had long deserved.

Meanwhile, new requirements have arisen from social, political and economic changes which the university has to examine and act upon where possible. The general sentiment seems to be that demands arising from those structural changes are almost entirely oriented towards the creation of new chairs or independent institutes; one gets the impression that it is not the issue as such which matters, but rather its outward form. However, the Foundation Committee of Bochum University has made it clear that chairs and institutes are not always the most appropriate answer. In some cases the title 'study group' (*Arbeitsgemeinschaft*) was chosen, to indicate that some modern problems can only be solved by a joint effort of different disciplines. In Bochum, for example, a 'study group in journalism and communication' was established which initially was attached to the chair for practical pedagogy.[20] Obviously these disciplines pose a variety of educational questions which have hardly been tackled so far. Consequently, the study group did not restrict itself to 'newspaper science' but dealt with the educational, psychological, sociological and political motives and implications of mass communications in general, thereby presupposing wholehearted interdisciplinary co-operation. This notwithstanding, such effort is generally initiated by a representative of a particular discipline who takes a special interest in the promotion of the new field. Journalism as an academic study has so far not become established in the majority of West Germany's universities,[21] possibly due to the false assumption that the acceptance of such a discipline would imply the actual training of future journalists. As far as I can see, nobody representing this field has ambitions of that sort. The study of journalism proves its value through the kind of research it fosters and in the collaboration with other disciplines. The *Arbeitsgemeinschaft* has of late developed into a semi-autonomous 'section' which seems to be a reflection of its present stage of theoretical advancement.

The Bochum example shows how a new university can adapt to changed conditions by making its academic resources available for the solution of current questions. Although other areas call for a similar, scientifically oriented treatment at university level – like the study of labour – it must again be emphasised that some demands currently imposed on the university cannot justifiably be met as far as their institutionalisation is concerned, even if the university finds itself thereby rejecting financial aid generously made available for such a purpose.

On aggregate, during the first reform phase the universities have been actively engaged in meeting justified new demands without stiffly insisting, as occasionally alleged, on the retention of obsolete traditions. Any attempt to extrapolate these tendencies into the next two decades would have to rely on guesswork rather than concrete prognoses. The multitude of existing projects[22] will almost certainly be reduced after consideration of their financial feasibility and the lack of adequate academic personnel. However, it is safe to predict a continuance of current reform, and certain tentative prognoses receive additional support from the fact that some problems are not exclusively national any longer; possibilities of reform and opportunities for it develop on international lines at least in the highly industrialised countries. Problems of practical organisation seem to attract most public attention, the issue of 'interior' university reform being of less concern.

STUDENT NUMBERS

From the abundance of problems facing the universities as a result of external pressures and their own shortcomings, I will start with a brief statistical reference to university development in the Federal Republic. At the beginning of the sixties the rapid increase of student numbers was threatening to overthrow not only the traditional university system but the classical idea of a university altogether. It was hoped, however, that this unstable situation would become controllable in the early 1970s when lower intakes of students were expected. At one stage, the *Wissenschaftsrat* had predicted some 250,000 students for the 1970s. Alternatively, given an increased intake of pupils in secondary schools and a higher proportion of 'successes', 380,000 students was thought to be the highest figure likely. Partly as a result of these rather modest targets – apparently these figures were already off course when the prognosis was published – the founding of new universities has hardly been speedy. In accordance with the recommendations of the *Wissenschaftsrat*,[23] new universities were established in the mid-sixties in Bochum, Dortmund, Regensburg, Konstanz and Bremen. Bochum – in contrast to some more conventional creations such as Berlin, Mainz and Saarbrücken – has been characterised as a project of 'modest reform aspirations'.[24]

At present, students total more than 380,000, and seem likely to reach some 800,000 in the not too distant future. There are a variety of causes for the underestimate of student numbers. No reliable prognostic instrument was available in the 1960s by which this rate of growth could have been anticipated. Also, the educational reform effort was concentrated on the field of secondary education. In his bleak, pessimistic account of the German educational system, Georg Pickt[25] has tried to prove that in the Federal Republic equality of opportunity was far from optimally realised and that the numbers of students – on a per capita basis – were considerably lower than even those in small underdeveloped countries. The quintessence of such doubtful methods of interpreting statistical figures, frequently the victim of prejudicial attitudes and false conclusions, was eventually summed up in the formula 'Send your children to better schools'. Reform concepts of this nature merely touch parts of the problems involved. The upper secondary schools have widened their range of intake and will go on doing so if comprehensive reorganisation gets fully under way. The rate of university expansion has been unable to keep abreast with the developments in secondary schools and, indeed, could hardly have done so, considering the difficulties of finance and of recruiting enough academic teaching personnel.

Finally, it should be noted that the *Fachschulen* sector (ie the colleges of specialised professional training) has only recently been promoted to join the structural complex of an integrated comprehensive university. Student numbers have exploded due to a variety of factors, and they in turn condition new structural models and alternative training facilities.

Building a university has become an increasingly standardised procedure,[26] so that nowadays a fully fledged university can be designed and finished within a decade. With the exception of Bochum, the newer foundations have in the main preferred to limit their research and teaching scope to certain disciplines or interdisciplinary aspects, a development which will almost certainly continue in future.

As a whole, the tertiary sector is approaching a stage of considerable expansion, as already indicated in Hessen and North Rhine Westphalia[27] – primarily because of the extension and reorganisation of higher education institutions into *Gesamthochschulen*, kind of enlarged polytechnics with university status. In North Rhine Westphalia, West Germany's most populous state, teacher-training colleges (*Pädagogische Hochschulen*) have been combined with colleges of advanced professional studies (*Fachhochschulen*) since 1972 to form the organisational 'crystallisation' centre for this type of comprehensive institution. Obviously neither a simple addition of higher-education institutions nor their administrative association will secure a true comprehensive form of tertiary organisation. Therefore it is planned to design appropriate short-term and long-term study units with varying degrees of practical and theoretical orientation. The traditional universities, too, are being affected by this development, although their place within an integrated network remained uncertain.

In terms of numerical expansion, the current reform tendencies have already produced some striking results: whereas in the mid-1960s only just over thirty universities and technical universities were represented in the West German conference of vice-chancellors (*Westdeutsche Rektorkonferenz*), by 1972 that number had risen to nearly seventy and it will continue rising as more and more teacher-training colleges are fully recognised and new comprehensive universities are founded. Even so, the additional study places cannot keep abreast with the fast-rising numbers of new students.

The main structural trends of university development can be summarised thus: student numbers swelling to over a million; an increase in the numbers of university establishments; and, finally, a transformation of higher-education institutions into comprehensive universities. Some proposed structural reforms on the other hand, seem to be little else than cosmetic treatments which will not reduce the deficit in the provision of study places and teaching personnel. The modification of the semester cycle – a study year of ten months' duration instead of two semesters with seven months' teaching time – seems to me a fruitless operation. This 'sensible, economical utilisation of existing space' will surely fail to provide additional study places unless significant changes in the management of teaching resources and a limitation of the maximum length of permitted university 'residence' accompany it. Since even 'smaller' universities approach student populations of 15,000–20,000, the problem of how to secure adequate study facilities for the present student generation while simultaneously trying to meet the increasing demand for more places will in future challenge the university with ever-growing force.

Current ambitions to reorganise the distribution of power within university policy-making bodies constitute another significant problem for the structural future of the university. Springing from the 'extra-parliamentary opposition' by the student generation of the late 1960s there are now claims that the university should reconstitute itself on democratic lines, modelling its inner structures and *modus operandi* on quasi-political prototypes.[28] The 'democratisation' of the university set-up is supported in principle even by 'modest' reform advocates; students will not however participate in all matters of university policy, most likely being limited to certain functional categories. As experience shows, this kind of participation not only meets the demands for greater openness but also secures the degree of stability which academic establishments need for the retention of their qualitative standards.

TWO-TIER COURSES

Some reference should be made to the revision of what may be called the idea and substance of university education in Germany. It has already been mentioned that the German idea of a university found its classical manifestation in the Friedrich-Wilhelm University of Berlin which Wilhelm von Humboldt had founded in 1811. With some rare exceptions[29] university reforms have been united in their conviction that even large student numbers provided no argument against the retention of the traditional principle of unified research and teaching. Although it can hardly be disputed that research and teaching exercise an influence of reciprocal relevance,[30] there is reason to believe that where a university training is predominantly oriented towards the practical requirements of a particular profession, the needs of original research become of secondary importance. As a rule, students make their first contact with research when they have virtually reached the final stages of their course, or more specifically whilst engaging in self-conducted work at post-graduate level. Indeed, can it realistically be expected that with a student population nearing a million a cross-fertilisation of research and teaching is still feasible? On the other hand, Max Weber's remark that a 'scientific self-conscience' can only be created by a detailed penetration into the spheres of specialised research[31] still deserves careful examination today, which again adds to the general uncertainty about the direction in which university reform will eventually move. In the natural sciences, where the bulk of research work is now carried out by specialised institutes for scientific investigation (Max Planck Institutes), the break between *Forschung* and *Lehre* has already been strikingly illustrated. As more and more disciplines experience a similar degree of differentiation, that long-cherished ideal will eventually degenerate into a symbol of merely ornamental value.

It is safe to predict, therefore, that in the long run the introduction of two-tier study courses will become unavoidable. Here a phase of intensive research activity would be clearly distinguished, but not necessarily institutionally separated, from a preparatory 'learning' stage which might re-establish a link between academic training and vocational reality. It is widely held in business circles that a university education no longer qualifies a candidate for a leading position in industry. The promotion of *Fachschulen* into an integrated branch of comprehensive universities has further minimised the degree of practical orientation, and has left a vacuum where traditionally an advanced vocational training based on preparatory, theoretical instruction has been given. In Germany the ambiguous relationship between theory and profession has always tended to stigmatise the pursuit of applied and practical studies as inferior and unscientific. Today there is every justification to repeat the 1920s demands that the German academic world should develop a greater sense of social service and pragmatic orientation.

CURRICULAR CHANGES

In view of this, let us finally expand our thoughts on the prospective 'interior' reform of higher education referred to above. As this interior reform, mainly meaning curricular innovations, has in recent years been accorded less importance than structural problems and the democratic distribution of power, one can fairly say that the central issue of university reform has hardly yet been tackled. It is true that there has been a shift of gravity within and between disciplines: new subjects have joined the ranks of established studies—social sciences, labour studies, business research, labour market policy, adult education, to name but a few. Yet very few moves have been made to orient the existing disciplines towards students' professional interests.

To illustrate this point let me cite a particular German example. The training of secondary-school teachers in Germany is the responsibility of the university, which equips them primarily with an academic course of study in their particular subject accompanied by seminars intended to familiarise them with the scope and nature of their future professional activity. Recently there has been more desire for closer ties with educational practice through the establishment of special chairs for the didactic aspects of each discipline, designed to illuminate the process of transforming academic knowledge for classroom purposes. However, no significant distinction is made in specialised subject instruction between future school teachers and those who decide to remain in university life. Both categories of students receive, until the end of their first-degree course, a virtually identical education. Should the weight of specialised knowledge required by an aspiring university teacher also fall upon the shoulders of the secondary-school teacher? For the scholar of German, Old and Middle High German is, of course, indispensable, but one feels that the ordinary teacher of German should be spared such rigorous demands. On the other hand, aquaintance with such matters as a systematic teaching of grammatical principles is postponed to the second phase of training which is combined with practical teaching activities. If, as has been suggested, a two-tier system of university study were to be adopted, the curricular consequences would be a differentiation between professional and purely academic training. Of course even to hint at consequences which would tend to reduce the study course to a purely vocational dimension is regarded as heresy in Germany.

The conclusion can, therefore, only run as follows: a reduction in the amount of offered information and knowledge and a better-structured curriculum. I am convinced that the universities in West Germany can only escape the vicious circles of high student numbers, low recruitment figures for academic personnel, limited amount of study places and, finally, of being committed to a simultaneous engagement in research and teaching, if they are prepared to revise the traditional outlook. By means of a structural reshaping of the study course, the universities should be able to bring about a closer alliance between the academic world and the professions, proving that the claims of academic investigation and those of professional preparation can co-exist satisfactorily. In the long run, the universities will be expected to prove their open-mindedness towards new social requirements and problems which ask for clarification at an academic level. Such open-mindedness has been demonstrated in past years when several universities and teacher training colleges have established chairs for adult education. These do not just represent a special field of educational study but fulfil a wide spectrum of tasks stimulated by problems in the practical field. There are indications that a step in the direction of 'university extension' will be taken in the near future, although hardly with such scope and variety as the English extension model.[32]

This account has been restricted to some of the tendencies and potential changes of university development; important aspects such as the relationship between the university and the upper level of secondary schooling (*Sekundarstufe II, Kollegstufe*) have had to be neglected. Whether the developments anticipated above will actually take place is not solely dependent upon the clear-headedness of academic institutions, nor upon their readiness to take decisions, since in the end the decisions, whether planned or just 'unavoidable', are primarily of a political nature.

Although the prospects opened up by the decisions reached to date[33] are not exactly encouraging, there remains a hope that clear political majorities will foster the kind of self-confidence which does not shrink from taking unpopular measures designed to 'correct' the weight and relevance of tradition. A great deal will be expected from the universities in coming years; for political decisions and their implications – such as the problem of 'over-qualification' – they obviously cannot accept the sole or even the greater responsibility. The innovations which have been predicted above will, however, only be produced if the parliamentary-political decision-making process is accompanied by and co-ordinated with a change of attitude on the part of the universities themselves.

9

The University in the Soviet Union

J. J. TOMIAK

The October Revolution, because of its character and nature, was bound to influence profoundly the aims, the extent and the general characteristics of higher education in what had formerly been the Russian empire. Clearly, the time element was important. There was an immediate and clear-cut change in the newly declared and openly advocated norms and objectives. Many years had to elapse, however, before these could be properly realised in life in a country devastated by years of war and civil strife, in a society lagging behind in practically every respect, and particularly in education.

In 1914 Russia had 105 higher education establishments, with 127,400 students. Most of them were to be found in some twenty major urban centres in European Russia, particularly in Petersburg and in Moscow. In West and East Siberia and in the Far East there existed only four higher education institutions, three of them in the city of Tomsk. There were twelve universities with 40,776 students.[1]

The immediate impact of the revolution was to affect the concept of the role of the institutions of higher learning. From an important element in the general socio-political system based upon autocracy, orthodoxy and nationalism, within which they had been striving with only a limited success for a greater measure of autonomy, they had to transform themselves into a key element within the new communist society, politically committed to the support and strengthening of the new order and oriented towards radical social change and the promotion of sustained economic growth in the country.

Right from the start, and with a growing emphasis as time went by, important measures were introduced to ensure the political commitment of the students through the introduction of a complex of socio-political disciplines (the principal of Marxism-Leninism, dialectical and historical materialism, political economy and scientific communism) as a compulsory ingredient in the courses of studies and through intensive *Komsomol* activity in all institutions of higher learning. Other measures served to expand educational opportunities at this level through the opening of new universities, polytechnical and monotechnical institutes, the introduction of evening and part-time courses, through linking the number of students trained in the different fields of specialisation to the manpower requirements of the economy and making higher education accessible to the children of the workers and to women, with the assistance of state scholarships and grants. Educational planning became an integral part of a rigorous pattern of economic planning as the country's progress was speeded up under a series of five-year economic plans and accelerated further after World War II.[2]

The number of universities increased to forty in 1960 and to fifty-one in 1970, while the numbers of students in them doubled during that decade, reaching just over half a million in 1970. In that year 96,039 students were enrolled, 56·7 per cent of them for day courses, 16·4 per cent for evening courses and 26·9 per cent for correspondence courses.[3] In the same year the 805 higher-education establishments in existence (including universities) had 4,580,600 students; 911,500 were enrolled, of whom 54·9 per cent entered day courses, 14 per cent evening courses and 31·1 per cent correspondence courses.[4]

HIGHER EDUCATION ESTABLISHMENTS IN THE USSR,
ACADEMIC YEARS 1960–1 AND 1970–1

	1960–1	1970–1
All types	739	805
Of which:		
Industry and construction	169	201
Transport and communications	37	37
Agriculture	96	98
Economics and law	51	50
Health, medical services,		
physical culture and sport	98	99

L

	1960–1	1970–1
Education (including universities)	241	268
Art and cinematography	47	52

Source: Tsentralnoe Statisticheskoe Upravlenie, *Narodnoe obrazovanie, nauka i kultura v SSSR* (Moscow: 1971), p 168.

Higher education in the USSR today is characterised by features which had already manifested themselves in earlier times, but in recent years there have been important changes in the demographic, economic and social determinants of educational reality, leading to interesting shifts and changes in emphasis.

First, there have been important demographic changes. The overall birth rates have declined dramatically from 44 per 1,000 of population in 1926, 31·2 in 1940, 26·7 in 1950, 24·9 in 1960 to 17·4 in 1970. In consequence the age structure of the population has changed also. The 5–9 age group has declined as a proportion of total population from 11·7 per cent in 1959 to 8·5 per cent in 1970.

The differential birth rates for the different ethnic groups have, however, fully retained, indeed often increased, their significance. In 1970 the birth rate in the RSFSR was 14·6, in Latvia 14·5 and in the Ukraine 15·2 per 1,000 of population; in the same year it was 33·5 in Uzbekistan, 34·7 in Tadzikstan and 35·2 in Turkmenistan. The population rates of growth in the different Union republics showed in 1970 even greater variation, due to the impact of differential death rates. The rate of population growth in Estonia in 1970 was 4·7, and in Latvia 3·3 per 1,000 of population; but it was 28·6 in Turkmenistan.

There has been an improvement in the standard of health, nourishment, and sanitation, reflected in a substantial reduction in infant mortality rate from 182 per 1,000 infants born in 1940 to 25 in 1970,[5] as well as in an increased life expectancy, and in the consequent increase in the proportion of old people in the population.

Economically, there has been a rise in the material standard of life and an increase in the income per head of population in real terms. The official statistics claim the ability of the country to double its national income every decade, a rate that clearly cannot be maintained permanently, but it may signify a considerable improvement at present. The average proportion of urban population has increased from 39 per cent in 1950 to 57 per cent in 1971, though, significantly, it varied in the latter year from 63 per cent in RSFSR, 66 per cent in Estonia and 63 per cent in Latvia to 36 per cent in Uzbekistan and 32 per cent in Moldavia.

The structure of the economy has been changing too, with consequent changes in the occupational structure: the proportion of people gainfully employed in agriculture and forestry has rapidly declined, from 48 per cent of the labour force in 1950 to 39 per cent in 1960 and 27 per cent in 1970; the proportion of people working in industry and building has increased from 27 per cent in 1950 to 32 per cent in 1960 and 37 per cent in 1970. Less spectacular changes took place in the fields of transport and communications, but the proportion of people employed in services of all kinds has very significantly increased from 20 per cent in 1950 to 22 per cent in 1960 and 28 per cent in 1970. The absence of cyclical fluctuations in production has ensured the absence of large-scale unemployment.

Capital equipment has replaced certain kinds of labour and there have been advances in mechanisation and automation in the productive process. Labour efficiency has increased, although the differentials between the different branches of the economy still tend to vary greatly. There has also been a reduction in the working hours per week in Soviet industry from the average 47·8 hours in 1955 to 41 in 1961, and 40·7 in 1970. In 1967 a five-day working week was introduced for most of the working urban population.

Prices have been changing little, while the average earnings have increased from 80·6 roubles per month in 1960 to 122·0 roubles in 1970.[6]

Geographically, new industrial centres began to appear in the Ural and the Asiatic parts of the USSR after 1945, and have been growing rapidly ever since. Between the population censuses of 1939 and 1959, population increased in the USSR by 9·5 per cent, but in the Ural area it grew by 32 per cent, in Western Siberia by 24 per cent, in Eastern Siberia by 34 per cent, in the Far Eastern area by 70 per cent and in Kazakhstan by 52 per cent.[7] The rate of growth of the medium-size and large urban centres in the Ural and Siberian territories has been quite high.

The official figures concerning social structure indicate only the broad division of Soviet society into workers, including all working in the service sector of the economy, on the one hand, and collective farm peasants and craftsmen on the other. As a proportion of the total population the former have increased from 68·3 per cent in 1959 to 80 per cent in 1970 (est) and the latter have declined from 31·4 per cent in 1959 to 20 per cent in 1970 (est). The proportion of all people employed in the services (included in the first set of figures) increased from 20·1 per cent in 1959 to 25 per cent in 1970 (est).[8]

What is significant here is, however, the important question whether behind all this still operate, in a differential way, the influences based upon family background and size, parental occupation and income, life styles, aspirations and expectations. Certain sources tend to provide the evidence that this is so and indicate that it may well go on in the future.[9] The Soviet analysts tend to reject this proposition, but one must nevertheless take into account the fact that the sons and daughters of well-educated and highly qualified parents naturally tend to be proportionately over-represented in higher-education institutions. The problem is a real one, as objective selection norms to discover the future potential of a young boy or girl are not easily found. 'Concerned for their children's future, parents tend to "stuff" them, that is, train them to to a point where it is almost impossible to distinguish the truly gifted youth from the one who is simply well-informed. That is the main problem we face in picking out the right material for scientific training.'[10]

HIGHER EDUCATION IN THE SOCIALIST ECONOMY

In discussing the present position and the future of higher studies in the Soviet Union it is useful to bear in mind that 'higher education in the USSR constitutes and develops as an organic component of the unified system of socialist economy'.[11] Its growth and development is intimately related to, and depends upon, the planned expansion of the particular branches of industry, transport and communications, agriculture and the service sector of the economy. In addition, 'the contents and the form, the scale as well as the structure of higher education evolve according to the changes in the development of science and technology'.[12] In consequence of this approach, the directives of the Twenty-Fourth Congress of the CPSU on the five-year economic development plan for 1971–5 defined the educational tasks at this level as follows: 'to develop higher and specialised secondary education in accordance with the requirements of scientific-technological progress, to improve the quality of training and to better the ideological and political education of the future specialists; to train about nine million specialists with higher and specialised secondary education, having given special attention to the preparation of specialists in new fields of science and technology for the rapidly developing branches of industry and the services'.[13]

The principal factors which are bound to influence the universities and their growth and development in the USSR in the remaining quarter of the twentieth century are:

(1) The reduction in, and the stabilisation of, the overall rate of population growth in the country.

(2) The speeding-up of the process of industrialisation of the country, and of scientific and technological progress, favourably conditioned by the presence of large natural resources and a determined policy to make a much greater use of them.

(3) Adherence to centralised planning as an indispensable means for assuring a controlled and synchronised growth in all aspects of national life, including education; in particular relating the expansion in higher education, specialised secondary education and vocational training to the manpower requirements of the economy.

(4) The awakening and growing aspirations of the younger generation to take the fullest possible advantage of the opportunities available to them through education.

(5) The continued determination of the political authority to insist upon ideological commitment of the students and their active participation in the process of construction of a communist society.

All these are important factors, operating in the long run. They make, as the recent debates have made clear, for concentration upon three principal issues and complexes of problems: those connected with expansion, equality of opportunity and efficiency in higher education.[14] Because of the composite nature of the system of higher education in the USSR there are, however, also important questions of the precise nature of the role the universities are to perform *vis-à-vis* the other institutions at this level, and particularly in the field of scientific research, its organisation, content and methods.

EXPANSION

Nine new universities were opened in the course of the Eighth Five-Year Plan (1966–70). Even more are to be added before the completion of the Ninth Five-Year Plan in 1975. About 10 to 11 per cent of all students in higher education study in the universities and this proportion is not likely to change in the years to come. What is likely to change is, however, the proportion of students in the universities studying full-time. It will tend to increase and claim more than half of the students as a result of the researches analysing the effectiveness of part-time studies, discussed below.

What is also of interest here is the way in which the new universities are being created. Most have formerly been either branches of the older, often well-known universities, or else pedagogical institutes. This duality of background is often reflected in the orientation in studies prevailing in the new university, as well as in the relative strength of the more highly qualified teaching staff. It inevitably constitutes a differentiating element in the category of universities taken as a whole. Indeed, the older and well-established universities with large teaching staffs have the right to prepare their own individual curricula, which may differ from the model curricula elaborated by the ministry of higher and specialised secondary education and accepted by the younger universities. As the numbers of applications for admission clearly indicate, the universities differ in terms of renown and prestige, an aspect which may well intensify as the total number of universities increases.

An important element is the rapid expansion of upper secondary education in recent years, which is exerting a growing pressure upon the institutions of higher education. In 1928 nine out of every ten complete secondary-school graduates entered the day departments of higher-education establishments in the country; in 1940 five out of ten; in 1950 eight out of ten; in 1960 fewer than three out of ten; in 1970 only two out of nine.[15] The demand from this quarter is certainly becoming greater every year.

The pressures from the economy to expand higher education are no less. If the high economic growth rates demand an addition of 10 per cent to the existing number of scientific workers every year, then the realised additions over the last two decades indicate the dimension of the problem: in the period 1950–4 the average annual increase was 12·3 per cent; in 1955–9 it was 10·1 per cent; in 1965–70 it declined to 8·6 per cent.[16]

If the economy as a whole demands substantial expansion of opportunities in higher education, so does the educational system itself; 52·7 per cent of secondary-school teachers had higher education in 1970.[17] The schools, oriented towards modernisation of the curricula and rapid scientific advancement, need thousands of new teachers graduating from the universities and pedagogical institutes. This applies not only to complete secondary schools of general education, but equally so to the specialised secondary-education establishments in the country, particularly as compulsory complete secondary education for all up to the age of seventeen becomes imminent.

EQUALITY OF OPPORTUNITY

The desire to eliminate the basic kinds of inequalities in education, between men and women, among the different ethnic groups, between urban and rural areas, between the children of the professional, highly skilled workers and the semi-skilled and unskilled workers, has always played an important part in Soviet education policy. Although progress has been made in many ways, much more has still to be done to eliminate all aspects of inequality in opportunities for higher education. A very substantial measure of equality has been achieved between the sexes with respect to higher as well as secondary general and specialised secondary education, even though it is still much easier for a man to reach the top echelons in the different professions. The differences between urban and rural areas still persist and the prospects for the entry to and the completion of higher education vary substantially among the different Union republics and the different ethnic groups.

In the years to come, the policy of opening up new universities and other institutes of higher learning in the hitherto underprivileged territories, regions and republics will no doubt be reinforced, so that the smaller national groups will get a fair chance of being proportionately represented.[18] The differences between the rural and urban areas will only be eliminated in the longer run through a substantial increase in mechanisation and automation in agriculture and a parallel improvement in the quality of life in more remote rural areas.

Socially, a significant element in the policy towards greater equality of opportunity within the field of higher education are the so-called preparatory departments, which are coming into being in an increasing number of universities and other institutions at this level. On 20 August 1969 the Central Committee of the CPSU and the Council of Ministers of the USSR adopted a Resolution On Organising Preparatory Departments Affiliated to Higher Education Establishments. The regulations allow for admission to the preparatory departments of outstanding workers in industry and collective farmers with at least one year of productive employment behind them, as well as soldiers demobilised from the Soviet armed forces, who have completed the full course of secondary education, and have secured recommendations from the Party, *Komsomol* or trade-union organisations. The students follow a full-time course lasting eight to ten months and then take a university entrance examination. In the academic year 1969–70 over 20,000 young men and women were studying in the preparatory departments, while the plans were being prepared to increase their numbers to 100,000 in the middle 1970s. The students in the preparatory departments were receiving state scholarships of 35 roubles per month or, sometimes, direct scholarships from their factories, collective farms or industrial establishments, which were 15 per cent higher (according to the resolution by the USSR Council of Ministers No 1099 of 18 September 1959). In September 1972 they were all increased by 25 per cent.

In the University of Moscow the following faculties had preparatory departments in the academic year 1971–2: mechanics-mathematics, computer mathematics and cybernetics, physics, chemistry, biology and soil sciences, geology, geography, history, philosophy, economics, journalism, psychology and the Institute of Eastern Languages. In addition to the preparatory departments, the University of Moscow operates a whole range of preparatory courses in the evening and by correspondence for young workers in industry and agriculture, in all the above-mentioned faculties as well as in the faculties of philosophy and law.[19]

EFFICIENCY

The immediate result of the quick adoption and recognition of economics of education as an important field of study was, in the early 1960s, not only a series of studies concerned with the contribution of education to economic growth and productivity of labour, but also a critical examination of the effectiveness of learning, particularly in higher education.[20]

It was B. M. Remennikov who examined critically the real cost of the alternative types of study in the universities, full-time, evening and correspondence, in his *Ekonomicheskie problemy vysshego obrazovaniya v SSSR* in 1968, and exposed the unexpectedly high cost in real terms of study by correspondence. Taking into account the high drop-out rate (reaching 50 per cent), a much longer average length of study (exceeding sometimes the officially stipulated length by two years), a very generous provision of time off work for study and preparation for examinations and the consequent withdrawal from productive work, he estimated the cost of study by correspondence as amounting to 45 per cent of the cost of study in a full-time course.[21] This and similar studies served to pave the way for the revision of extensive use of study by correspondence in higher education. It was suggested that a better selection of students should be attempted, preference being given to those with some relevant industrial experience behind them; also that certain kinds of specialisation should be excluded from correspondence studies and only narrower fields of specialisation should be taught, leaving wider fields for full-time study. There has already been a decline in the number of students studying by correspondence and in the evening. This is likely to continue, particularly as the opportunities to study full-time increase.

At the same time much attention has been given to the need for the updating of curricular patterns and syllabuses, in order to take immediate advantage of the newest achievements in the fields of science and technology. Clearly, what is wanted is a more permanent means for a continuous review of the programmes of study. This is where the large-scale application of modern audiovisual aids comes in: films, closed-circuit television, teaching machines and carefully programmed learning with the help of well-equipped laboratories, instruments and apparatus. Intensive use of all of these in the future is certain.

In addition, new discoveries and new knowledge are already drawing new subjects into the courses of study, eg electronics, cybernetics, information science, engineering psychology, astrophysics, computer technology. This also is a permanent feature – many more new subjects will have to be accommodated into courses of study in the future.[22]

THE NEW ROLE OF THE UNIVERSITIES

Between 1 and 4 February 1972 there took place one of the regular consecutive conferences of university rectors in the USSR which at the same time was the first meeting of the newly constituted Universities Council. It was devoted to the problems of development of university education in the country. It was generally accepted that each university constitutes a major scientific centre supporting a very wide range of interests among the university staff. A modern university, in the words of V. P. Yelyutin, minister of higher and specialised secondary education, is 'a centre for fundamental scientific research which must go on developing quickly in order to serve as a base for the preparation of all kinds of specialists required by the economy and the educational system'.[23] It is in the universities that real opportunities exist for scientists working in the fields of social and natural sciences as well as in technology to work closely together and to benefit from each other's experience. It is in the universities that the heavy concentration of scientists can be found: 43,100 professors and lecturers teach in the universities; 10·8 per cent of all students in higher education study there, but 22 per cent of all Doctors of Science and 15·4 per cent of all Candidates of Science work there. In the four universities of Moscow, Leningrad, Kiev and Tbilisi are employed more than half of all the Doctors of Science working in institutes of higher learning.[24]

It is therefore imperative that a better distribution of talent is introduced, that the younger universities, often situated in areas which have just been opened up for more intensive economic development, all receive a fair share of well-qualified scientists. It is also important that the university scientists do not squander their energies on too numerous research projects of minor importance, but concentrate their attention on the study of fundamental problems of knowledge. What is particularly needed is much closer collaboration between the university staff on the one hand and the Academy of Sciences and its scientific branch institutes on the other. This should lead on to the co-ordination of effort and to the rationalisation of all scientific research involving all higher education establishments, the Academy of Sciences, specialised research institutes of all kinds, the State Committee for Science and Technology and the State Planning Commission.

The individual science centres should be guided in their complex scientific research and teaching work by the universities upon which they are based. The best example of it is the rapidly expanding University of Novosibirsk and the integration of its work with that of the neighbouring research institutes, remaining under the Siberian branch of the USSR Academy of Sciences, and specialising in mathematics, hydrodynamics, nuclear physics, automation and electronics, chemical kinetics and combustion, organic and inorganic chemistry, cytology and genetics, geology and geophysics, economics, history, philosophy and philology. This pulsating and vigorous science centre with its 7,500 scientific workers, including 1,500 university professors and lecturers, constitutes a model which is being recreated in the emerging science centres in North Caucasus, the Urals and the Soviet Far East, and which will be recreated in other, similar complexes in the future.[25] No doubt these will, in the next two decades, come into existence in the Asiatic, and so far very much underdeveloped, parts of the Union: 'the centre of industrial development is gradually shifting to the east of the country; Eastern Siberia must, under these conditions, become a unique proving ground for the scientific planning of the structure of the economy'.[26]

In the whole galaxy of subjects studied in the universities and covering the full range of human knowledge, the study of economics seems to receive a special stress and will do so in the future. Courses on the scientific organisation of production, rationalisation of effort, productivity, management, statistics and planning, principles of research design and computerised control systems are proliferating, while the mono-technical economic higher-education institutes have been showing the fastest rate of growth of all institutes at this level in the 1965–70 period.[27]

The problem which is rapidly becoming the centre of attention is the determined attempt to reduce the technological gap, ie to shorten the time interval between a scientific or technical discovery and its application in production on a large scale. Indeed, a new invention or a new idea is seen as the best guarantee of increasing productivity and making a fuller use of the abundant natural resources available. To achieve this, close collaboration, within each branch of science and technology, between the universities pursuing pure research, the specialised scientific institutes pursuing applied research and the industry based upon it, is necessary. This *sui generis* scientific vertical integration, intimately integrating scientific research with industrial production, is becoming a very important feature of the Soviet economy which will receive even greater prominence in the remaining decades of this century and largely facilitate the processes of continuous modernisation and maximal mechanisation and automation.

What will also be needed from the new graduates are the qualities of flexibility and adaptability, a forward outlook and the ability to take decisions based upon carefully considered evidence. In the words of I. Obraztsov, minister for higher and secondary specialised education of the RSFSR: 'what we need, are not specialists who have been orientated and trained for work in the fields, and with the help of methods, decided upon in advance, but specialists who are capable of selecting and formulating problems independently and creatively as well as of finding effective means for their solution; we need specialists with fundamental theoretical knowledge oriented towards a continuous up-dating of their knowledge'.[28] If this is the model of the Soviet scientist of the future, he will not differ from his counterpart in the West.

There remains, however, a very important element of political commitment which should be properly appreciated. Education in the university as well as in any other institution of higher learning in the USSR necessarily involves political education. 'The Soviet specialist today is a man who has thoroughly mastered the principles of Marxist-Leninist theory, sees clearly the political objectives of the Party and the country, has a wide theoretical and practical background and has a full command over his specialisation,'[29] declared Mr Brezhnev in his speech in the All-Union Students' Congress in 1971. His words were reiterated by Vyacheslav Yelyutin, minister of higher and specialised secondary education of the USSR: 'All work in the institutions of higher learning, the ethical basis of the relationship between teachers and students are subordinated to one task – education in the spirit of communist morality, the foundation of which is the struggle for the building of communism.'[30] It is in the climate of an intimate union between science, technology and political commitment that the Soviet universities are to educate their most talented youth, in whose hands will rest the future of the country and the system in the closing years of the twentieth and the opening years of the twenty-first century.

UNIVERSITIES IN THE USSR AND THE NUMBER OF STUDENTS, 1970

University	Number of students			
	Total	Day	Evening	Corre-spondence
Bashkir State (Ufa)	7,016	3,374	1,335	2,307
Voronezh State	11,717	6,111	2,328	3,278
Gorky State	10,111	5,915	2,939	1,257
Far Eastern State (Vladivostok)	6,351	3,907	416	2,028
Daghestan State (Makhachkakla)	8,092	3,784	1,383	2,925
Irkutsk State	10,084	5,104	1,235	3,745
Kabardino-Balkar State (Nalchik)	9,039	4,529	537	3,973
Kazan State	9,007	5,340	1,561	2,106
Kaliningrad State	4,307	2,034	229	2,044
Kalmysh State (Elista)	2,541	1,064	296	1,181
Krasnoyarsk State	2,384	1,162	239	983
Kuban State (Krasnodar)	7,403	3,355	350	3,698
Kuibyshev State	563	563	—	—
Leningrad State	19,785	10,584	4,951	4,250

University	Number of Students			
	Total	Day	Evening	Corre-spondence
Moscow State	26,769	18,109	6,195	2,465
Mordovia State (Saransk)	16,043	6,579	2,925	6,539
Novosibirsk State	3,805	3,491	314	—
Perm State	9,993	4,752	1,985	3,256
Petrozavodsk State	6,802	3,912	656	2,234
Rostov State	9,452	4,597	1,721	3,134
Saratov State	9,366	5,130	2,795	1,441
North Ossetia State (Ordzhonikidze)	6,908	2,399	—	4,509
Tomsk State	9,965	5,594	929	3,442
Ural State (Sverdlovsk)	6,384	3,108	966	2,310
Chuvash State (Cheboksary)	6,897	3,604	1,351	1,942
Yakut State (Yakutsk)	6,498	4,126	249	2,123
Yaroslavl State	302	302	—	—
Dnepropetrovsk State	12,311	6,186	3,109	3,016
Donetsk State	13,204	4,598	2,280	6,326
Kiev State	19,036	8,022	3,630	7,384
Lvov State	12,075	5,446	1,739	4,890
Odessa State	11,333	4,230	2,218	4,885
Uzhgorod State	10,780	4,114	1,232	5,434
Kharkov State	12,992	6,693	2,415	3,884
Chernovtsy State	9,533	3,442	1,321	4,770
Byelorussian State (Minsk)	16,941	9,137	3,121	4,683
Gomel State	4,825	2,798	—	2,027
Samarkand State	12,305	4,784	2,342	5,179
Tashkent State	15,498	7,408	4,064	4,026
Kazakh State (Alma Ata)	10,008	5,046	1,327	3,635
Tbilisi State	16,019	8,348	5,254	2,417
Azerbaidzhan State (Baku)	11,466	4,826	2,986	3,654
Vilnius State	15,682	6,991	3,069	5,622
Kishinev State	8,056	4,154	—	3,902
Latvian State (Riga)	8,702	3,979	1,735	2,988
Kirghiz State (Frunze)	13,996	6,031	1,311	6,654
Tadzhik State (Dushanbe)	12,300	5,382	2,447	4,471
Erevan State	11,871	6,963	2,920	1,988
Turkmen State (Ashkhabad)	9,880	5,158	1,035	3,687
Tartu State	6,273	4,184	—	2,089

10

The University in Japan

K. NARITA

The rapid expansion of *Daigaku* – the most relevant term in use relating to the Japanese higher-education institutions which can be taken as equivalent to the English 'university' – seems to reflect the competitive social mobility for better living standards and status. The Central Advisory Council for Education estimated in a report submitted to the minister of education in June 1971 that the enrolment ratio will be as high as 40 per cent by 1980.[1] This indication of the trend towards mass higher education is taken as the basis for a consideration of the university's future role in Japan.

SOME CHARACTERISTICS OF THE JAPANESE UNIVERSITY

In general, the university in Japan has been the centre of higher learning, as in every other country. But, let us have a brief review of some of the national peculiarities which characterise the Japanese universities. The characteristics appear to result from certain complicated conditions, of which, to avoid detail, some explicit ones are shown below in respect of first the historical background, secondly the legal and institutional bases and thirdly the sociological dynamics.

The first national university along the modern or Western pattern was established in 1877, the University of Tokyo, renamed the Imperial University in 1886. Since the Meiji Restoration brought Japan into full international contact, it was inevitable that the government should wish the young national university to educate scholars and technocrats in modern Western knowledge and skills. There followed the second Imperial University of Kyoto (established in 1897), and by 1910 two others; three more were added between the two world wars. All were elitist universities, whose graduates, with very rare exceptions, obtained the top-level positions in any professions.

Apart from these imperial universities there were no private universities until 1918, although the first one in its embryo form had its origins far earlier than the national university: the celebrated Keio University was set up in 1858, as a private academy of Dutch and English studies, by Yukichi Fukuzawa, then one of the most far-sighted and progressive scholars in Japan.

In the 1880s and 1890s a number of private institutions for professional training or foreign studies were started, for there was an increasing demand for second-rank professionals as Japanese society gradually evolved to a more modern form. In 1903, under the regulation issued that year, twenty-nine such private institutions were officially recognised as colleges. The deep-rooted desire, however, to share university status was repeatedly expressed, as most of them matured and gained a reputation for academic quality, so eventually the University Code of 1918 was revised. The new code created voluntary corporations and the local government was empowered to set up the universities, subject to approval by the minister of education, in terms of their financial stability, academic standards, the creation of facilities, etc.

Thus, historically, there were, and still are, three sections among the Japanese universities, the national (including former imperial), the private and the local public, according to who the founding bodies were. Until the entire reorganisation of the educational system during and after 1947, they continued to work as an elitist system. Only a few per cent of each age group were selected through the stratified and streamed school system, discrimination by sex being also a characteristic of this selection. There were forty-eight universities altogether in 1946, of which eighteen were national (including seven former imperial universities, the biggest), three local public and twenty-seven private. The student numbers in 1946 totalled 112,992, of whom only 328 were women.[2]

As a part of the drastic educational reform after World War II, the system of Japanese higher education was entirely reviewed and more democratic access to it assured. The newly promulgated School Education Law of 1947 provided the primary legal base for the new system of higher education, replacing the University Code of 1918 and other former regulations. This law defines the aim of a university as being the academic centre for teaching and research to develop the student's intellectual and moral capacities. The university shall usually be constituted as several faculties – exceptionally, where necessary, as only one. The undergraduate courses run for four years normally (the faculties of medical and dental sciences have six-year courses). The Ministry of Education has created the University Chartering Committee which is responsible, prior to the minister's approval, for the establishment of any institutions at the university level. Additionally, as far as the establishment, modification or close-down of the national university system or its constituent institutes is concerned, confirmation through legislative measures at the National Diet must be obtained.

It should be noted here that two major educational changes took place as to the institutional structures. First, the common secondary-school system, with the raising of the legal school-leaving age to fifteen, superseded the former stratified and streamed one. This makes access to the upper secondary stage, and then to higher education, much easier. The new university system which started in 1949 was open to application from those who graduated from the upper secondary school. Secondly, the universities newly instituted under the School Education Law were, in practice, not necessarily entirely new, but came to incorporate most of the former higher-education institutions such as the colleges of technology and economics, teachers' training colleges, and the senior departments of higher schools which were substantially preparatory to the imperial universities. This enabled the depressed country to more than triple the 1946 number of institutions (to 178 in 1949) though the number of students, 126,868, was only a 10 per cent increase.

Owing to these changes, it can be said that the university system of postwar Japan was prepared to move towards mass higher education.

Sociologically two kinds of strain need noting. First, the internal strain from the pressure of numbers is marked. Second are the pressures from outside.

A rapid increase in student numbers took place during the 1960s, as in most of the advanced countries. Numbers more than doubled from 700,700 in 1960 to 1,648,500 (including junior college students, whose numbers rose from 83,500 to 263,200). In May 1973 1,529,000 were in universities, 288,000 in junior colleges. Peculiarly to Japan, this expansion was attained by burdening the private sector most heavily. The official report of the Ministry of Education pointed out: 'The increase was especially large in private universities and junior colleges. The proportion of students enrolled in private universities and junior colleges increased from 66% in 1959 to 78% in 1969. Seventy-five per cent of the university students and 90% of the junior college students were enrolled in private institutions in 1969.'[3]

Compared with the relatively steady expansion of the national universities, the private institutions therefore faced problems, for instance the inferior staff-student ratio – on average 31·5 students per full-time teacher in 1973, as against 8·3 in a national university;[4] equipment and facilities were inferior, and so on. Teachers in the private universities are forced to carry much heavier teaching loads than those in the national sector. Private universities are supported by the fees paid by their students, who have to support an expensive college life.

The pressure from outside comes from various quarters. Tight state control over the universities, either national or private, was a dominant feature until the end of World War II. Under the present regime the universities are thought to enjoy considerable autonomy, although the state has fiscal control over the national ones. More significantly, however, the powerful financial lobbies have imposed their opinions upon educational policy since their rapid economic recovery in the early 1950s. It was as early as 1954 that the Japan Federation of Business Managers, the most prominent of such lobbies, produced their *Suggestions for the Reform of the Educational System*, calling for the diversification of the upper secondary stage and the higher-education institutions with immediate expansion in the fields of science and technology. The manpower policy which followed and persisted through the 1960s placed the emphasis basically on the same line. That this was closely related to the accelerated economic growth of the decade is unquestionable.

The explosion of knowledge, the growth of the sciences, the rapid development of mass communication, growing mobility and the urban concentration of the population are also outside factors. It is often said that the Japanese universities are not in the main successful because of their organisational rigidity based upon the traditional chair system and departmentalism. They have not adapted well to the changing circumstances.

DIVERSITY AND EXPECTED UNIVERSITY CHANGES

There is a saying in Japan that 'all the cats and scoops', which means 'one and all' in a sarcastic sense, 'go to the university'. As has already been seen, Japan is among the countries now on their way to mass higher education. Against this trend there is an argument that there should be 'noble' institutions and 'less noble' ones within the system of higher education.[5] Surprisingly, there is only one nomenclature for higher-education institutions in Japan, mentioned at the beginning of this chapter, ie the *Daigaku*, so that even the junior college is called, as it were, the shorter-cycle *Daigaku*. (The exception is the technical college, which combines the upper secondary and junior college stages.) The university system, therefore, is thought of as uniform, but is expected to become more diversified.

The general structure of the university system is four tiered. First, the undergraduate course is divided into two. All students are required to take general education subjects during their first two years. After that they proceed to the specialised courses leading to the first degrees, normally four years' schooling altogether (six years in medical and dental sciences). Secondly, the graduate school is divided into two grades, one for master's degrees (a two-year course) and another for the pre-doctorate (five years, of which the first two years are the equivalent of the master's course). All the national universities, and a good many of the private universities, follow this general structure, although there are universities with faculties which are not qualified to set up the pre-doctorate graduate course, and many of the smaller private universities have no graduate schools at all.[6]

In the meantime the Central Advisory Council for Education suggested in its report that, 'In order to diversify Japanese higher education in the future, institutions for higher education must be categorised according to students' qualifications and the number of years for the completion of an average course of studies.' The categories proposed were as follows:

(1) Category I (provisionally to be called 'university') would include institutions providing three or four years of education for graduates from upper secondary schools, and would consist of three types: (a) the comprehensive type for non-specialist careers; (b) the academic discipline type, systematically providing basic academic knowledge and skills;

(c) the professional job-oriented type providing the theoretical and technical training for particular professional occupations.

(2) Category II (provisionally 'junior college') would be similar to present junior colleges, but would be divided into the 'general culture' type and the 'occupational' type.

(3) Category III (provisionally 'technical college') would again be similar to the existing one.

(4) Category IV (provisionally 'graduate school') would provide advanced academic education for two or three years for the graduates from the 'universities' and for those whose ability was recognised as equivalent to or higher than the former.

(5) Category V (provisionally 'research centre') would be for those pursuing an advanced level of research worthy of a doctor's degree.

Categories IV and V appear much like the two grades of the present graduate school, but more distinctly separated.[7]

This proposed categorisation, which certainly shows the mode of diversification, has two dimensions, horizontal and vertical. There can be, as a matter of course, horizontal diversification, although it has not been made clear yet whether there might be some ranking gaps between the 'university' and the 'junior college'; while the categorised structure as a whole would produce the vertical diversification. My own view is that with this vertical diversification in mind the 'university', in particular the type (b), and the categories IV and V, represent the 'noble' institutions, and the others the 'less noble' ones.

As previously shown, an overwhelmingly large proportion of students attend the private-sector institutions. Two things should be noted.

Firstly, in theory the standard of any private university is never inferior to that of the national (or the local public) one. Indeed, a good many of the distinguished private universities have a remarkable academic heritage. There is, however, in reality a wide variation in size, financial basis – the most vital condition for the private institutions – provision of facilities such as libraries and laboratories, staffing, etc. Mainly for financial reasons most of the private universities have been forced to admit far more students than the 'recognised' number of places and to overload their teaching staff with rather poorer facilities. It is said that therefore they do not attract the more distinguished scholars. And it cannot be denied that a number of institutions are weak in academic standards.

The second point relates to the balance of studies or the student distribution by faculties. Some figures are given below.

PERCENTAGE DISTRIBUTION OF UNIVERSITY STUDENTS BY
FACULTY IN JAPAN, 1959 AND 1969

	Year	All faculties %	Literature %	Law & economics %	Science & engineering %
Public	1959	100·0	10·1	15·0	28·8
	1969	100·0	9·4	16·6	37·7
Private	1959	100·0	17·5	51·9	19·3
	1969	100·0	19·0	46·6	21·8

	Year	Agriculture %	Medicine, dentistry and pharmacy %	Teacher training %	Others %
Public	1959	8·4	6·6	23·6	8·1
	1969	8·1	5·6	21·9	8·6
Private	1959	2·6	3·3	0·9	4·5
	1969	2·3	3·3	1·4	5·6

Source: Ministry of Education, Japan, *Educational Standards in Japan* (1970), p 29, Table 10.

The table (above) shows that the private sector tends to absorb far more students in the fields of humanities and social sciences than in science and technology, probably due to the higher cost of the latter and also to the fact that, to economise on resources and facilities, the humanities and social sciences can be taught through the lecture with larger student groups. Furthermore, except for the comparatively small proportion of highly reputable ones, the private institutions confer less prestige on students leaving after graduation to seek their careers.

These factors have made the position of the private universities at large very difficult. Although they have educated a good many of the qualified professionals and many distinguished scholars, it is also true that they have played a major role in the recruitment of rank-and-file clerical workers or sales people in the course of the country's rapid economic growth.

To raise substantially the standards of private universities, in staffing, facilities and level of academic quality, including the capacity for research, is of urgent importance, but this will not mean slowing down the trend towards mass higher education. The private sector will grow further, absorb more clients, and open wider the opportunities for higher education in the 1980s and after.

Even though the egalitarian incentive pushes mass higher education further towards the phase of universal access, there persists a strong feeling for excellence. According to my view, the national universities do not inevitable become the 'noble' institutions, nor the private universities inevitably the 'less noble' ones. But there may well be more institutions in the private sector than in the local public sector which cannot improve their standard enough to attain equality with the national ones. With both this and the proposed categorisation of higher-education institutions in mind, then, even with groupings of universities (ie national, local public and private) there might be gaps between the 'noble' and the 'less noble'. In consequence, the students will be sorted out at the thresholds of the universities by some selection measures, based upon their achievement in the entrance examination, their scholastic aptitude-test results, or the attainment report from their secondary schools. Is this any different for the students from the present selection procedure for admission to the upper secondary school? Despite a seriously critical review, made by an OECD specialist group in 1972, of the highly competitive selection from the level of the post-compulsory stage up to university matriculation,[8] and despite the increased accessibility to the university henceforth, the presumed stratified structure of universities in the near future will still be biased towards social selectivity. In other words the educational selection process begun with the schools would end with the university but at the same time the latter, with its various categories of institutions, would begin a process of social selectivity.

A UNITED COMPREHENSIVE CENTRE OF HIGHER LEARNING

This seems the way along which the Japanese higher-education system is likely to go. Since the structure of the system has educational and social implications, I have tried to mark the role it will play in its projected shape. Owing to the vertical diversification, together with the social selectivity, the contradiction of disparity among the various institutions also may not disappear. I do not believe that at the beginning of the 1980s all the graduates of the upper secondary schools – it is expected by the Central Council for Education that these will amount to 97 per cent of the age group – could be competent for the studies expected from them at the proposed academic type of university. But it will not be exceeding expectations if, during the last two decades of this century, Japan reaches the phase of universal tertiary education, or at least universal access to higher education; is, therefore, this categorised or separately stratified system the only possible choice? Will there not be any alternative or more suitable way by which the future university in Japan can fill its possibly more diverse role?

If tertiary education as provided by the formal universities and junior colleges (or any other facilities), and also by the arrangement of the 'televised broadcast university courses' now being projected separately, were to be made open to every member of the public, there would be students from every kind of social background, of both sexes, from eighteen (the normal age of entry to university at present) to probably more than forty-five years of age. Their motivations, aspirations, interests and needs would differ so widely that no single type of institution could meet them satisfactorily. Accordingly, at this stage, the higher-education institution would have to provide not only the traditional academic studies but also many other kinds of service.

Teacher education and training, for instance, has already been brought into the realm of the university function in Japan, while refresher courses for teachers of primary and secondary stages are now conducted by local education centres run by local authorities. It would be advisable to overcome this split. Teachers' in-service education could obtain a good deal from the university too.

The extension service and continuing education are further examples. The former has been the weakest function of the Japanese universities until now, and the latter, though not to be conducted only by the university, is a task to be tackled henceforth. The future higher-education institution will not be able to function without these services. There should be courses for professional education, as well as the re-education courses offered for mature people who have gained experience in their careers.

Besides these teaching and training functions, research has been and should be an indispensable element. Many argue that the separation between teaching and research is more reasonable and practical as the size and diversity of the student body grows larger: it seems that the idea of Cardinal J. H. Newman is still alive, affirming that 'to discover and to teach are distinct functions: they are also distinct gifts, and are not commonly found united in the same person'.[9] But I would not myself agree.

There are, of course, people in a university who have more inclination for teaching or student counselling than sitting amid a heap of books and written materials or engaging in studies of processes going on inside test-tubes. But the university, or any other higher-education institution, should not be entirely a teaching body, as the higher learning to be transmitted must be by nature and without exception based upon the latest findings of human intellectual creativity. The higher education institution without its research function will lack the basic momentum to attract students' creative minds.

Meanwhile, there are some people, mainly on the side of technology, who hold that the universities are incapable of meeting the growing needs of the big sciences. This view has some truth, as technology and the big sciences, interacting with each other, tend to develop rapidly and spend too vast an amount of money to be managed by a single university. They absorb a large number of scientists and technologists from the universities. But a fatal defect of research institutions when separated from universities is their lack of involvement in bringing up succeeding generations. In this respect they are fully dependent upon the universities. The implication is that research should not go alone, but side by side with teaching, although the balance of functions is the critical problem to be considered – for each member of the academic staff and for the institution as a whole.

A research information service should be also developed, with a branch in each disciplinary division of the higher-education institutions. Although the library service has been much improved recently in Japan, it still lags behind growing needs, in particular for research data and information. As international cultural communication and exchange is developed, the role of the university in this aspect is to be underlined.

Do 'excellence' and 'universalisation' stand as alternative choices? People who adhere to the sense of excellence conceive that the 'university' in Japan should be like the British or German one which retains the 'noble' position in the higher-education system. But, whether for good or for evil, Japan has, though rather complicatedly, mixed up various higher institutions in the name and form of 'university'. In spite of areas of inadequacy, to dissolve or to scrap and build anew would be countered by invincible resistance from the existing university side. Further, if we assume that we enter the transitional phase from mass to universal higher education in the 1980s and after (at least universal access to it is to be reached) it seems to me impracticable for the university to keep itself separate from other institutions, playing its role as the obviously obsolete ivory tower or the new type of elitist institution.

Instead, is it impossible for the university to embrace a many-sided role comprehensively, with a diversified structure of constituent colleges, schools and departments which carry different functions? My answer is probably 'yes'. Then, is it not reasonable that the comprehensiveness of the role requires organisational comprehensiveness? Moreover, if the rigidity of the Japanese higher-education system, something justly pointed out by Professor Ben-David,[10] has to be changed to a more flexible structure – a view recommended also by the Educational Ministry's Central Council for Education – the organisational comprehensiveness will work more successfully if the students and teachers can transfer between the intramural institutions.

This comprehensiveness should never exclude the function of advanced study, but the future university will and should attract a much greater number and variety of learned and professionally experienced people in order to meet the growing needs of advanced knowledge and high-level skills in various fields. The needs, however, arise from many sections of society. For instance, the different professions call for an annual supply of qualified men and women, and the industrial and business worlds demand certain types of university output. The university is not indifferent to these external needs. But in future the university will no longer stand alone as the last rung of the school ladder; it will rather become something like a learning-resources magazine from which anyone suitably qualified, young or middle-aged, without distinction of sex or social origin, either before or in service, can obtain benefit for his or her intellectual and professional needs at higher, specialised and advanced levels. Thus, indeed, it is to be hoped that the future university in Japan will play its role as the comprehensive centre for intellectual advance and professional improvement in the age of universalised higher education.

The argument underlying my sketch of the future role of the Japanese university has not been fully extended. The relationship between research in the university and that of non-university research institutes, the contribution and obligation of the university to the life of society, the role of the university as the bastion of intellectual liberty and academic freedom, and so on, are among the excluded questions of vital importance. But since the diversification of the higher-education structure is the current focal issue in Japan, as in some other countries, I have been at pains to emphasise this.

I am aware of being apparently egalitarian, but I do not stand for rigid uniformity in education. There should be a much greater diversity and flexibility in the future university, both as an institution and as a system at large. This, however, should not detract from the basic principle of the students' or the people's equal rights to higher education and a greater equality in the standard of each institution. In order to bring these about, each existing university will have to take vigorous and persevering steps for its own reform and improvement.

II

The University in China

R. F. PRICE

In discussing the role of the university in modern China, it will be necessary to consider institutions with a much narrower function than that associated with the English university. Nor should a process of simple translation be adopted. The Chinese word *daxue*, originally 'great learning', is applied to a number of institutions which according to their standards would not rate as universities. A famous example is the *Gongchanzhuyi Laodong Daxue* in Kiangsi Province, better translated as the Communist Labour College, an institution training technical personnel for agriculture. On the other hand, a number of institutions called *xueyuan*, variously translated as institute, academy or college, resemble single-faculty universities, and must be considered in any discussion of the university in China. For the sake of simplicity the word 'university' will be used unless it is specially necessary to distinguish institutions.

The justification for this choice of the range of institution will become clearer as the discussion proceeds. It should be noted that after the establishment of the People's Republic of China in 1949, all educational institutions were rapidly brought under state control, at either national, provincial or more local level. All third-level educational institutions come under the jurisdiction of the Ministry of Higher Education, and the specialised institutions are often jointly supervised by other ministries.[1]

European-style universities were gradually established in China when the ancient Imperial Civil Service Examination system was finally ended at the turn of the century. Peking University was established as the

186

National University of Peking in 1898. Early models were Europe, as refracted through Japan, and then the USA. Universities established and staffed mainly by foreign missionaries, totalling nineteen in 1949, played an important role both as educators and as models. In the immediate post-liberation reorganisation the Soviet Union became the model and universities were in some cases split up and their various departments merged in specialised institutes.[2] An idea of the range of institutions and the increase in their numbers over the years is given in the table below.

NUMBERS AND TYPES OF TERTIARY INSTITUTIONS IN CHINA

	1940*	1950	1953	1965
General universities	39	—	13	43
Polytechnical institutions	}54	}31	20	52
Monotechnical institutions			26	162
Agriculture, forestry and water control	—	18	29	98
Medical schools	—	29	32	87
Politics, law, finance and economics	—	—	11	33
National minority institutions	—	—	—	10
Foreign language institutes	—	—	—	14
Fine arts, music, film	—	—	—	36
Physical education	—	—	—	15
Teacher training	—	30	34	113
Totals:	143	207	182	663

Sources: Because of differences of classification figures vary from one author to another. The 1940 figures come from the *China Yearbook*, those for 1950 and 1953 from S. Fraser, *Chinese Communist Education*, p 134 (quoting Minister of Education Ma Xu-lun), and those for 1965 are from *China Monthly* (Nov and Dec 1965), in Chinese. C-S. Tsang gives an erroneous total of 664 which was copied by the present writer in *Education in Communist China*, p 144.

* The blanks for 1940 and other years indicate ignorance rather than total absence of institutions. Authors say whether state, provincial or private, rather than mentioning specialisation. Partial data indicates specialised colleges to be rather few for these years.

For detailed information on 490 research and development institutions, including many teaching institutes and universities, see the *Directory of Selected Scientific Institutions in Mainland China* (Surveys & Research Corporation: 1970). Institutions founded before 1949 include 16 universities, 1 teacher training institution, 3 agricultural colleges, 3 colleges of engineering and 16 medical colleges.

With the reorganisation of the early fifties, all third-level institutions became instruments of state policy. The Common Programme of the Chinese People's Political Consultative Conference in 1949 had as main tasks the 'training of personnel for national construction work', the 'developing of the ideology of serving the people', and the stressing of technical education. The student's choice has remained largely limited to his initiative in seeking a place, and if he is lucky in the subject-area studied. But during the past twenty-three years tertiary education has been used to train a relatively small proportion of the age group for those jobs considered nationally relevant. 'Tertiary education for (nearly) all', a slogan which might be applied to the countries of Europe and North America, can be only a distant possibility in a country which has not yet made primary education fully universal. At the same time some of the mind-broadening aspects associated with a university education are expected to be developed in the course of the widespread moral-political education which is a feature of factory and farm life in China today.

COMMUNIST PARTY LEADERSHIP AND POLICY DIVISIONS

The influence of the Communist Party on university affairs increased rapidly after 1950 until by the end of the decade it was all-pervasive and decisive. At one level it acts through Party members in their capacity as state officials. But perhaps more important, the Party itself sets out policy and gives the lead at national and local levels. Major policy is often initiated by joint statements of the Central Committee of the Party (CC CCP) and the State Council. Within the universities there are Party branches which meet separately and decide policy. As key posts, such as president and even departmental head, are often given to Party members with political reliability and administrative rather than high academic qualifications, there is the possibility of friction between the Party and the non-Party academics.[3] This conflict is part of the problem usually discussed in terms of the Party slogan which requires that the intelligentsia shall be both 'red and expert'.

While the CCP dominates education and the schools, it does not do this by mass enrolment of the schooled, and certainly not those with tertiary education. Figures given during the Third Plenum of the CC in 1957 showed only 1,880,000 intellectuals out of a total of 12,720,000 members. Considering that the term *zhishifenzi* includes persons with a secondary and technical training, this does not allow for a high proportion of university-level personnel. This is confirmed by data on the proportion of Party members among university staffs, where in spite of expressed fears of isolation the Party is not heavily represented.[4]

The CCP makes great efforts to train its members, both in the course of Party discussions and through various Party schools, both permanent and temporary. The Youth League and the People's Liberation Army can be considered to some extent a training ground for the Party. They are seen by many people in China as paths to influence and power.[5] All this is relevant to the future of the universities: on the one hand, if the custom of appointing managerial personnel from the ranks of the Party and the PLA persists, this makes unlikely the growth of schools of management and administration within the universities;[6] and on the other hand, and this seems unlikely, should the Party begin to recruit from the universities on a much greater scale, and to give more university-trained personnel positions of power, this could lead to changes in the kind of people applying for entry to university, as well as in the size of university enrolments.

The nature and role of the universities was a topic receiving considerable attention during the Great Proletarian Cultural Revolution (GPCR) of 1966–9. Teaching stopped for a period of some three years and campuses became a battleground for the various Red Guard groups. Particularly after the workers' teams had been sent in during the late summer of 1968, serious attention was given to the future of tertiary education. The *People's Daily* ran regular feature pages on the subject in which organisations and individuals aired their views. Attempts were made to clarify 'two lines', one proletarian, guided by Mao Tse-tung thought, and the other bourgeois-revisionist, the 'Liu line', after former premier Liu Shao-ch'i. If one sees these as two ends of a spectrum of emphasis the terminology can be a useful shorthand, but the issues are not simple, and certainly one should not too readily assume that either end represents the exact position of the man whose name is associated with it.

The main slogans under which the discussion was conducted had first appeared around 1958, and were repeated in the CC statement of the GPCR in August 1966. Education must serve proletarian politics; those receiving an education should 'become labourers with socialist consciousness and culture'; and education must be combined with productive labour. An additional slogan, training successors for the revolution, also appeared around 1965–6, later to be linked with the concept of 'red and expert'. The problem was to define these slogans in terms which could be applied to university reform, and to find the forces willing and able to carry it out.

Critics of the system 'dominated by bourgeois intellectuals' complained of discrimination against students of worker-peasant origin, of courses unrelated to the needs of the country (equated with production in the main), and of graduates who wished only for comfortable careers in the cities, rather than going to rural areas where skilled personnel were desperately needed. Much of the discussion was in terms of closing the three gaps: mental – manual labour; urban – rural; and between the classes.[7] But the problems associated with the need for time, for a certain amount of isolation, even 'individualism', if the necessary high standards were to be attained, could not be considered openly in the atmosphere of the time (later to be condemned as 'ultra-leftism'); on the contrary, anti-intellectual attitudes, so common everywhere in the world, were able to parade as progressive, and the lazy student was able to blame teachers for obscurity and irrelevance.

The majority interpretation of 'serving proletarian politics' and 'combining education with productive labour' was to concentrate further on the applied sciences. The Workers' Propaganda Team supervising changes at Fudan University proposed distributing biology specialities between agriculture, forestry and medicine. The team at Hebel University proposed keeping the division between the arts and science departments, but on the one hand combining art, history and philosophy, and on the other integrating the sciences with industrial, agricultural, forestry and medical departments.[8] They proposed transferring foreign-language teaching to the separate Foreign Language Institute. In the humanities, suggestions were made to abolish certain courses, eg journalism at Fudan. The genuine and difficult problems of the optimum use of scarce resources were only partially clarified by the statement by Chairman Mao, published in July 1968:

> It is still necessary to have universities; here I refer mainly to the need for colleges of science and engineering. However, it is essential to shorten the length of schooling, revolutionise education, put proletarian politics in com-

mand and take the road of the Shanghai Machine Tools Plant in training technicians from among the workers. Students should be selected from among workers and peasants with practical experience, and they should return to practical work in production after a few years' study.[9]

It is precisely the other subjects which are the really difficult ones when it comes to linking education with productive labour and serving proletarian politics.

The reforms in medical training, implemented early in the GPCR and widely publicised, are a good example of the obvious problem amenable to fairly simple solution. Emphasis was placed on the training of medical auxiliaries, aptly known as 'barefoot doctors' because those in the south worked at the same time in the paddy fields. Many of these were trained in crash-courses often organised in nearby high schools. The medical colleges, formerly concentrating on the production of city-oriented doctors trained primarily in Western medicine, now turned to the training of auxiliaries as well. The practice of sending teams of doctors and students into the rural areas to study while practising was extended and barefoot doctors were trained in the field by these teams. A number of references suggest that in the future the medical schools will recruit students from among these auxiliaries, a practice which would accord with another current slogan: popularisation first, then raise standards.

In teacher-training a similar practice of sending teams of teachers and students from the training colleges and institutes to the rural areas has been adopted. While not entirely new, the practice is on a much greater scale and may presage the pattern for the future.

The agricultural colleges exhibit another aspect of university reform yet to be solved. The pre-1949 concentration of tertiary institutions in the big coastal cities and Peking has continued, in spite of repeated murmurs about re-location. In the GPCR, Red Guards posted up quotations from Chairman Mao which included the following:

Why the deuce are agricultural universities run in cities? All agricultural universities should be removed to the countryside.

If a university course lasts five years, three years should be spent at the grass-roots level. The teachers should also go to the grassroots level to work as they teach. Isn't it possible to teach philosophy, literature, history at the grassroots level? Must teaching be carried out in modern buildings?[11]

But this is a long way from a full discussion of the most rational distribution of universities, which must include some consideration of the benefits of concentration of resources, human and other; which is not to say that they must remain concentrated in the coastal belt.

Another practice current during the GPCR was the 'open-door' method of running schools, contrasted with 'running schools behind closed doors'. This mainly concerned the admission of workers, peasants and soldiers as students, rather than choosing by examinations which favoured the children of the intelligentsia. But it also was connected with the slogan 'elevation through popularisation'. As the universities reopened after the GPCR they chose students of worker, peasant and soldier origin and experimented with courses of various length and purpose. The Shenyang Agricultural College ran short courses ranging from ten days to half a year with the aim of popularising simple techniques. Wuhan University described a very interesting experiment in which it combined teaching, research and production, training technicians alongside high-level research workers. A number of contributors in the *People's Daily* contrasted the new 'open-door' policy and role as populariser with former emphasis on training researchers 'to pioneer in science and technology'. No doubt the balance between these two functions will continue to plague educators and planners for decades to come, since both are necessary, and the personnel who can perform them are likely to remain centred in the universities.

TRAINING THEM RED AS WELL AS EXPERT

Chinese sources acknowledge Marx as the inspirer of the idea of linking education with labour. Often cited is the famous passage from *Capital*:

> From the factory system budded, as Robert Owen has shown us in detail, the germ of the education of the future, an education that will, in the case of every child over a given age, combine productive labour with instruction and gymnastics, not only as one of the methods of adding to the efficiency of production, but as the only method of producing fully developed human beings.[10]

Mao Tse-tung developed some ideas supporting this combination in his work *On Practice,* widely advocated for study in China. In January 1958, Mao wrote:

> As far as circumstances permit, all secondary vocational schools and skilled workers' schools should tentatively run factories or farms . . . Apart from carrying out production in their own farms, all agricultural schools may also sign contracts with local agricultural cooperatives for participation in labour, and send teachers to stay in cooperatives for the purpose of integrating theory with reality . . .[12]

This was taken further in the directive of the CC CCP and the State Council in September of that year:

> The Party line in education work seeks to make education serve the proletariat politically, and to unite education with productive labour . . . Marxist-Leninist political and ideological indoctrination[13] must be carried out in all schools to indoctrinate the teachers and students with . . . the viewpoint calling for the integration of mental labour with physical labour . . . The future direction is for schools to run factories and farms, and for factories and agricultural co-operatives to establish schools.[14]

Here schools meant all educational establishments from primary through to university. The directive was followed by wide-scale attempts to implement it, nearly all of which were abandoned after the hard years of 1960–1, and the consequent change of political emphasis.

While discussion of part-work schools is often hampered by insufficient clarity as to the exact nature of the *combination* involved, there is widespread recognition of the intended benefits.[15] The 1958 directive stated:

> There are facts to show that provided productive labour is well led, it is of advantage ethically, intellectually, or physically to the students. This is a correct way of training new personnel of all-round development.

The benefits might better be listed: moral-political; intellectual; and economic. The moral-political benefits expected concern mutual understanding between workers, peasants and intellectuals through working together, leading to the eventual extinction of essential class differences. The intellectual benefit is the old principle of learning by doing. Mao Tse-tung endorsed the economic benefit when he commemorated the third anniversary of the Kiangsi Communist Labour College:

> I completely endorse your cause. Part-work and part-study, running schools through the practice of working while studying, does not cost the state a cent ... Such schools are good indeed.

In 1964 when he met a teachers' delegation from Nepal, Chairman Mao complained that 'few people are for the new method, and more people are against it'. At the same time he developed some of the differences between the arts and sciences:

> Qinghua University has its workshops, and it is a plant of science and engineering. It won't do for its students to acquire only knowledge from books without working. However, it is not feasible to set up workshops in a college of arts, and it is not feasible to run workshops for literature, history, economics or novels. The faculty of arts should take the whole society as its own workshop. Its students should contact the peasants and urban workers, industry and agriculture. Otherwise they are not much use on graduation.[16]

The extent to which linking education with productive labour will radically alter the tone of the universities will depend on the nature of the work, the time spent, and the persistence of the policy. In the past, it is clear, for the majority of students work experience has been little more than that enjoyed by American and West European students during vacations, though it has taken rather different forms. Students have been expected to keep their institutions clean, and have taken part in general maintenance. In the institute at which I worked in 1965-7, staff and students constructed a swimming pool. At harvest time students, like office workers and other city dwellers, were organised to help. Work in factories was less common, except where linked with engineering courses, or during the 1958-60 and post-1966 periods.

Experiments like that at Wuhan University, reported in the *People's Daily* in June 1971, may have significance for the future, though it is early yet to be sure. At the same time they do nothing to help the humanities faculties. The science faculties set up ten production units within the university, including one making air-battery cells, one making transistor parts, and one to produce various chemicals from hog bristles. Links between factories outside and teaching-research specialities were the key. A number of workers were assigned to the university plants to keep them going during periods when students were required for other studies. To give students the necessarily varied experience, factories organised short-run production of certain well-established products, which were carefully selected to bring out as many principles and problems as possible.[17]

While universities like Qinghua and Wuhan have trained technicians in addition to technologists, colleges have been established in and by factories in many cities of China. At this stage it is impossible to predict the extent to which these will grow and what the mix will be between them, the specialised institutes and the general universities. Courses of study will almost certainly be narrower in the two former than in the latter, and one is tempted to think that standards will be lower in factory-run colleges. But this many Chinese will dispute, and only time will tell.

Guidelines for new curricula were laid down at an All-China Higher Education Conference in 1950. Based on work which had already begun in areas previously under Communist control, the *Decisions Concerning the Enforcement of Curriculum Reform in Institutions of Higher Learning* recommended abolition of politically reactionary courses, the introduction of 'revolutionary political courses of New Democracy', and a general simplification and rationalisation of 'overlapping' courses.[18] As a result institutions introduced compulsory political courses, usually consisting of foundations of Marxism-Leninism, the history of the Chinese Revolution, political economy and dialectical and historical materialism.[19] These occupied perhaps 10 per cent of the total time. Works by Chairman Mao, including *On Practice* and *On Contradiction*, have been studied and the title 'Mao Tse-tung thought' has either replaced or been added to Marxism-Leninism. The aim has been to encourage students to look outside their narrow academic discipline and understand their part in the task of building a socialist China. During the GPCR the phrase 'studying with problems in mind' became current, but no doubt all too often classes were a formal recitation of information and slogans more conducive to apathy and obedience than dedication or enthusiasm.

Throughout the past twenty-three years efforts have been made to increase the proportion of students coming from worker and peasant families. This was not so much from conceptions of social justice as from a desire to create a new intelligentsia which would more easily accept socialist ideas than students drawn traditionally from bourgeois, petit-bourgeois and landlord families. As elsewhere, selection of students by academic examinations tended to favour youth from just such privileged families. Teachers were also often unwilling, or unable, to adjust their teaching to students who lacked the traditional background. But the proportion of worker-peasant students increased: in 1952–3 it was only 20·5 per cent, and by 1957–8 was 36·4 per cent. It continued to rise during the sixties to 'about half'.[20] During the immediate aftermath of the GPCR, when students were recruited in increased numbers from the 'workers, peasants and soldiers', the proportion reached nearly 100 per cent. When enrolments stabilise again the figure is likely to be higher than before the GPCR. To what extent this will help to create a new intelligentsia is equally uncertain. Evidence both from China and outside suggests that while society is structured to produce social differences the schools reinforce rather than lessen these differences, and students from lower social classes absorb the attitudes of the higher. Looking to the future, the universities will certainly train a large number of the sons and daughters of worker and peasant families to be leaders in science and industry. In this way the individuals may be transferred from one class to another, but the decisive factors in changing the nature of class divisions and the proportions of people in the various classes will lie outside the universities.

THE UNIVERSITIES AND THE ECONOMY

As has been noted, the main role of the universities has been, and will continue to be, training the technical and managerial personnel required for the economy. Particularly it has trained personnel for the modern sector, mainly state-owned, large-scale, capital-intensive plants. Few if any tertiary graduates are to be found in the small-scale industry, some of it co-operative, to be found at provincial to commune level, or in agriculture.

An attempt is made to regulate student numbers in the different specialties to match the economy's projected needs. Students are also directed into employment when they graduate, with minimal arrangement for the expression of choice. Like all such attempts, success has been partial.

Since 1949 the demand for highly trained personnel has greatly increased, though at an uneven pace. In addition to the expansion of industries already developed before 1949, a number of totally new branches have been added to the Chinese economy. These include nuclear energy, electronics and, effectively, the chemical industry. The response of the educational system has been impressive. Between 1949 and 1963 China trained about 1·2 million tertiary graduates, 671,000 of whom were in the fields of engineering, science, agriculture, forestry and medicine. This compares with 70,000 graduates in the same subjects in the longer period 1928-48. In the same period, 1949-63, 8,000 Chinese students were trained in the USSR and East Europe. In 1963 graduate students totalled 15,000.[21]

The correlation between student specialisation and type of employment is important both for the economy, and for the individual's satisfaction. Unfortunately available data gives little information on how supply and demand have been matched. It is also mainly for the 1950s. For example, the distribution of tertiary graduates between subjects for the period 1948-9 to 1962-3 was:[22]

Engineering	33%
Education	27%
Medicine	10%
Agriculture	8%
Science	6%
Economics	6%
Other	10%

In the late 1950s, when Soviet methods of planning were being used, there were numerous complaints of the misuse of professional manpower – caused both by the enormous shortage and by poor work organisation.[23] Nevertheless, there was an improvement on the pre-1949 situation of technically trained graduates finding themselves unwanted.[24] To what extent the position changed during the 1960s is unclear. In twenty of the firms visited by Richman there was close agreement between the job held and the field of specialisation taken at university.[25] He reports that most of the tertiary graduates in the firms he studied 'were employed as department and section heads, vice-directors, workshop chiefs and their deputies in research, design, and development work, and as engineers'. He quotes a survey which showed that in 1955 only 6 per cent of industrial leaders were tertiary graduates. With 'leaders' interpreted as vice-directors, this compares with 25 to 50 per cent in Richman's sample. In all, 22 to 26 per cent of the engineering-technical-managerial personnel in the sample of thirty-one enterprises were tertiary graduates. But, as Richman points out, his sample is small and unrepresentative. It also does not answer the problem of how many graduates are not working in their special field.

The pattern of demand can to some extent be seen from the distribution of research scientists between the different fields.[26]

EMPLOYMENT OF RESEARCH SCIENTISTS, 1958

Industry and communications	45%
Basic science	18%
Medical science	7%
Agriculture and forestry	4%
Others	27%

A 1962 survey of 1,200 prominent scientists and engineers showed the following distribution by field:

Engineering sciences	20% plus
Physical sciences	c 33%
Earth and biological sciences	c 33%

Their distribution by type of employment was:

Chinese Academy of Sciences	46%
Institutions of higher learning	32%
Research institutes	10%
Government administration	2%
Public health	1%
Production enterprises	7%
Other	2%

Projection from figures like these is dangerous. Demand changes rapidly with changes in industrial techniques, the development of new branches of industry and the obsolescence of others. Nor is it clear what is the optimum proportion of tertiary-trained personnel in the work force. In Richman's sample of thirty-seven enterprises the proportion of tertiary graduates to total employment was 3·7 per cent. For all Chinese industrial enterprises he estimates a more realistic figure would probably be 1·5 per cent. The common assumption of management trainees and other vested interests that 'more is better' may be quite wrong, however. Similarly, the argument that 'skilled technicians and engineers are required to keep the costly machinery and equipment functioning properly' may be true, but that may not require that these people are university-trained.

The future pattern of the universities will be shaped to a considerable extent by the degree to which preference is given to graduates from the colleges within or closely linked with industrial enterprises. Richman reports that full-time graduates seemed to be preferred in heavy industry, chemical and drug firms, while graduates of spare-time programmes were in a majority in light industry. Enrolment in spare-time tertiary courses at several of the enterprises he visited in 1966 reached 5 per cent or more of total personnel. He went on to give the following examples:

At the Shanghai Steel Mill, 300 of its employees were enrolled in its own part-time higher school; at Shanghai Heavy Machine Tool, 400 were enrolled in its school; Nanking Chemical had 250 employees in its program; and Shanghai Sung Sing Joint Textile no. 3 had about 50 in its school. Peking Chemical Coke had about 100 of its employees enrolled in various spare-time higher schools.[27]

Obviously the growth of these classes would reduce the demand for university graduates, and if it did not reduce their student numbers, it would at least reduce their rate of growth.

RESEARCH AND GRADUATE TRAINING

Whatever may happen as a result of recent attempts to combine teaching, production and research, the universities will continue to concentrate on undergraduate teaching. Fundamental research is organised by the Chinese Academy of Sciences through its more than a hundred subsidiary branches and institutes. These include such institutions as the Universities of Science and Technology at Peking and Shanghai, but are typically non-teaching institutes. Faculty of universities and teaching institutes may conduct research independently or in co-operation with this Academy, or the Academies of Medical Sciences or Agricultural Sciences, both of which are also devoted to research and development. Various ministries, provincial and local government departments and industrial enterprises also run their own research institutes.[28] Increased spending on scientific research is therefore not likely to expand the universities directly, though it may do so indirectly.

Before 1949 Chinese universities awarded few higher degrees, and the practice of sending students abroad for this purpose continued throughout the fifties and sixties, with the majority going to the USSR.[29] In 1956 plans were announced for the granting of a degree to be called *fu-boshi* (associate doctor) but no lists of successful candidates have been published. Richman quotes a figure of 10,000 applicants for 800 places in 1963 and says that the number of places was planned to double in 1964. He also mentions meeting 'only four graduate-degree holders' in the enterprises he visited. It would appear to be consistent with a Maoist educational policy to emphasise practical studies, either in an institute or in the field, rather than the completion of what is so often a contrived academic exercise. Thus the early expansion of graduate training in the universities seems unlikely.

Several factors which might be thought to influence the development of university education have not been mentioned. Population increase, and with it the pressure of more young people to obtain higher qualifications will of course be present in China as elsewhere. Its exact effect will depend on the nature of political and economic decisions which we have discussed. The growing economic development of areas inhabited by the non-Han peoples will lead to a demand for tertiary education there, or its increase where it exists already, as in Xinjiang (Sinkiang). This may lead to demands for tertiary education in the native language, which may in turn spark off demands for the recognition of important Chinese dialects such as Cantonese, or the Min and Wu dialects, as proper vehicles for university studies. Some would argue, Japan notwithstanding, that the beautiful and rationally grounded Chinese script is also too great a burden for a mass-educated society to bear, and that this is a factor to consider when the universities' products are expected to play an active part in social production. But all this lies well in the future. It may only be noted that by 1957 China had adopted a substantial script reform and recently voices have again raised the question.[30]

The key to the future size and shape of the universities and institutes is the choice the Party will make of an economic model for building socialism. Oversimplifying, it will depend on the extent to which it follows a Soviet-type model which favours the Euro-American-type academic, urban-oriented elite, or successfully develops an alternative along lines advocated by Mao Tse-tung. In economic terms the latter model has recently been described as favouring limited investment in large industrial plants; encouraging the provinces to become self-sufficient; promoting the growth of small, self-reliant enterprises 'to be run by the "red masses" rather than the technocrats'; and generally putting participation and popularisation before expert leadership and the extension of knowledge beyond present bounds.[31] If the latter-type model is pursued there will be more stress on part-work and spare-time training and less on the full-time universities, though no doubt these would be encouraged to co-operate closely with the other types of schools, and themselves to develop further the 'open-door' principle mentioned above. It seems likely that elements of both will continue to be combined. It is also inevitable that there will be further changes of policy as different groups within the CCP assert their particular point of view, and as practice poses fresh problems and illuminates current theory.

Notes and References

Introduction

1 Lord Ashby, 'More Means Different', *Higher Education*, vol 2, no 2 (May 1973).
2 R. M. Hutchins, 'The Issues', *The University in America* (Chicago: Center for the Study of Democratic Institutions, 1967).
3 Report of the Departmental Committee on Intermediate and Higher Education in Wales (The Aberdare Report) (London: HMSO, 1881).
4 Ashby, 'More Means Different', op cit.
5 C. Carter, 'Costs and Benefits of Mass Higher Education', *Higher Education*, vol 2, no 2 (May 1973), p 145.
6 R. M. Hutchins, 'The Issues', op cit.
7 Report of Charles Carter, Vice-Chancellor, to the University of Lancaster Court (1973).
8 *The Learning Society*, Report of the Commission on Post-Secondary Education in Ontario (Toronto: Ministry of Government Services, 1972).
9 Ashby, 'More Means Different', op cit.
10 I. Illich, *The Convivial Society* (London: Calder & Boyars, 1973).

1 British Universities

1 B. Truscot, *Redbrick University* (London: Faber & Faber, 1943).
2 *Higher Education*, Report of the Committee on Higher Education (The Robbins Report) (London: HMSO, 1963).
3 *The Learning Society*, Report of the Commission on Post-Secondary Education in Ontario (Toronto: Ministry of Government Services, 1972).

2 The University in the USA

This assessment owes much to the publications of the Carnegie Commission on Higher Education. Pending publication of the commission's final report, looking to the year 2000, the best single source is Clark Kerr's address to the American Association for Higher Education National Conference, 8 March 1972.

1 A good summary of the origins and transformations of the system may be found in Christopher Jencks and David Riesman, *The Academic Revolution* (New York: Doubleday, 1968).

2 AMERICAN RESEARCH AND DEVELOPMENT EXPENDITURES

	Total (millions)	Federal govt share	Higher education amounts (millions)
1955	$6,279	(55·9%)	$589
1960	$13,730	(63·7%)	$1,185
1965	$20,439	(63·8%)	$2,451
1970	$26,287	(55·9%)	$3,593

Source: *Statistical Abstract of the United States 1972* (Washington DC: GPO, 1972), p 521.

3 The 'stud book' is of course the National Council on Education's periodic report on 'departments of distinction', reputationally ranked and accompanied by some data on other attributes of educational strength, supplemented (at least for faculty observers) by the American Association of University Professors annual report on salary levels.

4 Indeed, the Ford Foundation-funded *HEW Report on Higher Education* (1971) has a chapter entitled 'Everybody's Answer: the Community College', pp 57-61, although the report is sceptical about their ability to carry the heaviest load.

5 See Michael Marien, 'Higher Learning in the Ignorant Society', *The Futurist* (April 1972), pp 50-4 for the case that higher education must increase as *social* complexity increases.

6 This experiment represents a twenty-five college/university consortium pooling their educational research efforts with large-scale support from the US Office of Education and the Ford Foundation. See *The University Without Walls: a First Report* (Yellow Springs, Ohio: 1972).

7 And it will still have to meet the severe tests outlined in Kenneth Kenniston's *Youth and Dissent; The Rise of a New Opposition* (New York: Harcourt Brace Co, 1972).

8 See, for example, William T. de Bary's educational report for Columbia University, urging the new need for 'general education' across faculties and schools and levels of schooling: Columbia Reports (May 1973).

9 See Robert S. Morison, *The Contemporary University; USA* (Boston: Houghton Mifflin for Daedalus, 1966). Even in 1973, a poll showed that of all professions, university professors enjoyed their work the most.

10 Earl Cheit's *The New Depression in Higher Education* (New York: McGraw-Hill for the Carnegie Commission on Higher Education, 1971) documents this very well.

11 See *Urban Universities: Rhetoric, Reality and Conflict* (Organization for Social and Technical Innovation for US Department of Health, Education and Welfare, GPO, 1970) for case studies of the phenomena.

12 Alan Pifer's 'The Responsibility for Reform in Higher Education' (Annual Report of the Carnegie Corporation, May 1971) makes clear that the conventional assessment of great past successes and dire warnings about the future health of the system essentially resolve themselves into questions of finance.

13 This is the idea of the 'communiversity' of Samuel B. Gould, *Today's Academic Condition* (New York: McGraw-Hill, Colgate University Press, 1970), p 90.

14 See Stephen H. Spurr, *Academic Degree Structures: Innovative Approaches* (New York: McGraw-Hill for the Carnegie Commission on Higher Education, 1970).

15 See James A. Perkins (ed), *The University as an Organization* (New York: McGraw-Hill for the Carnegie Commission on Higher Education, 1973).

3 The University in Australia

1 See R. C. Petersen, 'The Australian Tradition', chap 2 in Warren J. Fenley (ed), *Education in the 1970s and 1980s* (Sydney: University of Sydney Department of Education, 1969).

2 See W. G. Walker, 'The Governance of Education in Australia: Centralization and Politics', *Journal of Educational Administration*, vol VIII, no 1 (May 1970), 17–40.

3 See A. R. Crane and W. G. Walker, *Peter Board: His Contribution to the Development of Education in New South Wales* (Melbourne: Australian Council for Educational Research, 1957).

4 See J. La Nauze, *Education for Some* (Melbourne: Australian Council for Educational Research, 1943), and W. C. Radford, *School Leavers in Australia, 1959–1960* (Melbourne: Australian Council for Educational Research, 1962).

5 For an interesting insight into the nineteenth-century university see University of Sydney, *One Hundred Years of the Faculty of Arts* (Sydney: Angus & Robertson, 1952).

6 For further details, see Colsel Sanders, 'The Australian Universities', chap VI in R. W. T. Cowan, *Education for Australians* (Melbourne: Cheshire, 1964).

7 Clark Kerr, 'The Speed of Change: Towards 2000 AD' in R. McCaig, *Policy and Planning in Higher Education* (St Lucia: University of Queensland Press, 1973).

8   See W. G. Walker, op cit and G. S. Harman, 'The Politics of Education in Australia', *Journal of Educational Administration*, vol VIII, no 1 (May 1970), pp 1–16.

9   R. T. Fitzgerald, 'Emerging Issues in the Seventies', *Quarterly Review of Australian Education* (Melbourne: Australian Council for Educational Research, September 1972), p 14.

10 These and other tendencies are discussed in W. G. Walker, *Theory and Practice in Educational Administration* (St Lucia: University of Queensland Press, 1970), pp 176–95 and W. G. Walker, 'Teacher Education: The Next Ten Years', paper read at Darling Downs Institute of Advanced Education, Toowoomba, 3 May 1973, mimeo.

11 D. W. Borrie, 'Demographic Trends and Education in Australia 1966–68', background paper, National Advisory Committee for UNESCO (Canberra: September 1968), mimeo. See also D. W. Borrie, 'The Demography of Higher Education', chap 5 in G. S. Harman and C. Selby-Smith, *Australian Higher Education* (Sydney: Angus & Robertson, 1972).

12 Government of South Australia, *Education in South Australia: Report of the Committee of Enquiry into Education in South Australia, 1969–1970* (1971), p 293.

13 E. H. and P. J. Jones, 'Aspects of Planning Future Tertiary Educational Institutions in Western Australia and some Political Implications' (Canberra: 1972), p 14.

14 See S. Durso, *Counterpoints: Critical Writings on Australian Education* (Sydney: Wiley, 1971).

15 Commonwealth of Australia, *Report on the Committee on Australian Universities* (Chairman, K. A. H. Murray) (Canberra: Government Printer, 1957).

16 Commonwealth of Australia, *Report of the Committee on the Future of Tertiary Education in Australia to the Australian Universities Commission* (Chairman, L. H. Martin) (Melbourne: Government Printer, 1964).

17 For a discussion of the Victorian and other agricultural colleges in transition, see University of New England Tertiary Agricultural Education Project, *Consensus and Conflict in Agricultural Education* (St Lucia: University of Queensland Press, 1973) and R. N. Farquhar, *Agricultural Education in Australia* (Melbourne: Australian Council for Educational Research, 1966).

18 For further information see University of New England, *Report on External Studies* (Armidale: University of New England, 1973). See also *External Studies: The First Ten Years 1955–1964* (Armidale: University of New England, 1965).

19 Barbara B. Burn, 'Higher Education in Australia', chap 6 in Barbara B. Burn, *Higher Education in Nine Countries. A General Report Prepared for the*

Carnegie Commission on Higher Education (New York: McGraw-Hill, 1971), p 130.

20 For an excellent discussion see P. H. Partridge, 'The Future of Higher Education: Problems and Perspectives', chap 11 in G. S. Harman and C. Selby-Smith, op cit.

21 Alec Lazenby, 'The Basis of Agricultural Education in the Next Decade' (Perth: May 1972), typescript, p 8.

22 Martin Trow, 'Binary Dilemmas—An American View', *Higher Education Review* (Summer 1964), quoted in Partridge, op cit, p 3.

23 Eric Robinson, 'Challenges Facing Australian Colleges of Advanced Education', in D. J. Golding *et al*, *Challenges Facing Advanced Education* (Melbourne: Hawthorne Press, 1970), p 14.

24 William Ginnave, 'Vivat Academia', chap 1 in S. Durso, op cit, p 9.

25 R. T. Fitzgerald, op cit, p 2. See also W. Gross, 'Organization Lag in American Universities', *Harvard Educational Review*, no 33 (1963), p 63, quoted by R. McCaig, 'Communication in Educational Organization: The University', chap 8 in W. G. Walker, *School, College and University: the Administration of Education in Australia* (St Lucia: University of Queensland Press, 1972), p 107.

26 Thorstein Veblen, *The Theory of the Leisure Class* (New York: Modern Library, 1931).

5 *The University in the Caribbean*
 1 (a) Data supplied by Consul General for Trinidad and Tobago in the Dominican Republic.
 (b) Data supplied by Cuban Ambassador to Trinidad and Tobago.
 (c) Council on Higher Education, Commonwealth of Puerto Rico, *Higher Education Facilities, Comprehensive Planning Study, 1971 Report* (June 1972), pp 22–3.
 (d) Data supplied by Trinidad and Tobago Ambassador to Haiti.
 (e) University of the West Indies, *Memorandum on Estimates of Needs for 1972–1975* (January 1972), p 32.
 (f) College of the Virgin Islands, Office of the President, 'A Fact Sheet for Interested Potential Faculty Members' (April 1973).
 (g) University of Guyana, Statement of *Development Policy for the Triennium 1972/73–1974/75* (July 1972).
 (h) Data supplied by the Netherlands Ambassador to Trinidad and Tobago.
 (i) Data supplied by the French Ambassador to Trinidad and Tobago.
 2 See Sir Eric Ashby, *Universities: British, Indian, African. A Study in the Ecology of Higher Education* (London: OUP, 1966).

3   H. Wells, *The Modernization of Puerto Rico. A Political Study of Changing Values and Institutions* (Cambridge, Massachusetts: Harvard University Press, 1971), pp 89–90.

4   *The Growth and Expansion of the University of Puerto Rico, a Brief Report* (Rio Piedras Campus, 1972). See also Wells, op cit.

5   From a report by the Government of Trinidad and Tobago on the University of the West Indies.

6   Ashby, op cit. See also S. R. Dongerkery, *University Autonomy in India* (Bombay: OUP, 1967).

7   Ashby, op cit.

8   J. A. Corry, *Farewell the Ivory Tower. Universities in Transition* (Montreal: McGill-Queen's University Press, 1970), p 34.

9   *The University, Society and Government,* Report of the Commission on the Relations between Universities and Governments (Ottawa: University of Ottawa Press, 1970), pp 116–17.

10 J. Suchlicki, *University Students and Revolution in Cuba, 1920–1968,* (Coral Gables, Florida: University of Miami Press, 1969), pp 104–12.

11 Corry, op cit, p 103.

12 See notes 1 (c), 1 (e) above.

13 Ashby, op cit.

14 University of the West Indies, *Scheme for Widening University Entrance to Day Courses in Arts and Social Sciences, on an experimental basis over a period of five years* (UWI Press, November 1971), pp 7, 9, 12–13.

15 Quoted in C. Drives, *The Exploding University* (London: Hodder & Stoughton, 1971), p 291.

16 Suchlicki, op cit, pp 129–30.

17 University of the West Indies, *Financial Summary, 1971/72,* pp 4–5; *Memorandum of Estimates of Needs for 1972–1975,* pp 50–1.

18 University of the West Indies, *Memorandum on Estimates of Needs for 1972–1975,* pp 31–2.

19 Ibid, p 54.

20 R. F. Arnove, *University Student Alienation: A Venezuelan Study* (New York: Praeger, 1971), p 145.

21 See note 1 above.

22 University of the West Indies, *Vice-Chancellor's Report to Council* (1972), pp 2–3.

23 See note 4 above.

24 O. E. Moore, *Haiti, Its Stagnant Society and Shackled Economy* (New York: 1972); Inter-American Development Bank, *Socio-Economic Progress in Latin America,* Annual Report 1971 (Washington DC: 1971), pp 226, 232–3.

25 Suchlicki, op cit, p 126.

26 B. Diederich and A. Burt, *Papa Doc: Haiti and Its Dictator* (London: Bodley Head, 1970), pp 381–2.

27 G. Henderson, *Emigration of Highly Skilled Manpower from the Developing Countries*, Unitar Report No 3 (New York: 1970), pp 167, 258.

28 University of the West Indies, 'The Number of Doctors Needed in the Commonwealth Caribbean' (UWI Press, 23 March 1972), p 2.

29 Central Statistical Office, Trinidad and Tobago, *International Travel Statistics*.

30 See D. Rodriguez Graciani, ¿*Rebelion o Protesta? La Lucha Estudiantil en Puerto Rico* (Rio Piedras, Puerto Rico: 1972). On Mexico, see J. B. Sierra, *Conversaciones con Gaston Garcia Cantu* (Mexico City: 1972); Dr Sierra was Rector of the university from 1966 to 1970 and therefore had to cope with the student protest of 1968.

31 Suchlicki, op cit.

32 T. Blackstone, K. Gales, R. Hadley and W. Lewis, *Students in Conflict, LSE in 1967* (London: Weidenfeld & N., 1970), pp 234–8. See also H. Kidd, *The Trouble at LSE, 1966–1967* (Oxford University Press, 1969).

33 Arnove, op cit, p 110.

34 See, for example, K. Ramchand, *The West Indian Novel and its Background* (London: Faber, 1970). This, however, is not true of G. R. Coulthard, *Race and Colour in Caribbean Literature* (Oxford University Press, 1962).

35 See, especially, 'Revolution on the Campus', *The American Scholar* (Autumn 1969). Blassingham's article 'Black Studies: An Intellectual Crisis' is on pp 548–61 and Brimmer's 'The Black Revolution and the Economic Future of Negroes in the United States' on pp 629–43. See also *Black Studies in the University: A Symposium* (held at Yale in 1968) (Newhaven: Yale University Press, 1969); T. Draper, *The Rediscovery of Black Nationalism* (London: 1970), chap 10.

36 Carlos Moore, 'Cuba: The Untold Story', *Présence Africaine*, vol 24, no 52 (1964), pp 217–18.

37 P. Theroux, *V. S. Naipaul, An Introduction to his Work* (London: Heinemann, 1972). Naipaul's comment was made in a BBC interview with Ronald Bryden.

6 *The University in South Africa*

1 J. L. Sadie, 'Population and Economic Development in South Africa', *South African Journal of Economics* (1973), pp 205–22.

7 *The University in Latin America*

1 R. J. Havighurst and J. R. Moreira, *Society and Education in Brazil* (Pittsburgh: University of Pittsburgh Press, 1965), p 199.

2 'Educacao (1) Diagnostico Preliminar' (Rio de Janeiro: IPEA, 1966), p 176.

3 *Economic Growth of Columbia: Problems and Prospects* (IBRD: Johns Hopkins University Press, 1972), p 391.

4 C. N. Myers, *Education and National Development in Mexico* (Princeton University, 1965), p 104.

5 The following table of salaries applied in October 1966 for faculties of federal universities in Brazil (US$ per month):

Full professor (*Catedratico*), 199; Associate professor (*Ajunto*), 186; Assistant professor (*Assistente*), 153; Instructor (*Instrutor*), 140. Information supplied by MEC, Rio de Janeiro.

6 C. C. Gill, *Chile: Education and Social Change* (Washington: US Department of Health, Education and Welfare, 1966), p 74.

7 B. Higgins, *Economic Development: Principles, Problems and Policies*, 2nd ed, rev (New York: W. W. Norton & Co, 1968), p 727.

8 B. Higgins, *Economic Development* (1968), p 411.

9 This scarcity situation is reflected in the full employment amongst the highly educated in Latin America. This contrasts sharply with the situation in India and parts of Africa where graduate unemployment is a pervasive problem.

8 The University in West Germany

1 C. H. Becker, *Gedanken zur Hochschulreform* (Leipzig: 1919). See also H. Schelsky, *Einsamkeit und Freiheit. Idee und Gestalt der deutschen Universität und ihrer Reformen* (Hamburg: 1963), pp 158ff; H. Heimpel, 'Probleme und Problematik der Hochschulreform', *Schriften des Hochschulverbandes*, Heft 8 (Göttingen: 1956), pp 5ff.

2 H. Gerber, 'Hochschule und Staat', *Schriften des Hochschulverbandes*, Heft 5 (Göttingen: 1953).

3 K. Kromphardt, *Vom Zukunftsauftrag der neuen Universität. Voraussetzungen und Möglichkeiten einer inneren Hochschulreform*, p 106: 'The required separation of a purely academic examination system and one supervised by professional and public bodies would necessitate a clear distinction between scientific preparation and pre-vocational education on the one hand, and a theoretical plus practical professional training on the other.'

4 Schelsky, op cit, p 312. See also: *Empfehlungen zum Ausbau der wissenschaftlichen Einrichtungen*, Teil I (Wissenschaftliche Hochschulen, Tübingen: 1960), p 55.

5 Cf: H. Wenke, 'Die Deutsche Hochschule vor den Ansprüchen unserer Zeit', *Schriften des Hochschulverbandes*, Heft 7 (Göttingen: 1955), pp 9ff; Heimpel, op cit, p 26; *Anregungen des Wissenschaftsrates zur Gestalt neuer Hochschulen* (Bonn: 1962), pp 73–4.

6 Wenke, op cit, p 10.

7 Heimpel, op cit, p 16.

8 For this cf: J. Ortega y Gasset, *Schuld und Schuldigkeit der Universität* (München: 1952), pp 73ff; L. Raiser, 'Die Universität im Staat', *Schriften des Hofgeismarer Kreises* (Heidelberg: 1958), p 11.

9 E. Baumgarten, *Zustand und Zukunft der Deutschen Universität* (Tübingen: 1963), pp 36ff.

10 Wenke, op cit, pp 13f.

11 Cf: *Denkschrift des Wissenschaftsrates, Abiturienten und Studenten* (Bonn: 1964), where estimates for the years up to 1980 are included which the actual developments have so far proved wrong.

12 *Studenten und Neue Universität* (Bonn: 1962). There is also a relevant contribution published in the *Deutsche Studentenzeitung* (Sondernummer zum 7. Deutschen Studententag, Bonn O. J.).

13 For a critical analysis of our current educational policy refer to some recent articles of mine in *Die Welt*.

14 'Empfehlungen des Wissenschaftsrates zum Ausbau der wissenschaftlichen Einrichtungen', op cit.

15 'Anregungen des Wissenschaftsrates zur Gestalt neuer Hoch schulen', op cit.

16 'Universität neuen Typs?' Vorträge einer Tagung in der Evangelischen Akademie Loccum, *Schriftenreihe des Hochschulverbandes*, Heft 11 (Göttingen: 1962) (W. Hahn, H. Wenke, E. Baumgarten, K. Müller, H. W. Rothe, H. Ohl, W. Klemm).

17 'Empfehlungen zum Aufbau der Universität Bochum.' Denkschrift des Gründungsausschusses (published by the Ministry for Culture in North Rhine Westphalia, 1962).

18 K. Jaspers, *Die Idee der Universität* (Berlin/Heidelberg: 2nd ed 1946).

19 Schelsky, op cit, p 219.

20 'Empfehlungen zum Aufbau der Universität Bochum', op cit, p 21.

21 Cf: W. Haacke, *Publizistik. Elemente und Probleme* (Essen: 1962); Hochschul- und Forschungsinstitute, Ausbildungsstätten, in *Internationales Handbuch für Rundfunk und Fernsehen* (1964), pp B15ff.

22 Now available as a comprehensive account: K. von Dohnanyi (ed), *Die Schulen der Nation. Zur Bildungsdebatte: Fakten-Forderungen-Folgen* (Düsseldorf/Vienna: 1971).

23 *Denkschrift des Wissenschaftsrates, Abiturienten und Studenten* (Bonn: 1964).

24 This phrase was coined by the former North Rhine Westphalian Minister for Culture to indicate the character of the new university foundation in Bochum.

25 Georg Pickt, *Die Deutsche Bildungskatastrophe* (Olden/Freiburg: 1964).

26 *Festschrift zur Eröffnung der Universität Bochum,* ed H. Wenke and J. H. Knoll (Bochum: 1965).

27 *Grosser Hessenplan, Hochschulentwicklungsplan,* ed the Ministry for Culture of Hesse (Wiesbaden: 1970).

28 For recent contributions see: L. Kroeber-Keneth, *Zuviel Akademiker?* (Freiburg: 1972); ORDO, *Jahrbuch für die Ordnung von Wirtschaft und Gesellschaft,* vol XXIII (Düsseldorf: 1972); René Ahlberg, *Ursachen der Revolte* (Stuttgart: 1972); H. Maier, *Zwischenrufe zur Bildungs-politik* (Osnabrück: 1972); W. Hennis, *Die deutsche Unruhe* (Hamburg: 1970).

29 H. Schelsky, *Abschied von der Hochschulpolitik oder Die Universität im Fadenkreuz des Versagens* (Bielefeld: 1969).

30 H. Wenke, *Die deutsche Hochschule vor den Ansprüchen unserer Zeit* (Göttingen: 1957).

31 In particular, I am referring to opinions expressed in the treatise 'Wissenschaft als Beruf'.

32 Klaus Künzel, 'University Extension. Eine Studie zur Entwicklung Universitärer Erwachsenenbildung in England', phil diss (Bochum: 1972).

33 *Zum Problem der Gesamthochschule. Berichte des Deutschen Industrie-instituts zu bildungs- und gesellschaftspolitischen Fragen,* vol 4, no 3 (Köln: 1972); Hochschulrahmengesetz, Synopse, Stellungnahmen, Dokumente (Friedrich-Ebert-Stiftung, Bad Godesberg: 1972).

9 *The University in the Soviet Union*

 1 Tsentralnoe Statisticheskoe Upravlenie, *Narodnoe obrazovanie, nauka i kultura v SSSR, Statisticheskii sbornik* (Moscow: 1971), pp 151, 158.

 2 Cf: N. P. Kuzin and M. I. Kondakov (eds), *Education in the USSR* (Moscow: 1972), pp 120–30; K. Nozhko *et al, Educational Planning in the USSR* (Paris: Unesco, 1968), pp 61–78; M. A. Prokofiev *et al, Narodnoe obrazovanie v SSSR* (Moscow: 1967), pp 267–98; J. J. Tomiak, *World Education Series: The Soviet Union* (Newton Abbot: David & Charles, 1972), pp 89–103.

 3 Tsentralnoe, op cit, pp 159–65.

 4 Ibid, p 187.

 5 Tsentralnoe Statisticheskoe Upravlenie, *Narodnoe Khozyaystvo SSSR v 1970 g* (Moscow: 1971).

 6 Ibid. See also A. Kosygin, *Directives of the Five-Year Economic Development Plan of the USSR for 1971–1975* (Moscow: 1971), p 29.

 7 A. D. Breiterman, *Ekonomicheskaya geografiya SSSR* (Moscow: 1968), p 83.

 8 Tsentralnoe Statisticheskoe Upravlenie, *Narodnoe Khozyaystvo SSSR v 1970 g,* p 22.

9 Cf: D. Lane, *The End of Inequality, Stratification under State Socialism* (London: 1971).

10 I. Nørlund, E. Zucker-Schilling and I. Sedivy, 'Letters from the Soviet Union', in K. I. Zarodov (ed), *Soviet Union Today* (Prague: 1972), p 110.

11 A. S. Shurnev and Ryakov, 'Vyssheye obrazovanie v devyatoy pyatiletke', in *Vystnik Vesshey Shkoly*, no 2 (Moscow: February 1972), pp 36–42.

12 V. P. Yelyutin, *Razvitie vysshey shkoly v SSSR (1966–1970)* (Moscow: 1971), p 18.

13 Ibid, p 1.

14 Cf: N. F. Krasnov, 'Novyy etap v razvitii vysshey shkoly', in *Vestnik Vysshey Shkoly*, no 10 (Moscow: October 1972); G. Maksapetyan, 'Gody studencheskie: Krugozor inzhenera', in *Pravda*, no 14 (Moscow: 14 January 1973), p 3; 'Nauchno-tekhnicheskiy progres i universitety (s pervogo zasedaniya soveta universitetov)', in *Vestnik Vysshey Shkoly*, no 4, (Moscow: April 1972), pp 7–14; 'Novye zadachi vysshey shkoly', in *Sovetskaya Pedagogika*, no 10 (Moscow: October 1972), pp 3–9; M. Anuchin, 'Zaochnik: slagaemye uspekha', in *Izvestia*, no 5 (Moscow: 6 January 1973), p 5.

15 P. Oldak and V. Grober, 'VUZ, shirokie dveri i tesnye stupeni', in *Literaturnaya Gazeta*, no 42 (Moscow: 18 October 1972), p 10.

16 Ibid.

17 Ibid.

18 N. S. Yegorov, 'Nauchno-tekhnicheskiy progres i universitety', in *Vestnik Vysshey Shkoly*, no 3 (Moscow: March 1972), pp 3–7.

19 V. I. Tropin (ed), *Spravochnik dlya postupayushchikh v Moskovskiy Universitet* (Moscow: 1971), pp 89–92.

20 Cf: S. G. Strumilin, 'Effektivnost' narodnogo obrazovaniya v SSSR', in *Ekonomicheskaya Gazeta* (Moscow: 2 April 1962), pp 28–30; S. I. Zinovev and B. M. Remennikov, *Vysshie uchebnye zavedeniya SSSR* (Moscow: 1962) and V. A. Zhamin and S. L. Kostanian, 'Education and Soviet Economic Growth' in *International Review of Education*, vol XVIII, no 2 (Hamburg: UNESCO, 1972), pp 155–71.

21 B. M. Remennikov, *Ekonomicheskie problemy vysshego obrazovaniya v SSSR* (Moscow: 1968), p 110.

22 Cf: *On the Main Trends in the Field of Education in the USSR in 1968–1970*, a report presented to the XXXIInd Session of the International Conference on Public Education in Geneva (Moscow: 1971).

23 Yelyutin, op cit, p 31.

24 Yegorev, op cit, p 3.

25 Cf: S. T. Belyaev and T. Golenpolsky, 'The State University of Novosibirsk, Experience and Problems', in W. R. Niblett and R. Freeman Butts

(eds), *The World Year Book of Education 1972/73: Universities Facing the Future* (London: 1972), p 255.

26 E. Zaleski *et al*, *Science Policy in the USSR* (Paris: OECD, 1969), p 238.

27 Tsentralnoe Statisticheskoe Upravlenie, *Narodne obrazovanie, nauka i kultura v SSSR*, p 153.

28 I. Obraztsov, 'VUZ semidesyatikh godov dlya nauki i proizvodstva', in *Izvestia*, no 290 (Moscow: 14 December 1972), p 5.

29 L. I. Brezhnev, *Rech' na vsesoyuznom slete studentov 19 oktyabra 1971 goda* (Moscow, 1971), p 9.

30 Yelyutin, op cit, p 62; cf also E. Tyazhelnikov, *Otchet Ts. C. VLKSM i zadachi Komsomola po vospitaniya molodezhi v dukhe leninskikh zavetov* (Moscow: 1970).

10 The University in Japan

1 Ministry of Education, Japan, *Basic Guidelines for the Reform of Education*, Report of the Central Council for Education (1972), p 65.

2 Statistics, unless indicated otherwise, from the Ministry of Education's annual statistics reports.

3 Ministry of Education, Japan, *Educational Standards in Japan* (1970), p 26.

4 The ratios were calculated from the numbers in statistics issued by the Ministry of Education for 1 May 1973.

5 In the course of discussion on the trend 'Towards Mass High Education' by the OECD Education Committee in 1971, these conceptions of 'noble' and 'less noble' higher education were put forward.

6 The number of universities providing graduate courses was as follows in 1972:

	No of universities	Universities providing courses for master and doctor degrees	Universities providing courses for master degrees only	Universities* providing courses for doctor degrees only	Total
Total	397	100	72	20	192
National	75	26	34	1	61
Local	32	8	4	7	19
Private	290	66	34	12	112
Grand total	794	200	144	40	384

* All of these are the medical or the medical-dental universities

7 Ministry of Education, Japan, *Basic Guidelines for the Reform of Education*, op cit, pp 28–9.

8 OECD, *Reviews of National Policies for Education*, pt II, chaps 1, 5 (Japan: Asahi, 1971).

9 Cardinal J. H. Newman, *On the Scope and Nature of University Education* (London: Everyman's Library ed, 1965), pp xxxii–xxxiii.

10 Joseph, Ben-David, *American Higher Education* (New York: McGraw-Hill, 1972), pp 8–9.

Chapter 11   The University in China

1 There was no Ministry of Higher Education before 1952 and between 1958 and 1964. Examples of joint control are: The Sian College of Highway Research, under the Ministry of Highways and Ministry of Higher Education; Changchun College of Geology under the Ministries of Geology and Higher Education; Colleges of medicine and agriculture come only under the Ministry of Higher Education.

2 Nanking Agricultural College was set up in 1952 by merging the agricultural colleges of Jin-ling University (a former Protestant institution established in 1913) and Nanking University. The Peking College of Aeronautical Engineering was set up in the same year by amalgamating the Departments of Aeronautics of Qinghua University, Amoy University, and six other colleges.

3 R. MacFarquhar, *The Hundred Flowers* (London: Stevens, 1960).

4 Chou en-Lai, in S. Fraser, *Chinese Communist Education* (New York: Wiley, 1965), p 227.

5 M. Oksenberg, 'Getting Ahead and Along in Communist China', in J. W. Lewis (ed), *Party, Leadership and Revolutionary Power in China* (Cambridge University Press, 1970), pp 304–50.

6 But see C. T. Hu, 'The Chinese People's University: Bastion of Marxism-Leninism', in *The World Year Book of Education* (London: Evans Brothers, 1972–3), pp 63–74.

7 Cf: Karl Marx, *Critique of the Gotha Programme*, where he talks about the 'higher stage of communist society' and F. Engels, *Anti-Duhring*, section 3, 'Production'.

8 *People's Daily*, 29 March and 24 April 1969.

9 S. Schram, *The Political Thought of Mao Tse-tung* (Harmondsworth, Pelican Books, 1971), p 371.

10 *Current Background*, no 888 (Hong Kong: United States Consulate General), p 80 and p 16.

11 K. Marx, *Capital*, vol 1 (Modern Library ed, London), pp 529–30.

12 *Current Background*, no 888, p 8.

13 The translation *indoctrination* carries a connotation not present in the original Chinese. Instruction or teaching might be better here.

14 S. Fraser, *Education and Communism in China* (London: Pall Mall Press, 1971), pp 454–566.

15 This is briefly discussed in R. F. Price, 'Making Universal Schooling Serve Proletarian Politics', *China After the Cultural Revolution*, vol 1 (Brussels: Centre d'etude du sud–est asiatique et de l'extreme orient, 1972), pp 172–3. Also R. F. Price, *Education in Communist China* (Routledge & Kegan Paul, 1970), pp 211–20.

16 *Current Background*, 888, p 10 and 891, p 47.

17 Survey of China mainland press (SCMP), 4935 (Hong Kong: US Consulate General, 13 July 1971).

18 C. F. C. Yang, 'A Study of the Educational Policies of the People's Republic of China', PhD thesis (New York University, 1965); Price, op cit, p 153.

19 I. Schlesinger and U. Z. Klepidov, 'New Curricula of the General Education School', *Science and Society*, 88 (13 February 1960), pp 72–4.

20 Fraser, op cit, p 17.

21 *An Economic Profile of Mainland China* (EPMC), studies prepared for the Joint Economic Committee, Congress of the US (Washington DC: Government Printing Office, 1967), p 545.

22 EPMC, p 533.

23 J. P. Emerson, 'Manpower Training and Utilization of Specialized Cadres, 1949–68', in J. W. Lewis, *The City in Communist China* (Stanford University Press, 1971), pp 183–214.

24 Y. C. Wang, *Chinese Intellectuals and the West, 1872–1949* (Chapel Hill: University of N Carolina Press, 1966).

25 B. M. Richman, *Industrial Society in Communist China* (New York: Random House, 1969), tables 3–20, pp 195–7.

26 EPMC, p 535.

27 Richman, op cit, p 200.

28 Surveys and Research Corporation, *Directory of Selected Scientific Institutions in Mainland China* (New York: Hoover Institution Press, 1970).

29 Wang, op cit, p 124.

30 Kuo Mo-jo, in *Honggi Zazhi*, no 4 (1972), trans in *China News*, no 24 (London: Society for Anglo-Chinese Understanding, August–September 1972).

31 E. L. Wheelwright and B. McFarlane, *The Chinese Road to Socialism* (London: Monthly Review Press, 1970), pp 163–4.

Index

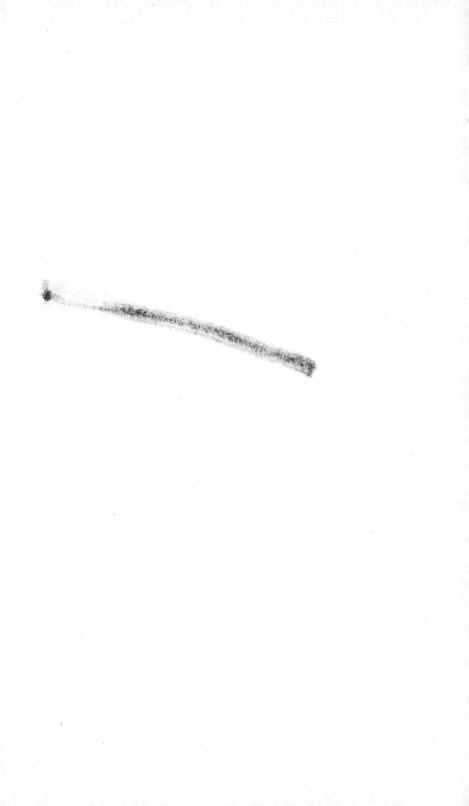